IMAGES of America

WILLIAMSTOWN

Williamstown 1858

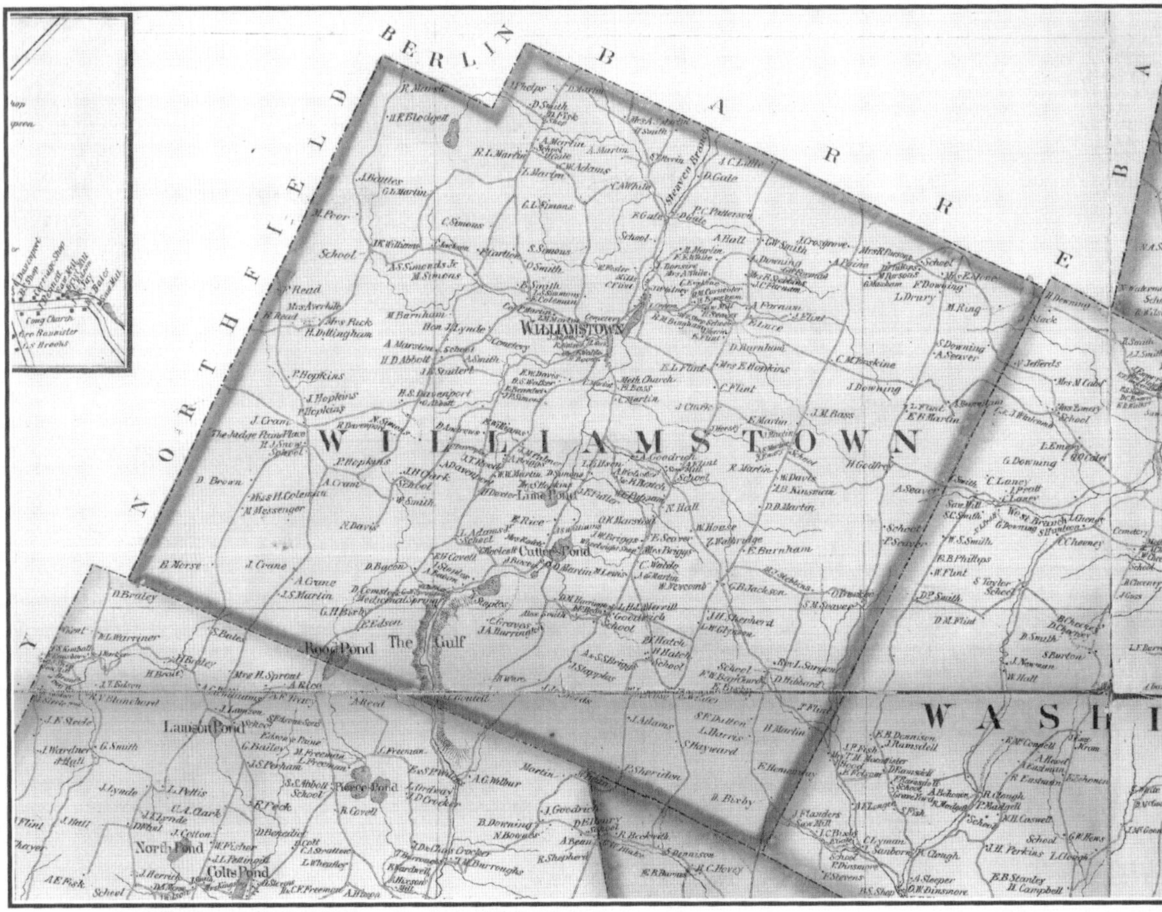

From the Map of Orange County, 1858 H.F. Walling Reprinted 2009 www.old-maps.com

Settlers came to Williamstown, Vermont, in 1784. By 1791, the population count according to the US Census increased to 146. This map from the 1858 F.W. Beers *Atlas of Orange County, Vermont* captures the farms, schools, and businesses as the settlement grew into a vibrant town, with a population increase to 1,452. (Courtesy of the Williamstown Historical Society.)

ON THE COVER: Pictured here are members of Williamstown's Rural Good Luck Club with their rowing boats headed out on the water at Berlin Pond. (Courtesy of the Williamstown Historical Society.)

IMAGES
of America

WILLIAMSTOWN

Doreen Chambers

ARCADIA
PUBLISHING

ISBN 978-0-7385-9769-0

Published by Arcadia Publishing
Charleston, South Carolina

Printed in the United States of America

Library of Congress Control Number: 2012939799

For all general information, please contact Arcadia Publishing:
Telephone 843-853-2070
Fax 843-853-0044
E-mail sales@arcadiapublishing.com
For customer service and orders:
Toll-Free 1-888-313-2665

Visit us on the Internet at www.arcadiapublishing.com

Contents

ACKNOWLEDGMENTS

Williamstown is a collaborative effort of individuals who share a common love and respect for the residents, land, nature, and history of Williamstown, Vermont. I would like to sincerely thank the Williamstown Historical Society, from whose collection most of these photographs were taken. I owe George Bosworth, photographer, for taking many of the scenic pictures and helping to preserve the images of our town as it looked around the turn of the century. I am indebted to the historical society director, and good friend, Becky Watson. For his technical assistance and categorizing the pictures, I would like to thank Paul Zeller.

For kindly donating photographs to use, I would like to express special thanks to Martha Aldous, Irene Walbridge, Teddy Hengstenberg, Fanny Martin Stewart, Bob Jarvis, Harriet (Murray) Ashland, Carrie Lewis, Evelyn M. Covell, Winston Chambers, and Rob Hepburn. For donating their picture albums to the historical society, I thank the following people: Irene Walbridge, Ora Whitney, Fanny Martin Stewart, Bertha Morgan, and Leo Edson. Thanks for helping with captions and proofreading go to Martha Aldous and Becky Watson of the Williamstown Historical Society. I would also like to thank my wonderful husband, Winston Chambers, for all his extra help and support during my long stretches on the computer. Finally, I would wish to express my heartfelt appreciation to Lissie Cain and Rebekah Collinsworth, Arcadia Publishing acquisitions editors, for their help, ongoing encouragement, and friendship across the miles. Unless otherwise noted, images appear courtesy of the Williamstown Historical Society.

INTRODUCTION

As the frontier grew, settlers staked their claim on a 230,040-acre piece of land called Williamstown. The land that had been granted was divided into eight-acre lots. Within three years, each proprietor had to plant and nurture five acres of land. To encourage families to settle into Williamstown, at the first proprietors meeting in Windsor, it was voted that the first three wives to settle in the town would be granted equal shares of land.

Early photographs and postcards begin with the adventurous lives of the first settlers. To get to their land, they climbed over mountains and through streams, fought wild animals, and tended to their own medical issues, finally arriving in Williamstown, which was basically an untouched wilderness, in June 1784. Elijah Paine, John Paine, Josiah Lyman, Joseph Crane, John Smith, and others were the first settlers to come. The wives remained behind while the men settled the ancient forestland. When they first arrived, they built rough log cabins from the forests on the West Hill. After spending many hard, dreary months working, they went back for their wives.

Vermont has sudden changes and varying extremes of climate. The *Gazetteer of Orange County* reported that when Josiah Lyman went to get his wife, Eunice (Tiffany) Lyman, in Randolph, Vermont, she and her household possessions had to be pushed and pulled through snow on a hand-held sled all the way back to Williamstown. They slogged 25 to 30 miles across frozen land. The man pushing the sled froze to death on the journey. The wives of Newell Deming, Josiah Lyman, and Joseph Crane achieved immortality in history as the first three wives to settle in Williamstown and get their shares of land.

Town records show that the first school was taught by Eleanor (Buck) Crane in Josiah Lyman's abandoned log house. When it became unfit for use, the school was moved into Lyman's hotel.

The Bicentennial Edition of the *Gazetteer of Vermont Heritage* includes a narrative on Williamstown that states "a great many of the first settlers were killed by falling trees. But the first settlers of Williamstown passed on from whiskey." The narrative also reports that "in Williamstown in August, 1839, there occurred an unusual incident: a local store was burned with all its contents, caused by spontaneous combustion of a hogshead of New England rum. It was said quite a number of townsfolk were sorely tried that the rum was wasted."

Early photographs end with Prince Edward, fourth son of George III and father of Queen Victoria. *Let Me Show You Vermont*, by Charles Edward Crane, states that the prince visited Williamstown in the early 1790s and stopped for dinner at Judge Paine's house. Prince Edward thought Vermonters were still hostile toward the British royalty and was also of the opinion that Vermonters were savages. To save him from possible poisoning, 20 armed men accompanied the prince to serve as food tasters. Prince Edward lightly joked with Sarah Paine saying, "I suppose, madam, you have never read anything but your bible and Psalm book." She replied, "Oh, yes, we do. We are very familiar with the writings of Peter Pindar." Peter Pindar (John Wolcot) was the writer of scorching satires on the characters and capacities of the royal family. So the prince departed with evidence that Vermonters were not as unsophisticated as he thought.

Williamstown land is hilly and after a few weeks of mud season, water rushes headlong down the mountains and into the Stevens Branch River that runs through the valley floor. According to the "History of Washington County" in the *Vermont Historical Gazetteer*, the Stevens Branch was named after a man whose body was discovered inside a cabin at the mouth of the river. Later it was determined that he came from Corinth and his name was Stevens. The Stevens Branch River played an important role in the life of the community. Here a prosperous area arose called Mill Village, named for its several mills.

Photographs in the second chapter begin with the development of Mill Village and show the movement of the settlement into the valley where the present-day village exists. Surrounding the village are hills known locally as East, West, and South Hills. The village is nestled in the valley of these hills. It is laid out in a linear configuration, in which everything is clustered in hamlets along the main road. It has one square pattern in the center of the village.

Under the soil of those hills is some of the most beautiful granite in the world. With the expansion of the Central Vermont Railroad and the granite quarry industry, people came to Williamstown from faraway places like Italy and France to work. These artists and craftsmen influenced Williamstown's historical building styles. Some building styles are loosely modeled on architectural traditions like pre-railroad Folk houses, Colonial, early Classical Revival, Italian, and Victorian. The large traditional farmhouse, built throughout the 19th century, can be seen throughout Williamstown.

Later photographs and postcards show the progression of human growth through the different eras of industrialism, romanticism (and tourism), and realism. Today, as visitors travel around this small rural town, they still do not face the crowds, congestion, and development seen in many cities. If one theme emerges from these images of Williamstown's past, it is the people of Williamstown and their love of the fresh countryside and Williamstown's beautiful landscape.

One

The New Life

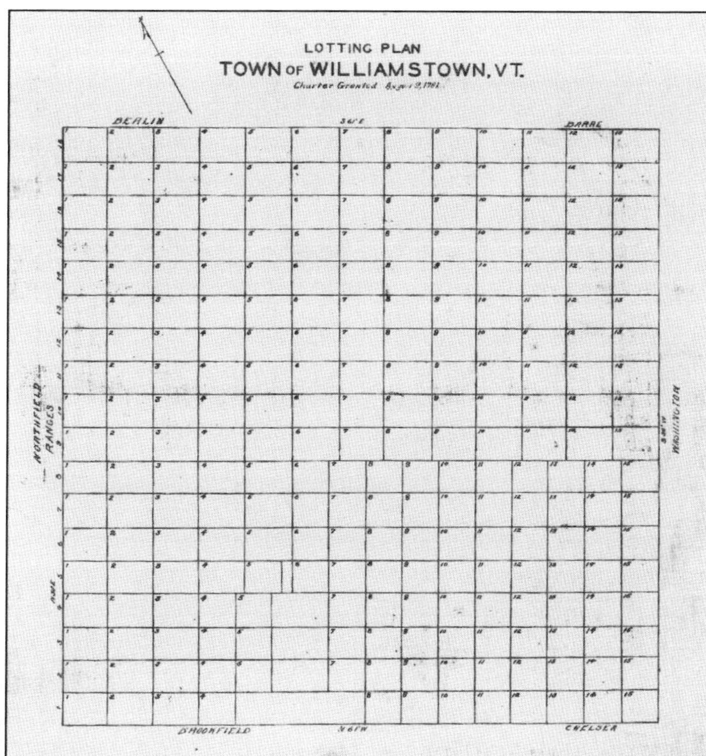

Early records show the town of Williamstown was chartered on September 30, 1781, to Samuel Clark and 74 others. The *Gazetteer of Orange County* reports that at a proprietor's meeting in Windsor in 1784, the men accepted the lotting plan and survey of Williamstown. At the first proprietor's meeting, it was voted to have the clerk tear up as many square pieces of paper as there were proprietors and number them according to the lots.

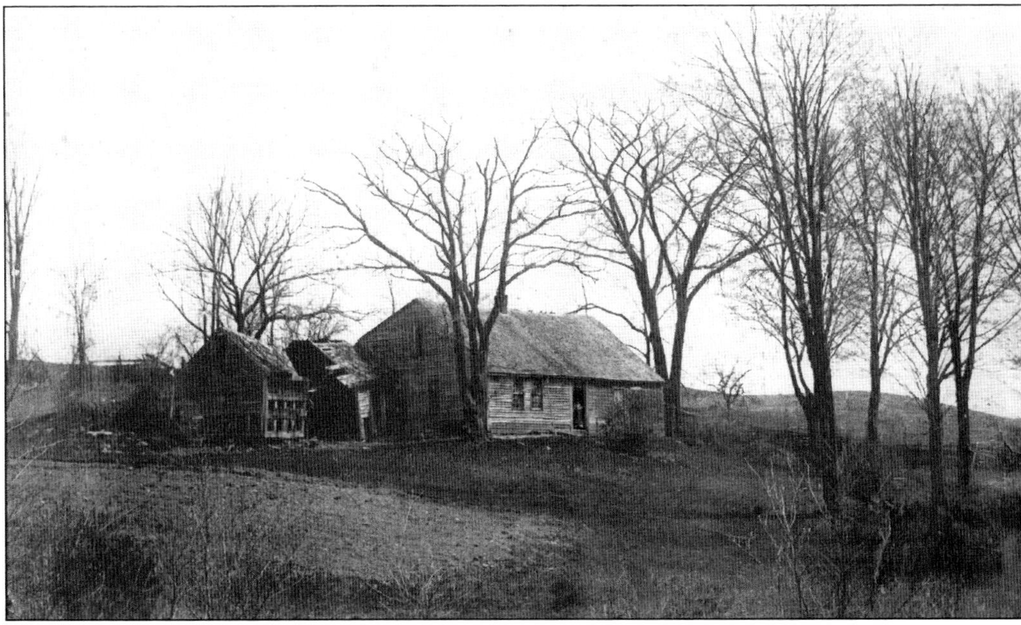

This was the first log cabin, built by Perley Howe. Later, it was known as the Jacob Martin place. When Elijah Paine, Joseph Crane, Josiah Lyman, and Pennell Deming arrived in June 1784, they used downed trees to build primitive log cabins for their families. Crude cabins were made with large logs and fastened with wooden pins. Spaces between the logs were filled with clay and mud, and the roofs were made of hemlock bark.

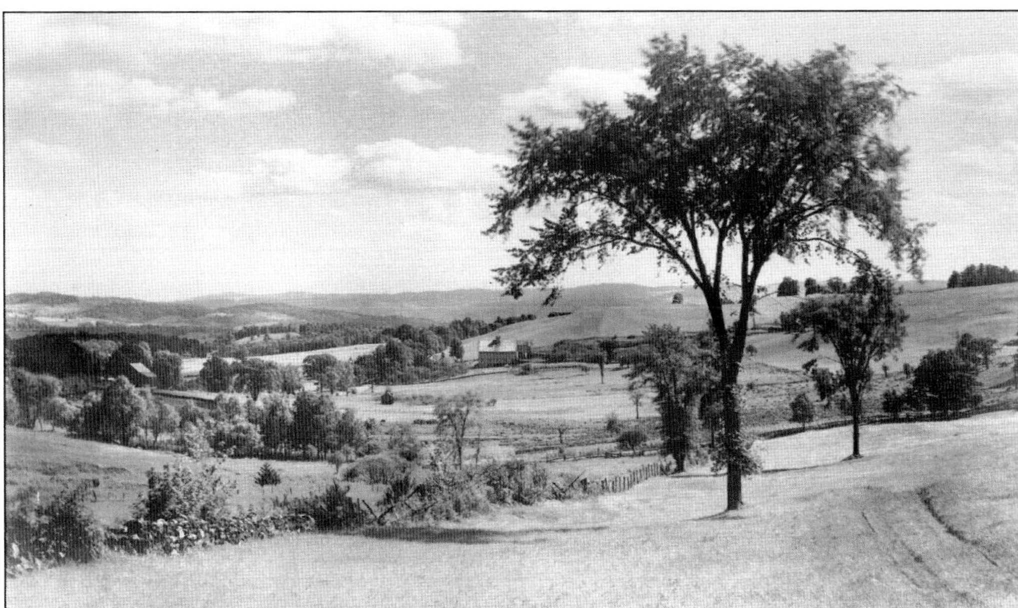

Elijah Paine's cabin stood near what is known as the early Clogston residence. The other cabins were built in the western part of the town. This idyllic landscape shows the view from West Hill looking toward East Hill. The photograph was taken in the early 1800s; by then, the land had been stripped of its trees and heavy cover. When settlers first arrived, the trees were enormous, thick, and tall.

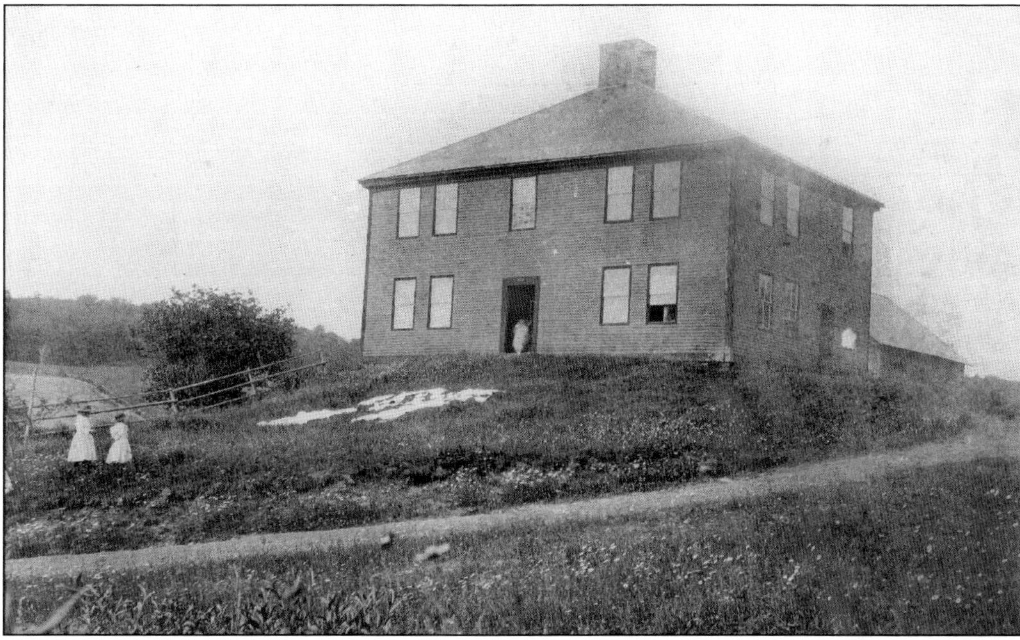

In 1788, Cornelius Lynde (1751–1836) married Rebecca Davis (1770–1840); it was the first recorded marriage in town. The home of Cornelius and Rebecca Lynde was built on the West Hill. This photograph shows where they tamed their lot and resided for many years. They had nine children. Rebecca Lynde is standing in the door of the house, with two of her children in the yard. The house and other buildings burned to the ground in 1932.

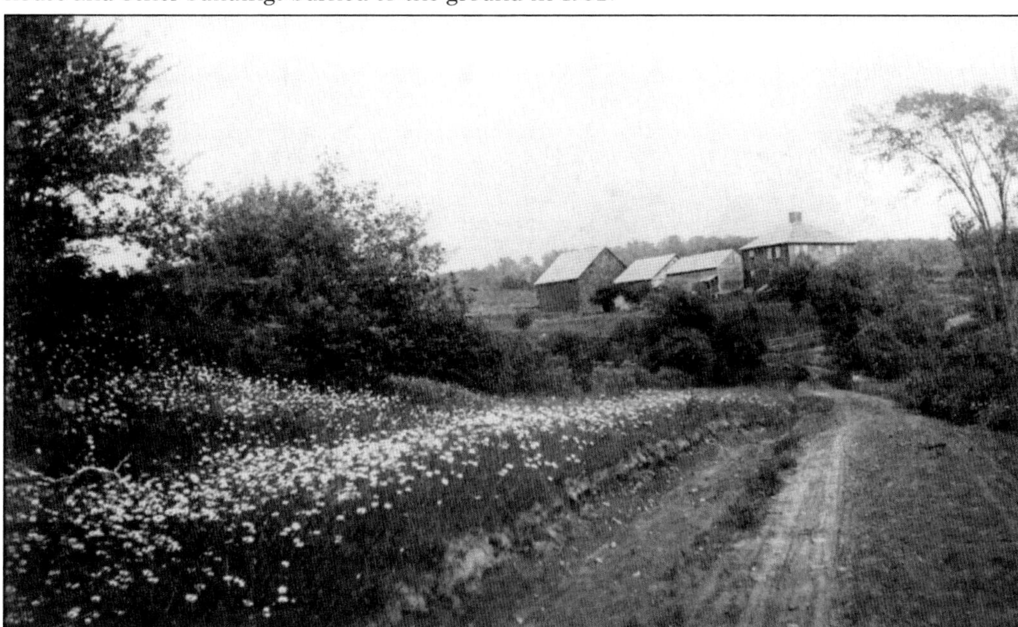

Cornelius Lynde was one of Williamstown's first settlers. He had a number of careers, including justice of the peace, town clerk, town representative, member of the state council, and assistant justice of the county court. He also built the first sawmill in town and was the first postmaster. Lynde's house is pictured here.

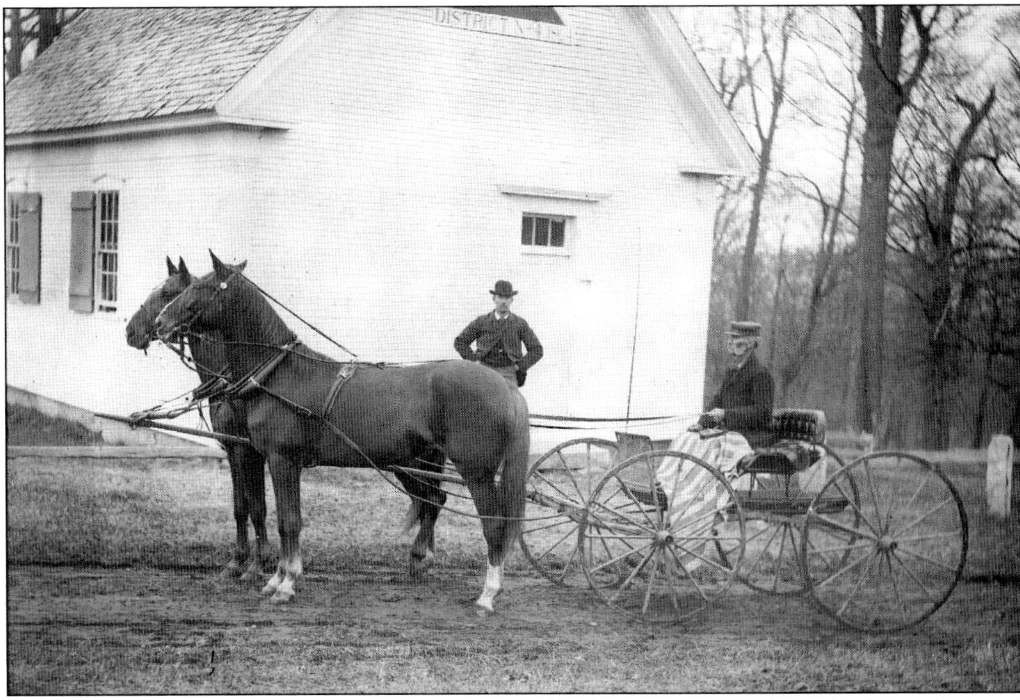

Dexter Jones is standing in front of Lynde School. The Lynde School was built in the Lynde District and was named for Cornelius Lynde, one of the first settlers in Williamstown. It was built on a tiny corner lot on Hebert Road, where the road makes a sharp 90-degree turn. The town's annual report shows the road to the Lynde School was impassible in the springtime.

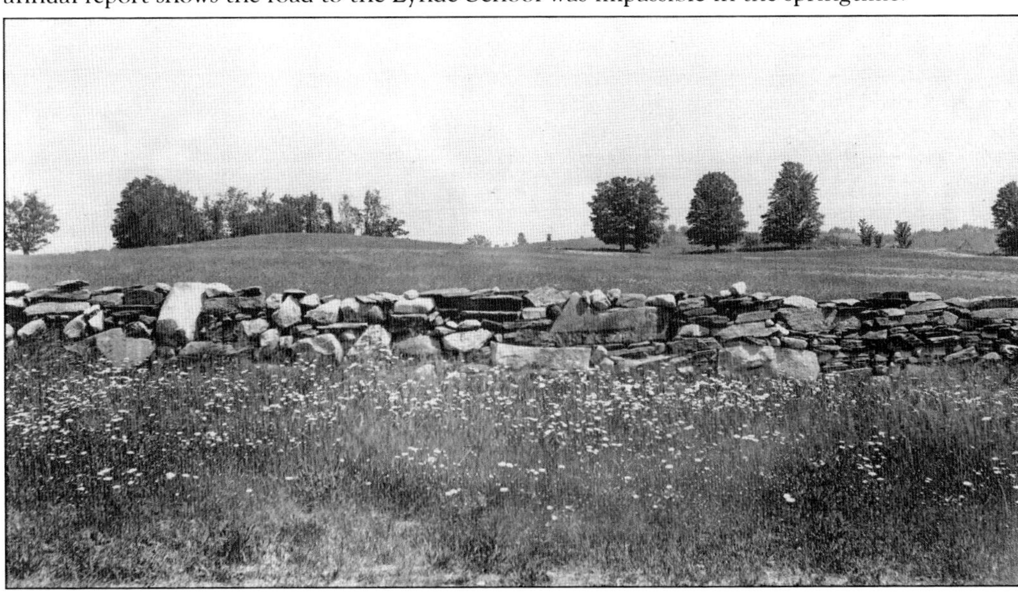

In March 1785, the men went back to get their families and returned to Williamstown. Penual, sometimes spelled Pennel, Deming (1739–1893) and Rebekah (Cheney) Deming arrived first. Taming the land involved considerable work in clearing rocky forests. The rocks were used to build stone walls that fenced in their pastures and marked their land boundaries, and also simply served as a way to dispose of the stone.

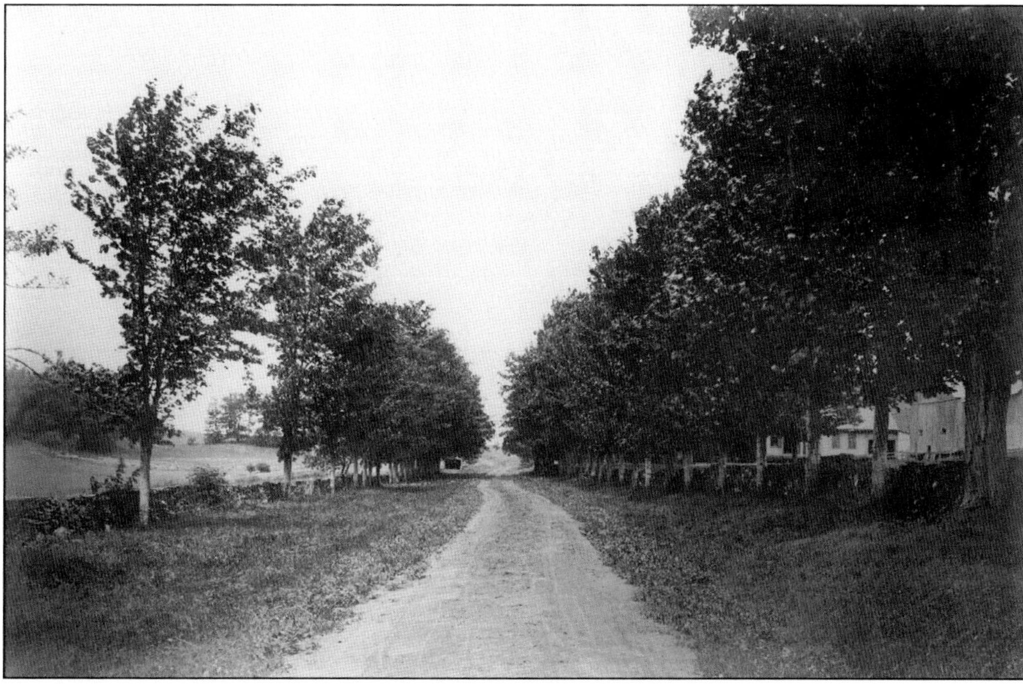

Joseph Crane (1759–1790) and Eleanor (Buck) Crane (1765–1832) arrived in Williamstown shortly after the Deming family. After moving out of their log cabin, they built the Crane Homestead, pictured here. The beautiful stone walls on both sides of this road were eventually dismantled and used for road construction. A load of hay caught fire on nearby Bear Hill, and the fire spread to the Crane property and burned the barn to the ground.

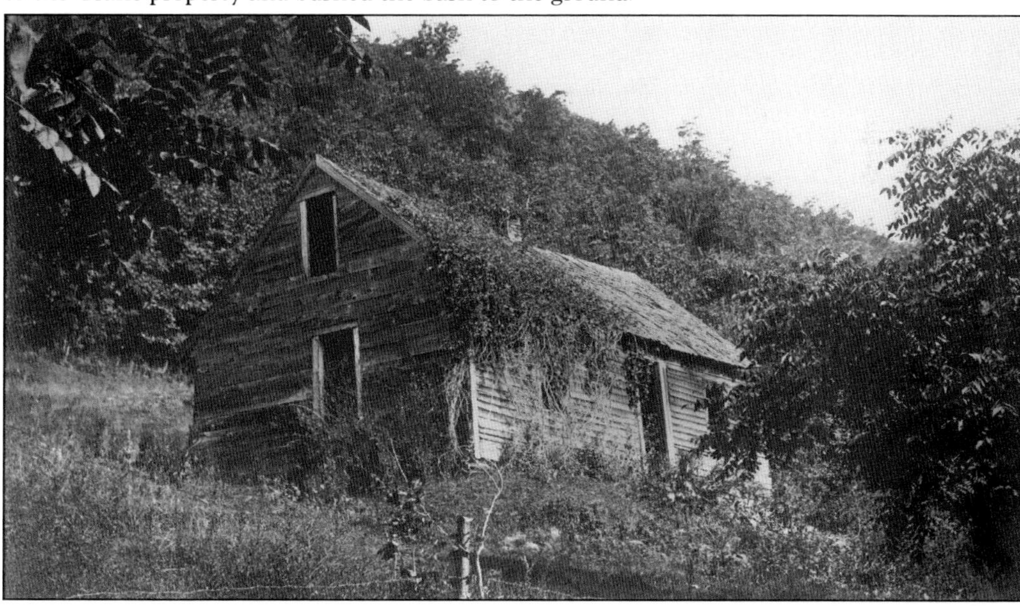

Another early settler in Williamstown was Josiah Lyman. In 1792, Lyman built the first frame house in town on the Lyman Lot. He married Eunice (Tiffany) Lyman, and they had a daughter named Apama Lyman. The first town meeting was held at the Lymans' house on September 4, 1787; the town was organized at this meeting. (Courtesy of Ruth Whitney.)

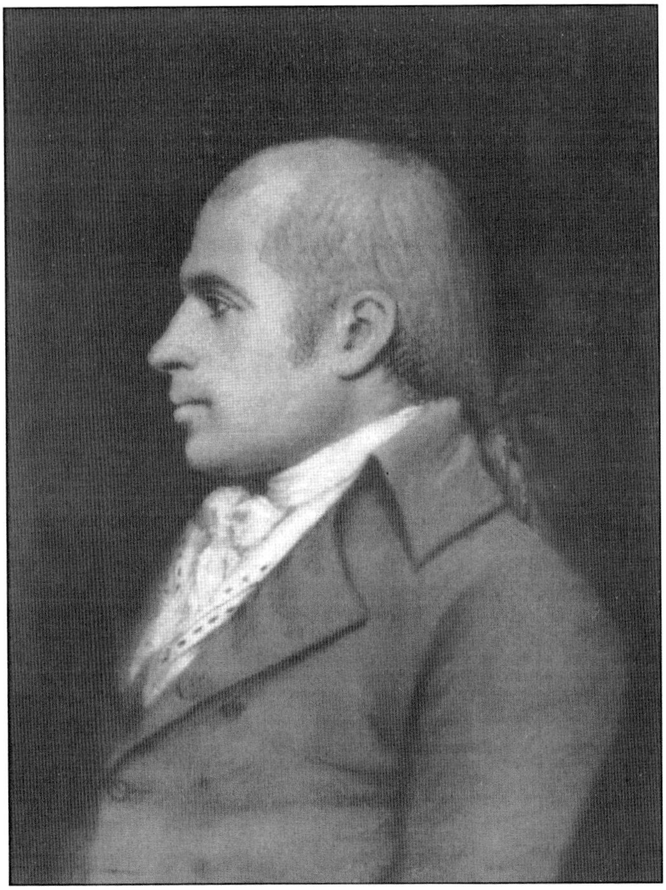

In 1781, Elijah Paine (1757–1842) began his journey from Windsor, Vermont to Williamstown. The *Gazetteer of Orange County* reports that he brought the first table to town in front of him on horseback all the way from Windsor. While living in Williamstown, Paine had a number of careers, including justice of the state supreme court, US district judge, US senator, and scientific farmer.

This barnyard scene shows an old farmer with a long, white beard holding a milk bucket. Early on, single cows were brought to the farms, making just enough milk to feed their families. Difficult rocky soil, marshes and wetlands, steep terrain, and the cold winters made living and working in rural areas difficult, but to many settlers, it was seen as the good life.

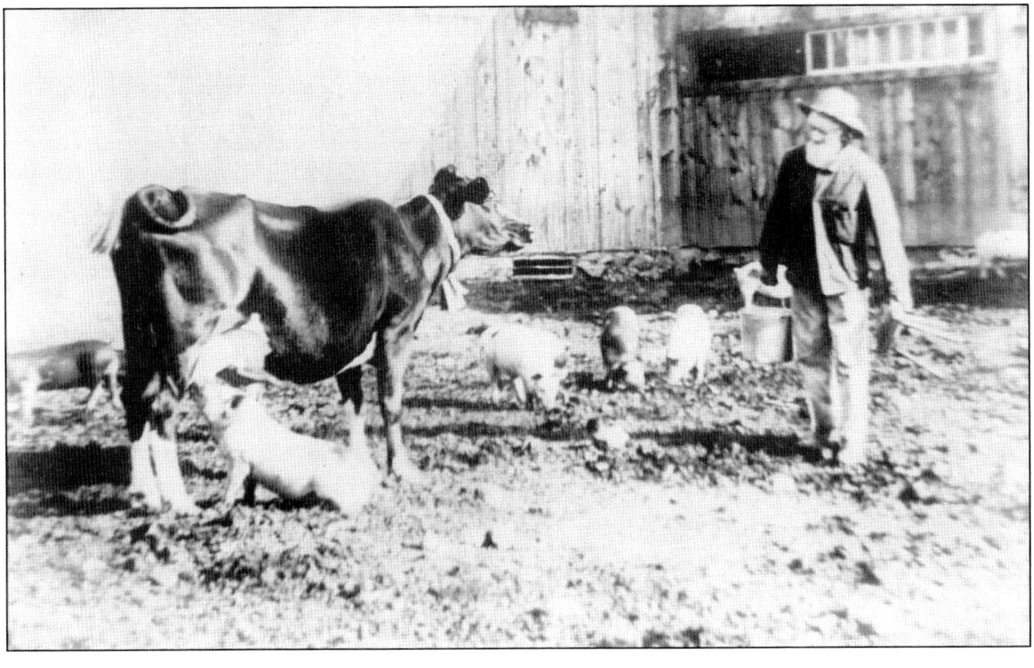

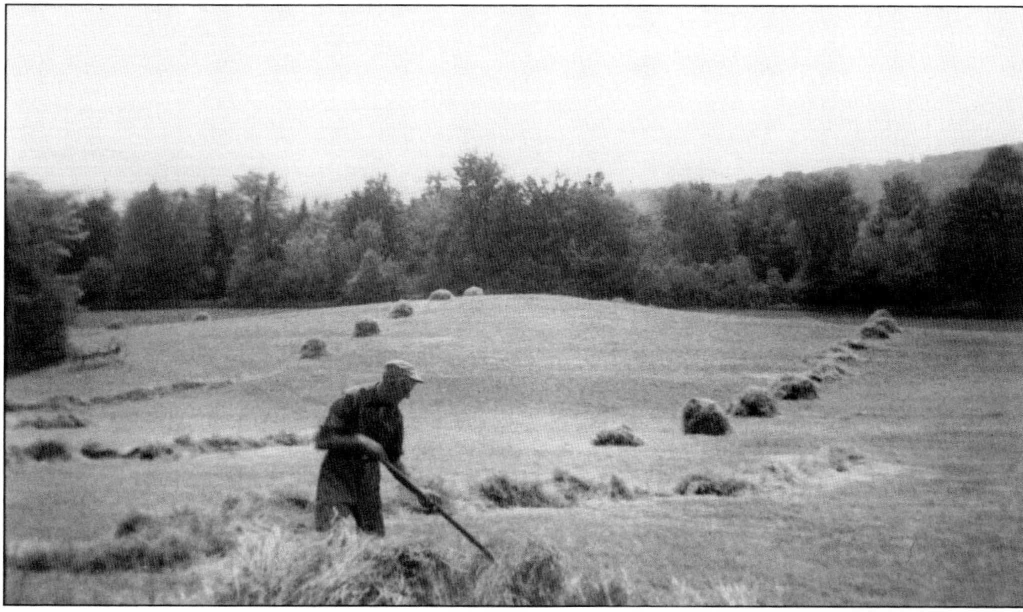

With man as the bearer of the burden, this photograph shows an unidentified farmer raking hay into stacks. Watering the animals, plowing and planting the field, chopping the wood, milking the cows, and sometimes bringing a premature calf into the kitchen for extra care, were all a part of the everyday life of a farmer.

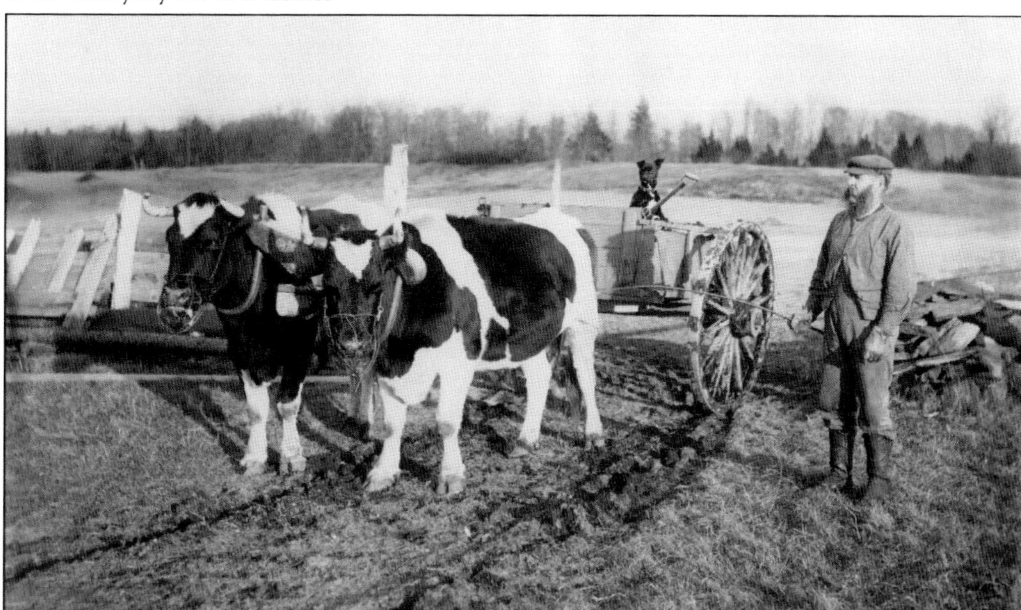

Later on, the horse, ox, goat, and dog helped bear some of the farmer's burden. This man was photographed next to his team of yoked oxen hitched to a wagon, which is partially full of chopped wood and a dog. Hiram Curtis on the Townsend-Desnoyers farm would make many trips to the forest and woodpile before the long, cold winter set in. To cut, split, and stack a cord of wood would take him a full day, and providing a family's winter heat required 20 to 30 days of labor and about 15 acres of woodland.

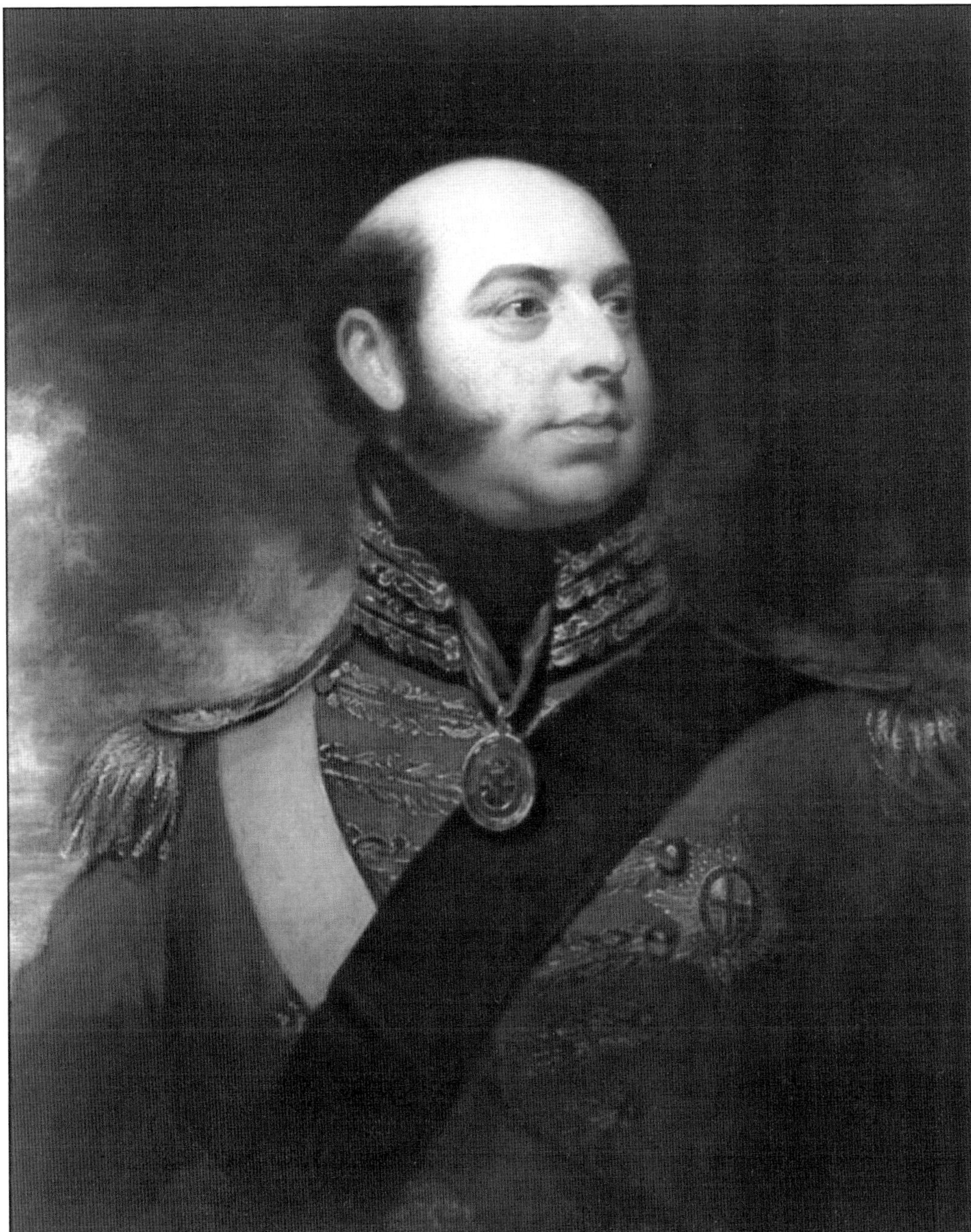

This 1818 portrait of Prince Edward is by Sir William Beechey. In *Let me Show You Vermont*, Charles Edward Crane reports that the prince visited Williamstown in the early 1790s, stopping at Judge Paine's home for dinner with his 20 armed men to serve as food tasters. On arrival, the prince secretly thought all Vermonters were savages, but upon leaving he understood Vermonters were well read and refined.

Two

Settlement Moves to the Valley

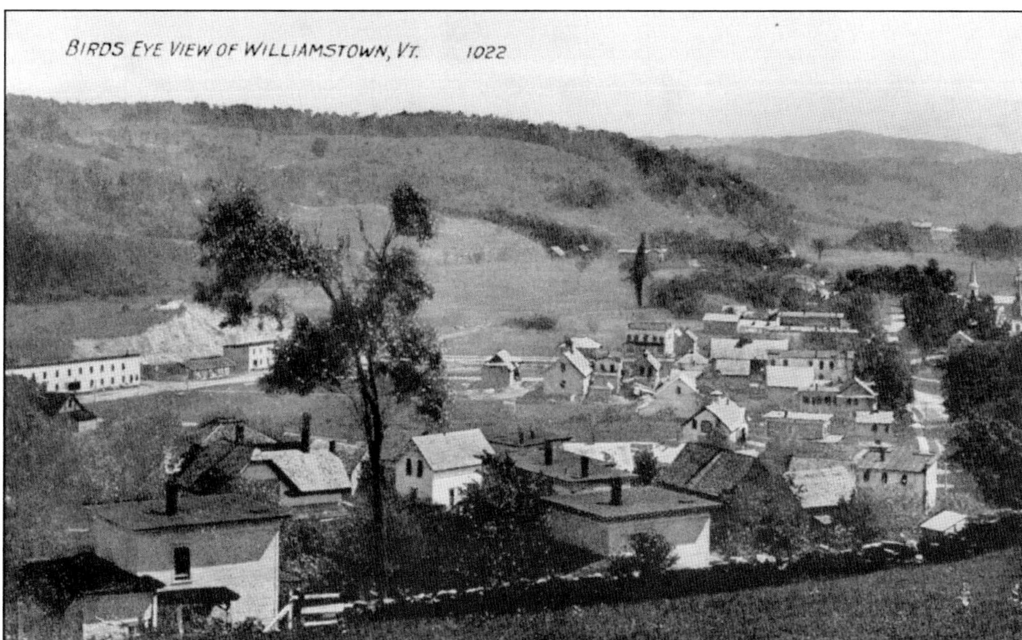

Not content with the isolation and self-sufficiency necessary for living in such a remote area, around the mid-1800s, settlers migrated from the hills to the valley. This move allowed them a better environment to develop their businesses. This bird's-eye view shows the hills in back of the valley, where the present-day village exists. (Photograph by Union Card Company; courtesy of Bertha Morgan.)

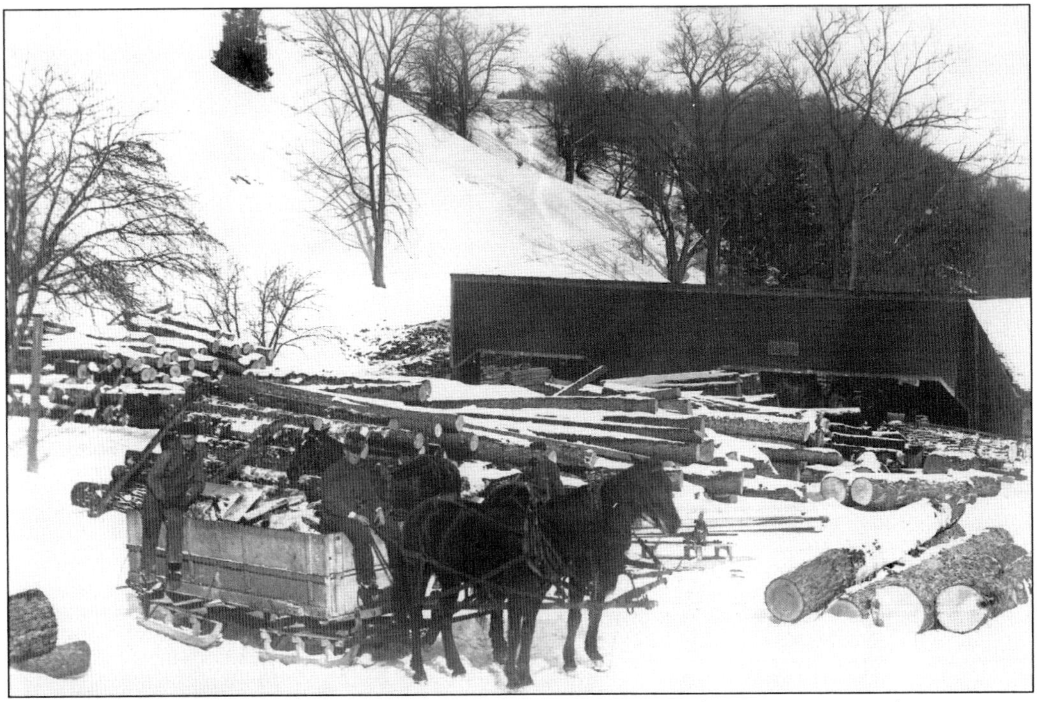

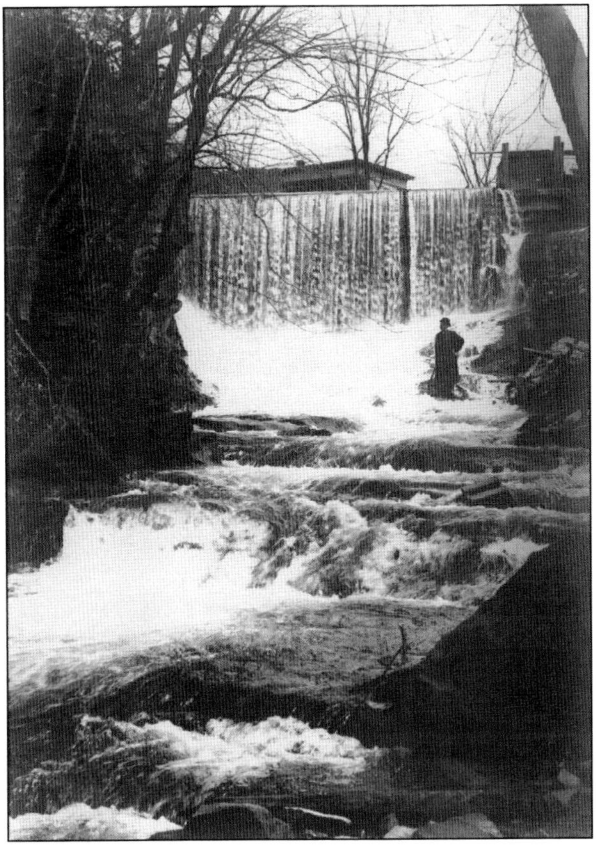

In 1785, proprietors voted to grant Elijah Paine a 100-acre lot on the condition that he build and operate a sawmill and gristmill; in 1796, Paine completed the mill, and the town prospered as a result. Before the advent of power companies, it was necessary to build an industry close to a river in order to use the waterpower via waterwheels, pulleys, and pipes to work the machinery. (Courtesy of Ruth Whitney.)

To harness the power of the water from the Stevens Branch River, a dam was built. Dam raceways carried water into the mill, and the excess was returned to the river by tailraces. The *Gazetteer of Orange County* reported that the gristmill had three grinding stones used for grinding grain (corn, wheat, and barley) for meal.

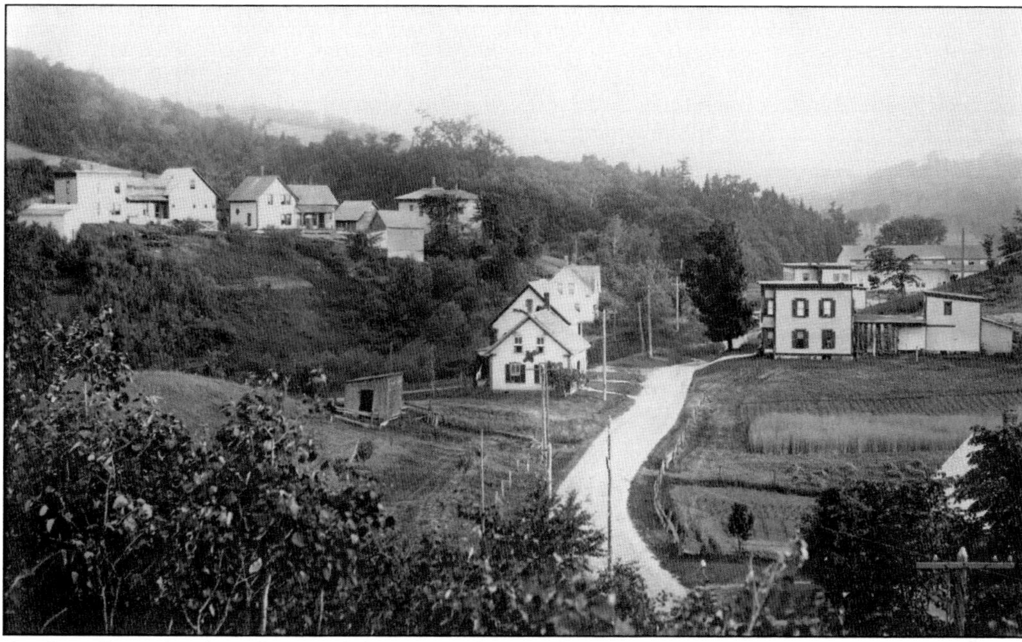

As the village developed around the water, about a dozen homes were built for the workers of the mill, and the commercial industries that relied on the river; the picture shows early Mill Village. The Nixon brothers' granite shop was also located in Mill Village. According to the *Gazetteer of Orange County*, in 1866, George Lynde and U.L. Cheney bought the gristmill and site and erected a sawmill and polishing mill. The polishing mill contained nine polishing machines. They also bought logs and sold lumber for building purposes.

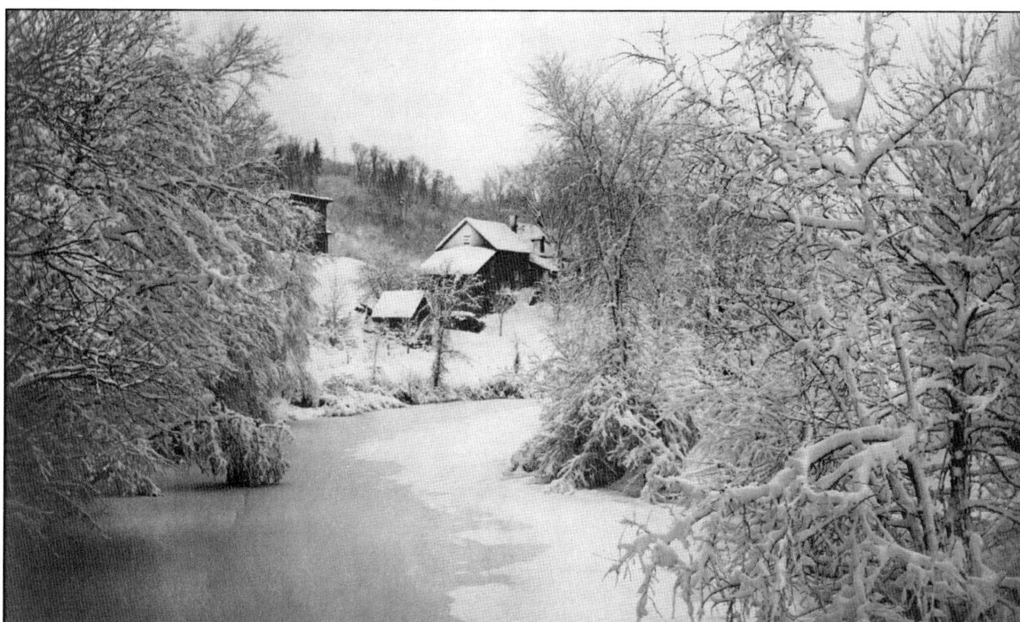

This photograph shows the millpond in the winter; this is the pond that formed after the dam was built. Both the dam and pond are gone, allowing the river to take its natural path through the village. (Courtesy of Ruth Whitney.)

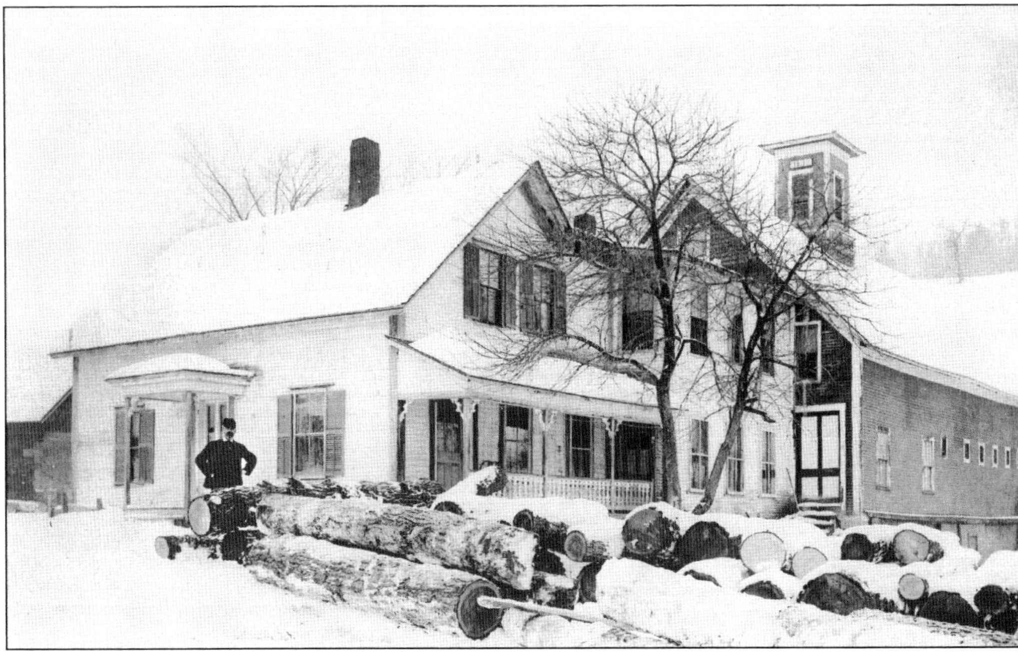

This photograph shows Dr. Reed standing in back of a stack of logs piled up at the old mill. The logs were sold for a variety of local building purposes. Large quantities of lumber were also exported across the country.

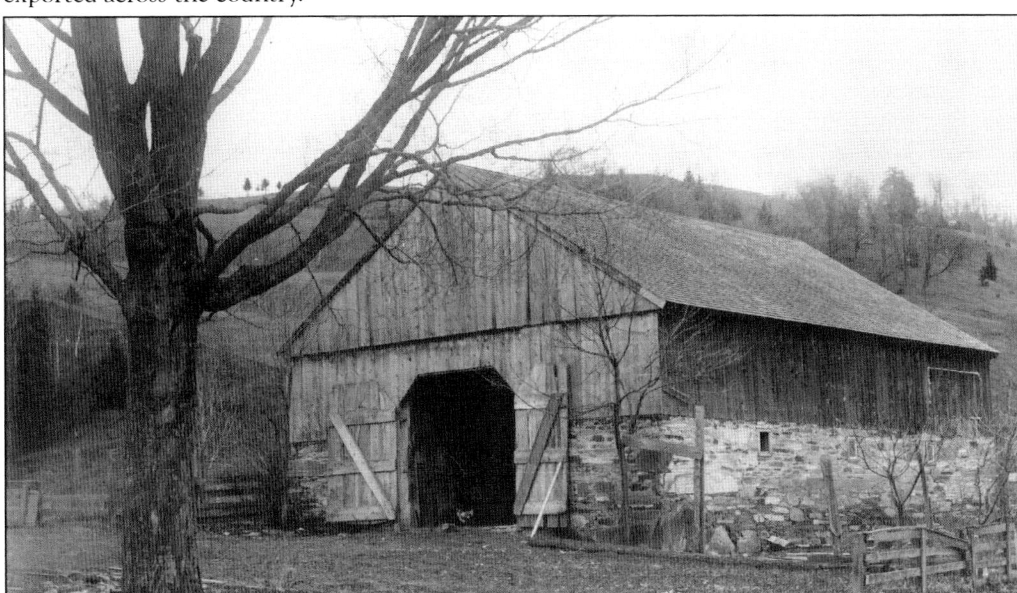

The Gen. Ebenezer Bass barn is shown here. A *Williamstown Herald* special edition reported that Judge John Chaffe, who settled on Moses Poor's farm, built the first barn. The judge promised a fun time at the barn-raising "bee." A joining of 40 neighbors showed up to help him, including 11 women and 6 babies. The women took turns babysitting, helping the men raise the barn, and dancing. They all had a grand time. Shortly after, the church reprimanded James Paul for "being tempted by the devil and wickedly playing the fiddle at a certain barn raising."

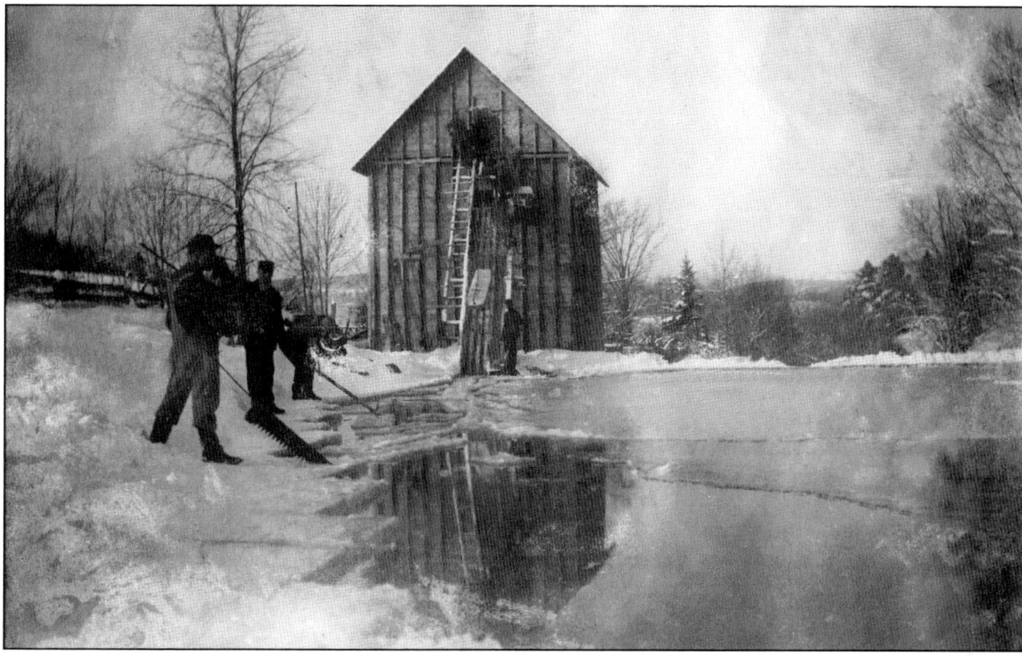

Five men are shown harvesting ice for Charlie Edson. Workers would begin by sawing ice from the lake surface into square chunks, which were then pulled from the lake with large ice tongs or poles that had sharp hooks. The ice was dragged or loaded onto horse-drawn sleds and brought to the icehouse in the background. (Courtesy of Bertha Morgan.)

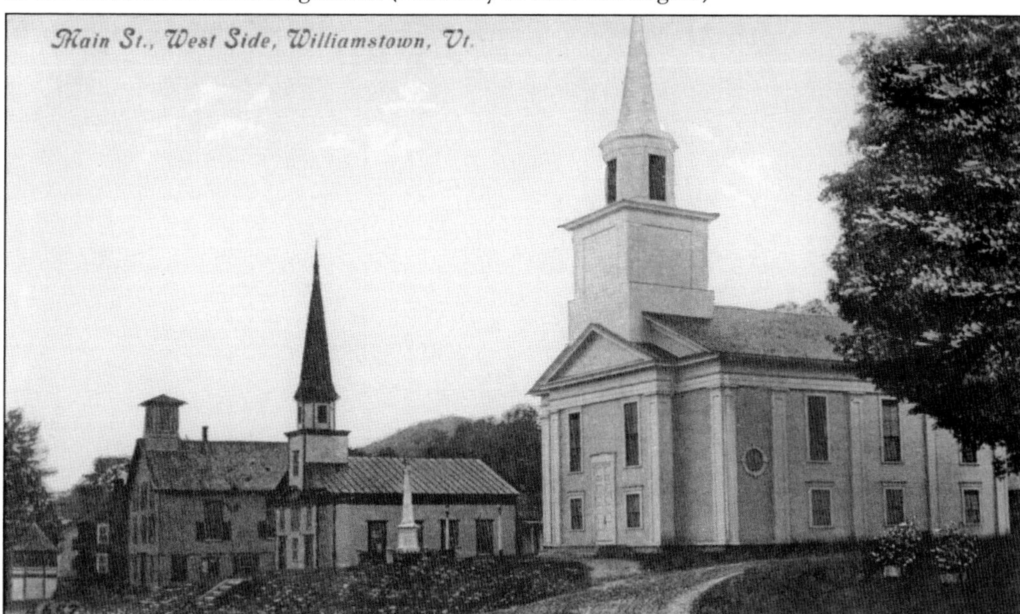

Located on Main Street, three of the village's best-known buildings are, from left to right, the Williamstown Town Hall, Universalist church, and the Congregational church. Also pictured is the marble Civil War Soldiers Monument. Elijah Lyman organized the Congregational church in 1795. It has granite stairs in front of the building with two potted flowers on the lawn. This photograph was taken in the early 1900s. (Courtesy of Bertha Morgan.)

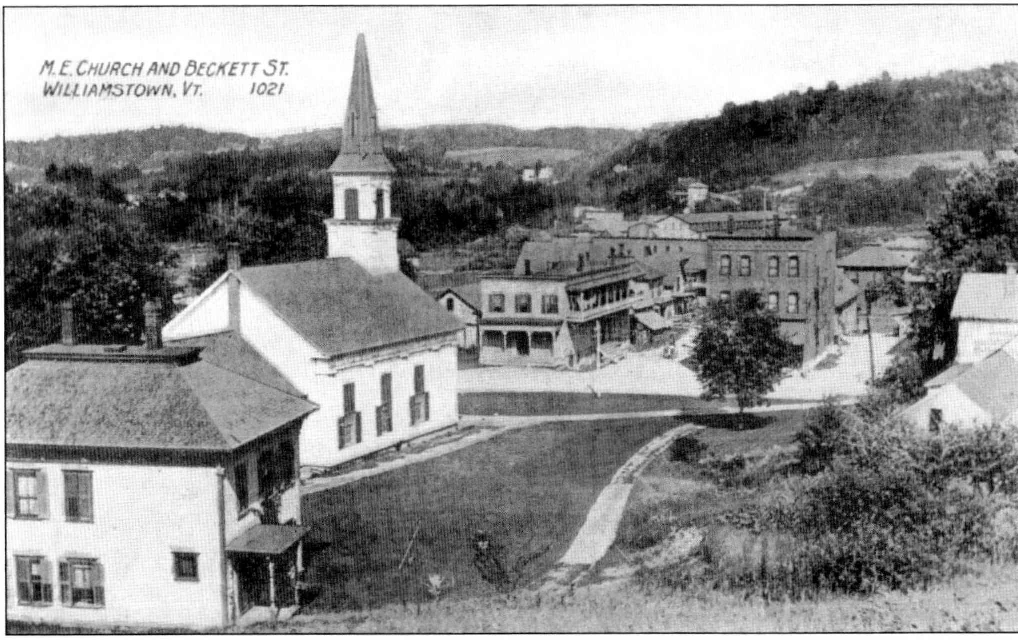

The Methodist church and Beckett Street are shown here. Zadock Thompson reported in the *Williamstown Herald's* special Williamstown edition that "in 1840 the town had three meetinghouses, one tavern, two stores, one tannery, several gristmills, a mechanics shop, and about 35 dwellings. There were also 17 school districts and eight sawmills." (Photograph by Union Card Company.)

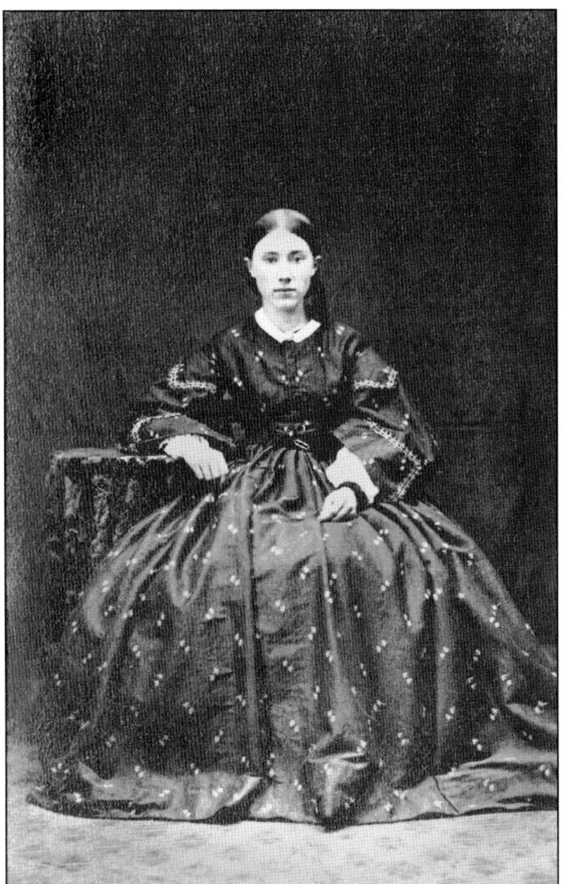

Cultural and social aspects of the early settlers' lives improved with their migration to the valley. Fashions also changed; for example, Laura Davis Lynde (1845–1897) is shown here wearing an informal entertaining dress characterized by beautiful material, full-gathered skirts, and sleeves. (Courtesy of Fanny Martin Stewart.)

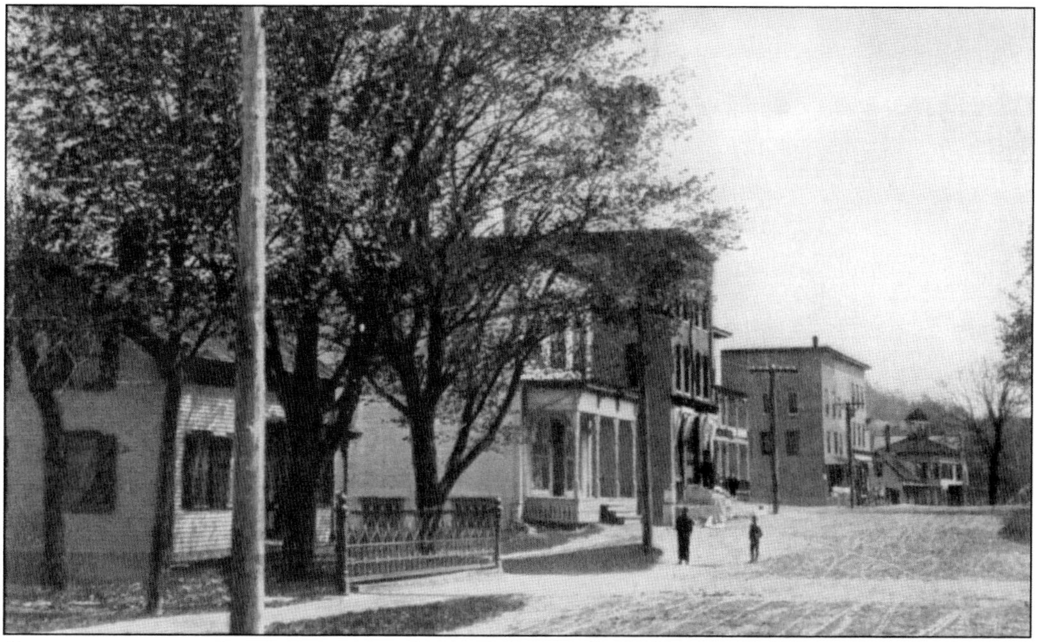

On a warm, sunny day, two men watch a woman in a long flowing pink dress as she makes her way up the stairs. Dresses with trains were fashionable during the Victorian era (the mid-1800s to early 1900s). This south view shows the wide dirt road of Main Street in the village. Note the wrought-iron fence used as side rails over the culvert of the Stevens Branch River. (Courtesy of Bertha Morgan.)

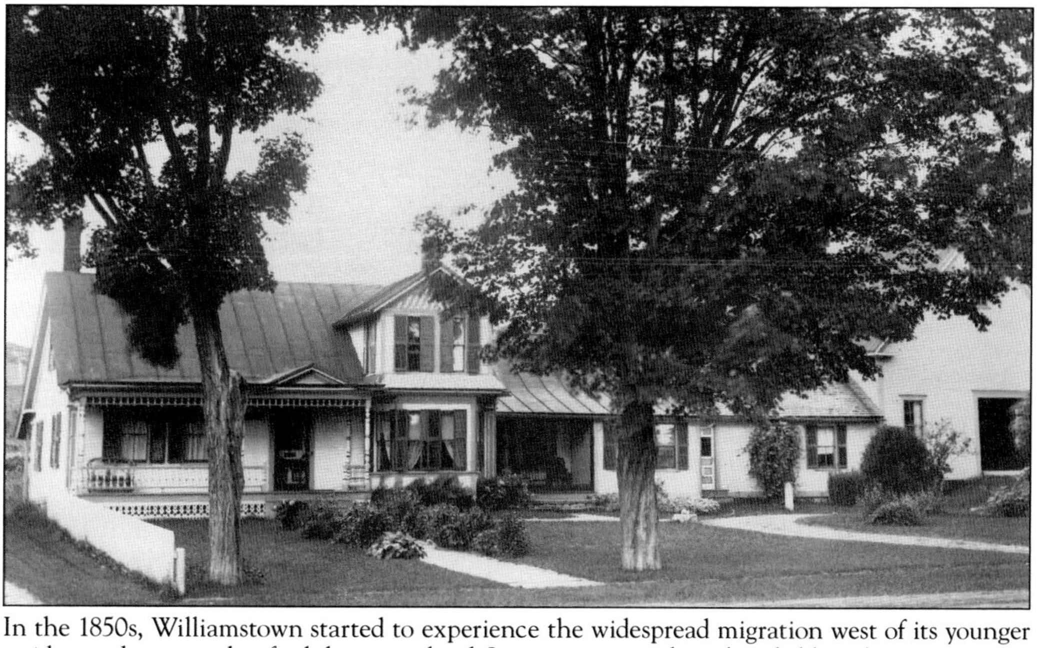

In the 1850s, Williamstown started to experience the widespread migration west of its younger residents who wanted to find their own land. In an attempt to keep his children from pioneering west, Perley Howe, one of the first settlers who came here in 1790, built each of his children a house in Williamstown. This photograph shows the house of his daughter Anna, who married Samuel Abbott. (Courtesy of Ruth Whitney.)

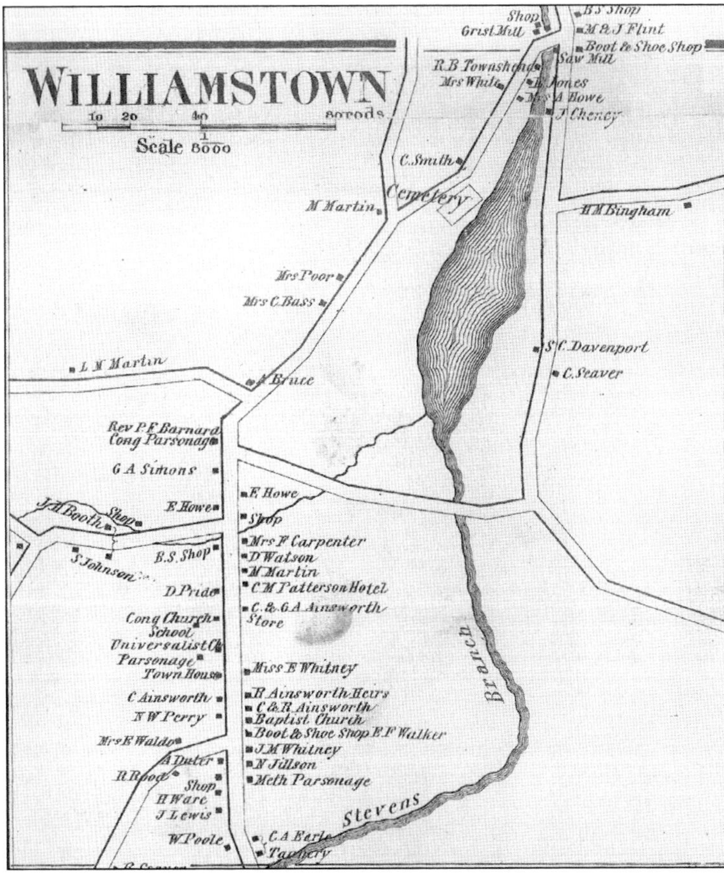

This 1858 F.W. Beers map shows the population of the village spreading along the Stevens Branch River. Mill Village was located north of the cemetery, where there is a dot showing the sawmill at the spot where the two roads merge into one.

The *Gazetteer of Orange County* summed up the village in 1886 as having "three churches, a blacksmith shop, three wheelwright shops, and about 35 dwellings." This photograph shows the first blacksmith shop in town, built by Burton Bruce. Later on, Joe Gregory sold it to Frank Hopkins. (Courtesy of Bertha Morgan.)

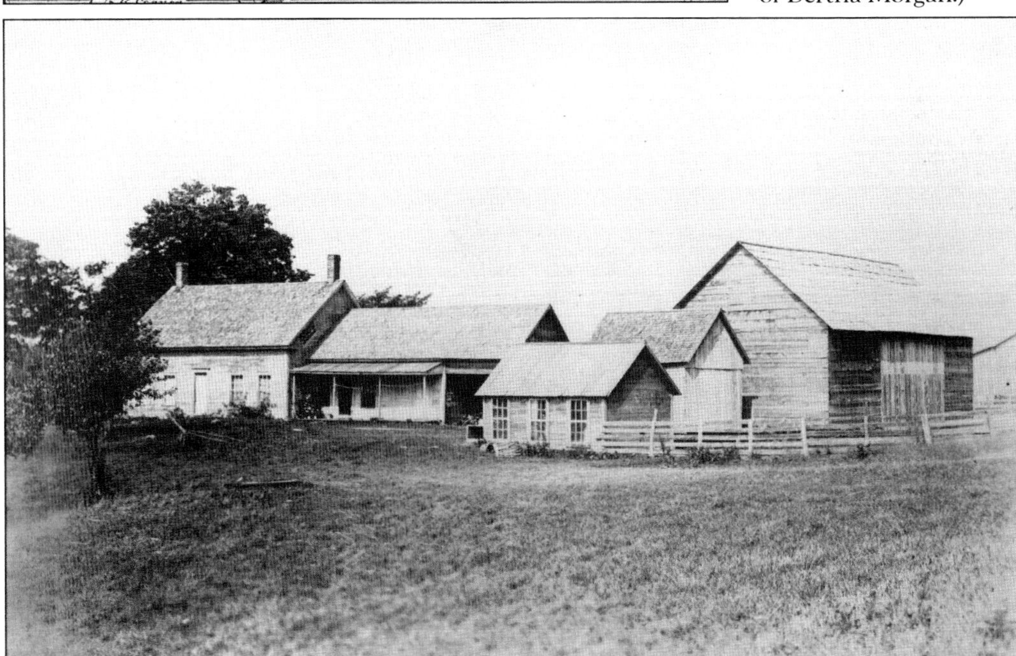

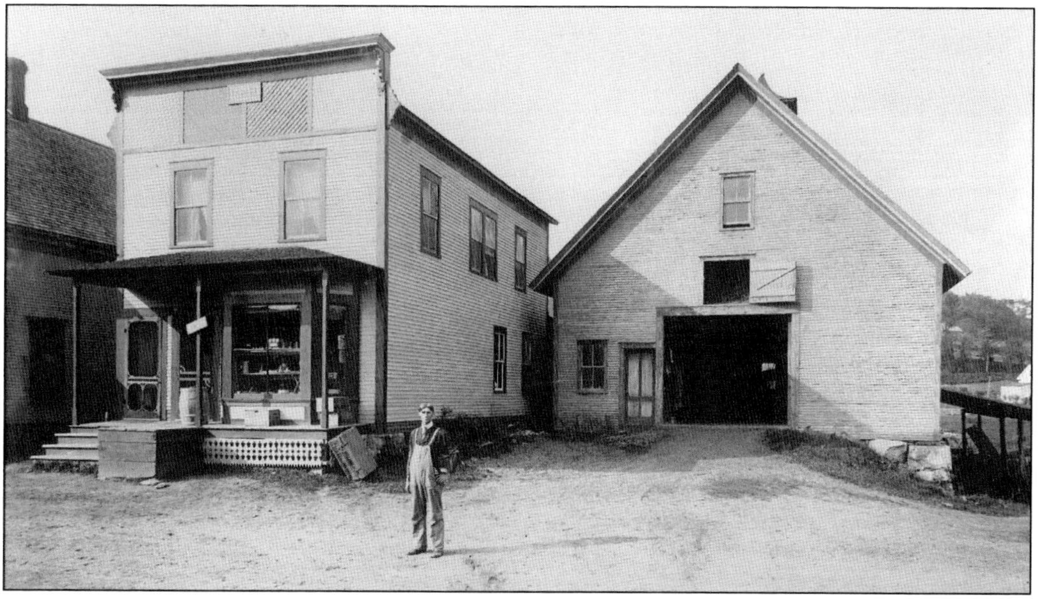

On September 8, 1921, about 11:00 p.m., a fire started in the barn at right and spread to the Texton and Brockway store in the village. Both burned to the ground, along with the meat market and a few other buildings. (Courtesy of Ruth Whitney.)

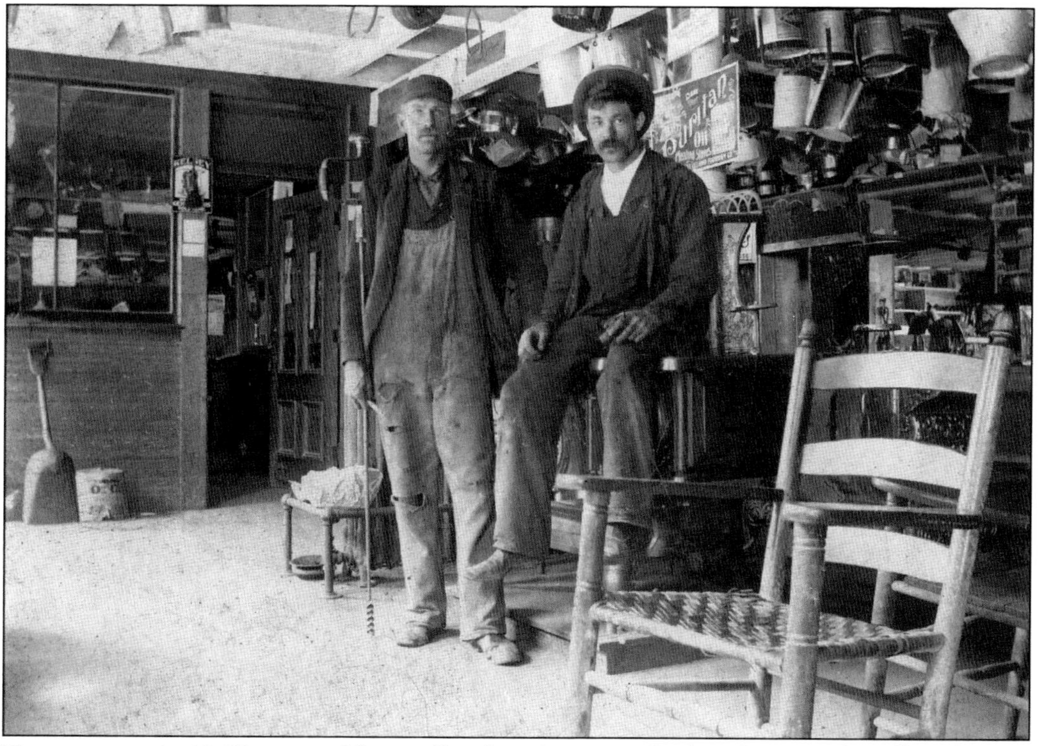

Two men pose inside Texton and Jerome Brockway's store on Beckett Street in the village, behind the old general store. The general store sold dry goods, household items, farming equipment, and food items that residents could not produce themselves. The store was also a popular meeting place for socializing and gathering the local news. (Courtesy of Bertha Morgan.)

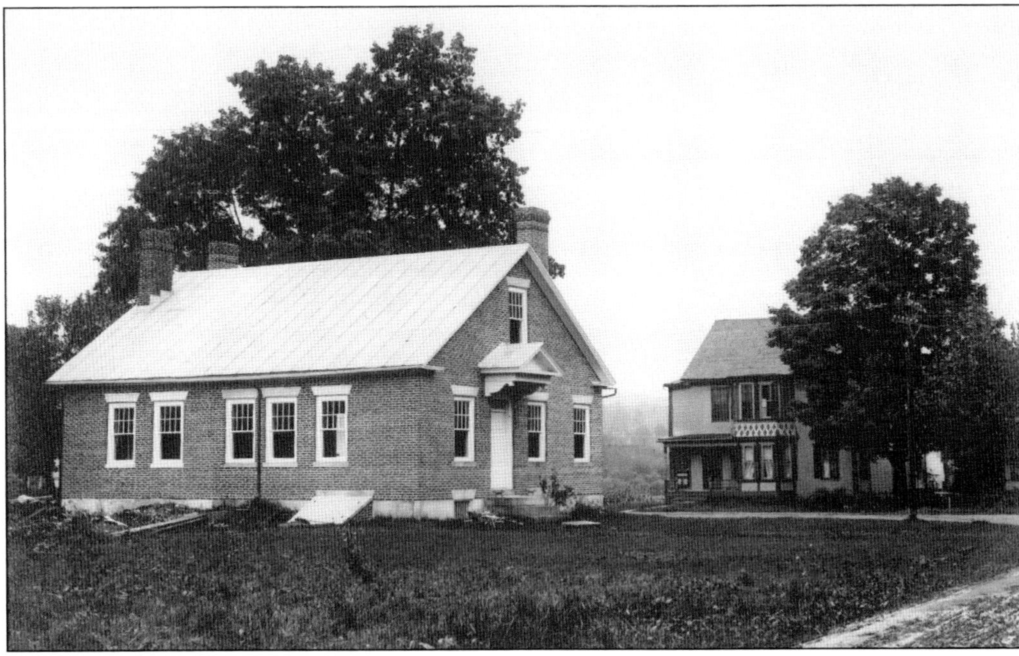

In 1833, Enoch Howe, a blacksmith and prominent citizen, built this redbrick home located in the village on Route 14. His second daughter, Abby (Howe) Pierce, and her son Albert lived with the Howe family for many years. Albert Pierce was one of the town's famous "baseball nine." (Courtesy of Bertha Morgan.)

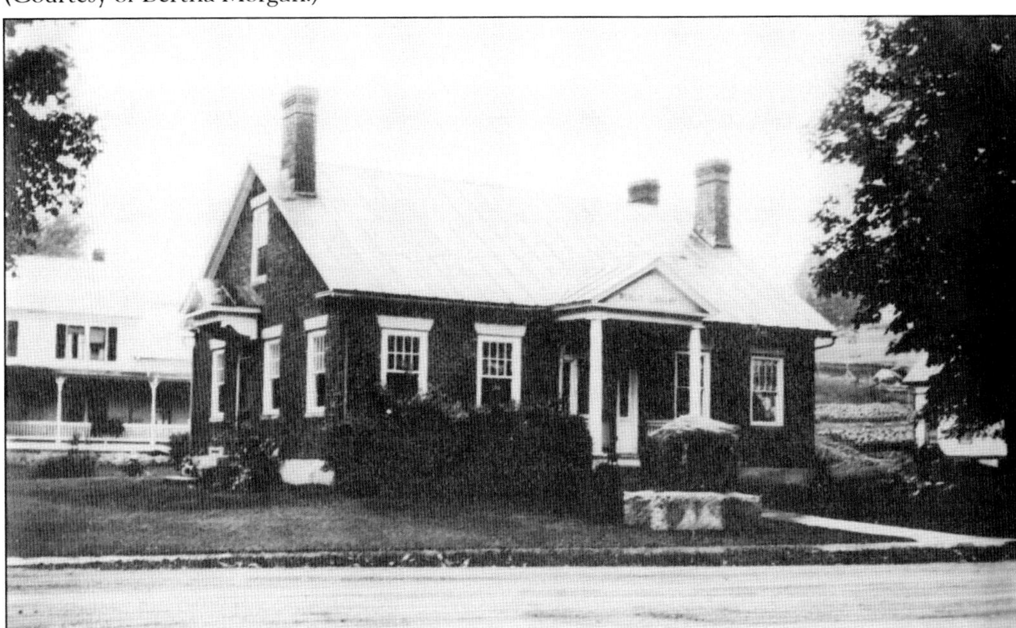

Known for her love of books, Laura Lucretia Ainsworth purchased the Enoch Howe residence and then donated it to the town to function as a free public library. In her honor, it was named the Ainsworth Library. A granite plaque was placed on the front lawn in 1983 to indicate that the building was originally built by Enoch Howe. (Courtesy of Bertha Morgan.)

Laura Lucretia (1836–1925) married James Edward Ainsworth on December 19, 1867. They had no children. Laura was a respected and important community leader who contributed much to the advancement of society in Williamstown. (Photograph by Rasmussens's Portraits; courtesy of Bertha Morgan.)

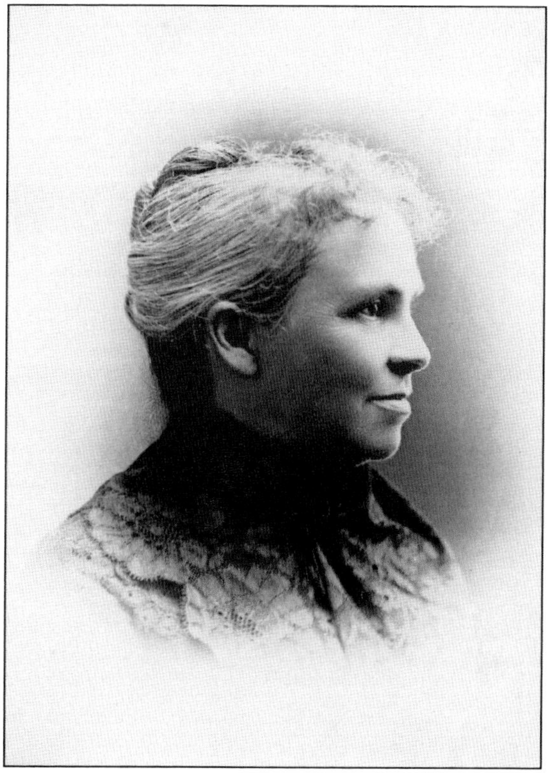

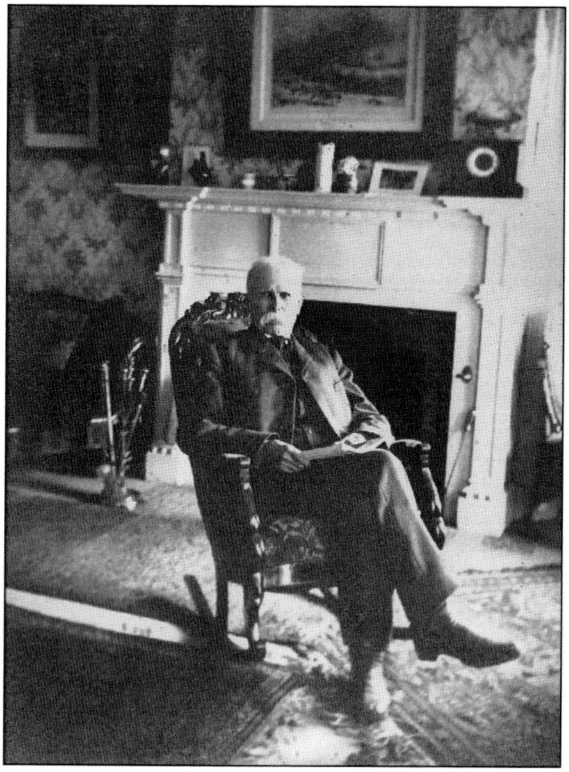

Shown here is James Edward Ainsworth (1831–1909) sitting in the parlor of his home. In times of early settlement, families owned few books. At one point, the books were gathered together and circulated among the settlers; these were often called parlor libraries. (Courtesy of Bertha Morgan.)

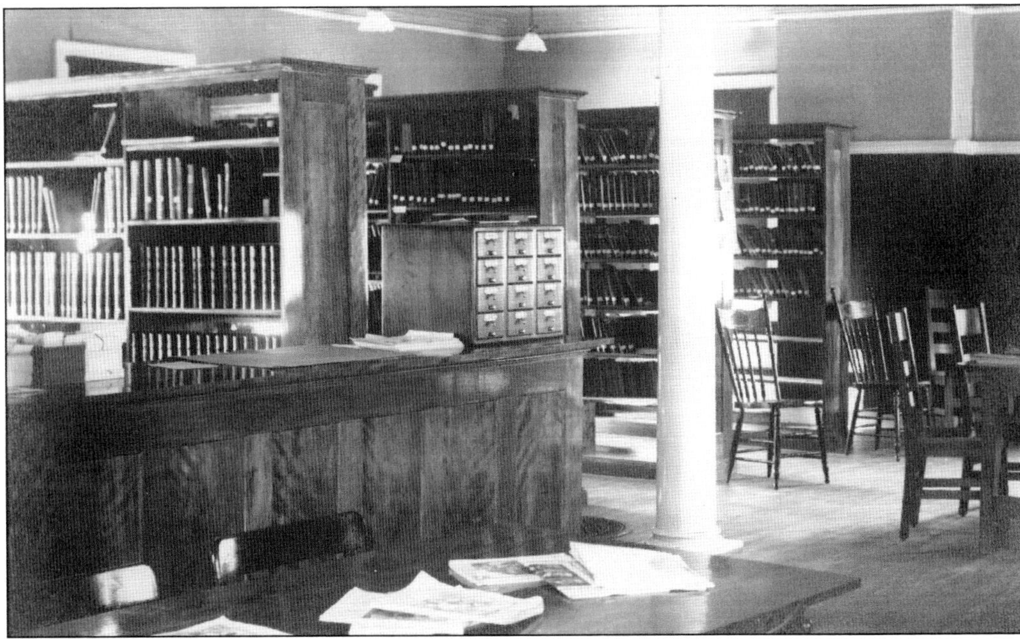

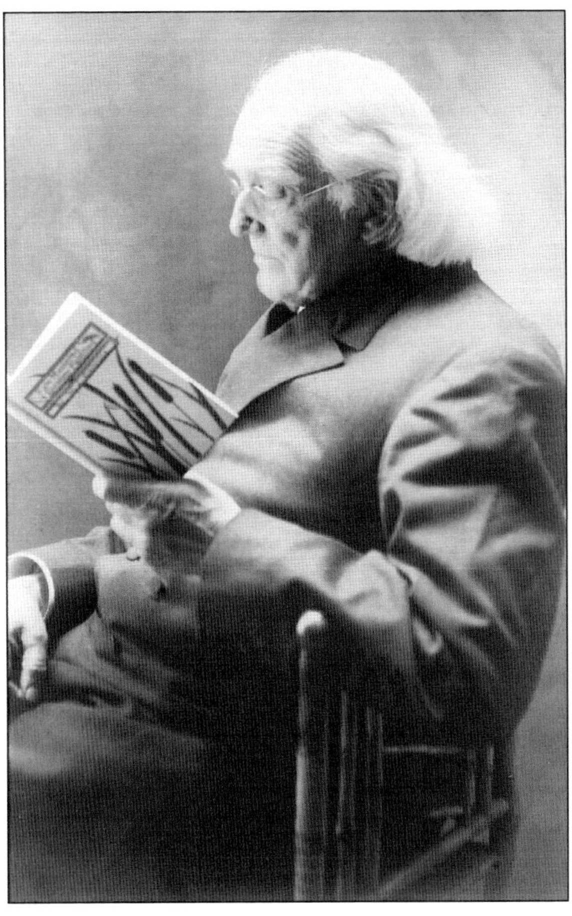

Books fill the shelves of the Ainsworth Public Library. On August 27, 1930, the *Barre Daily Times* reported that a valuable book was presented to the library, titled *George Martin of Salisbury, Mass, and His Descendants*, by Elliot Burnham Watson and Rev. Alven Martyn Smith, both natives of Williamstown. (Courtesy of Bertha Morgan.)

During the long winter months, a favorite pastime was reading books. In the summer, residents got up with the sun, worked a full 10 hours, and read books until sundown. (Courtesy of Bertha Morgan.)

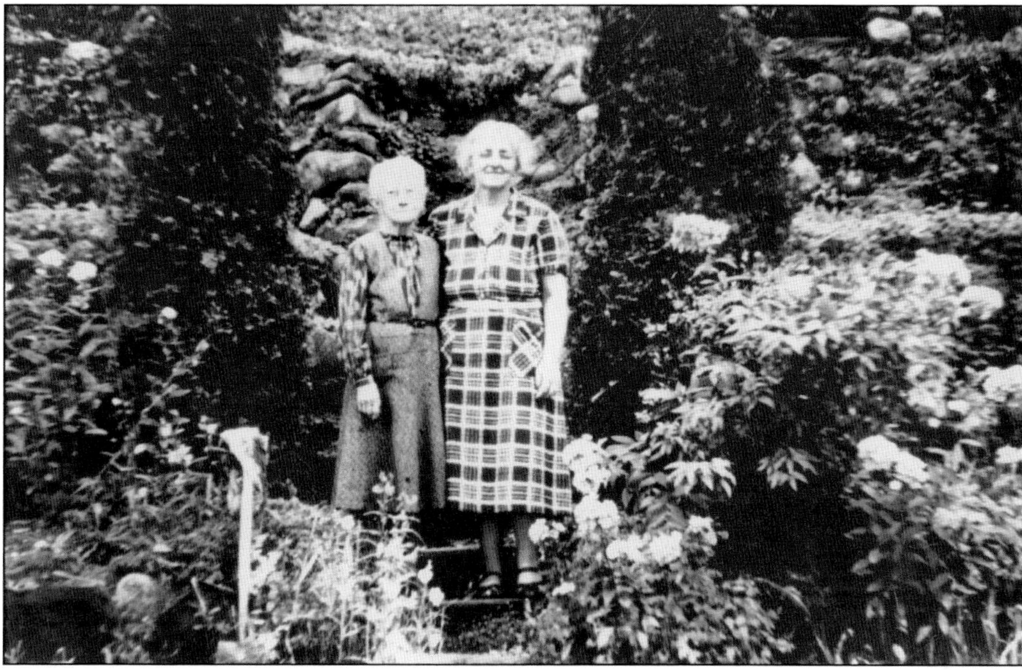

In the summer, people moved outdoors to enjoy the natural beauty, and some even made their natural surroundings more beautiful. The Robinsons put their heart and soul into landscaping their elaborate gardens. This photograph shows Belle (left) and Mattie Robinson. Note the flowers along these stairs in back of their house. (Courtesy of Rob Hepburn.)

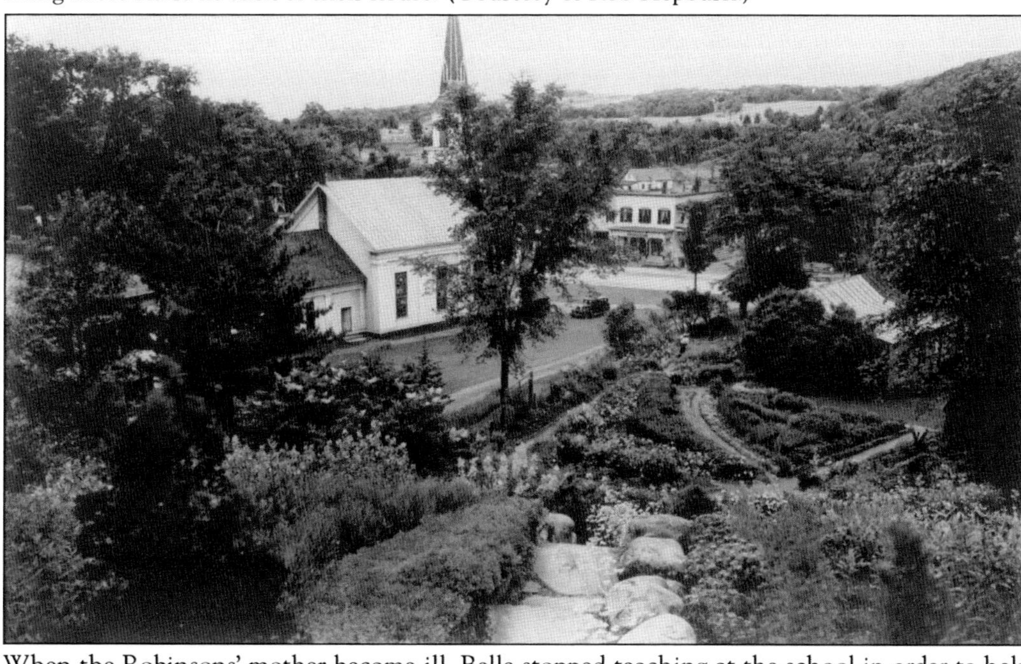

When the Robinsons' mother became ill, Belle stopped teaching at the school in order to help and ended up turning the gardens into a very profitable business. The Robinson girls also made and sold fine wool braided rugs. Their brother Burt had a tin shop in a shed attached to the house. (Photograph by E.T. Houston; courtesy of Ruth Whitney.)

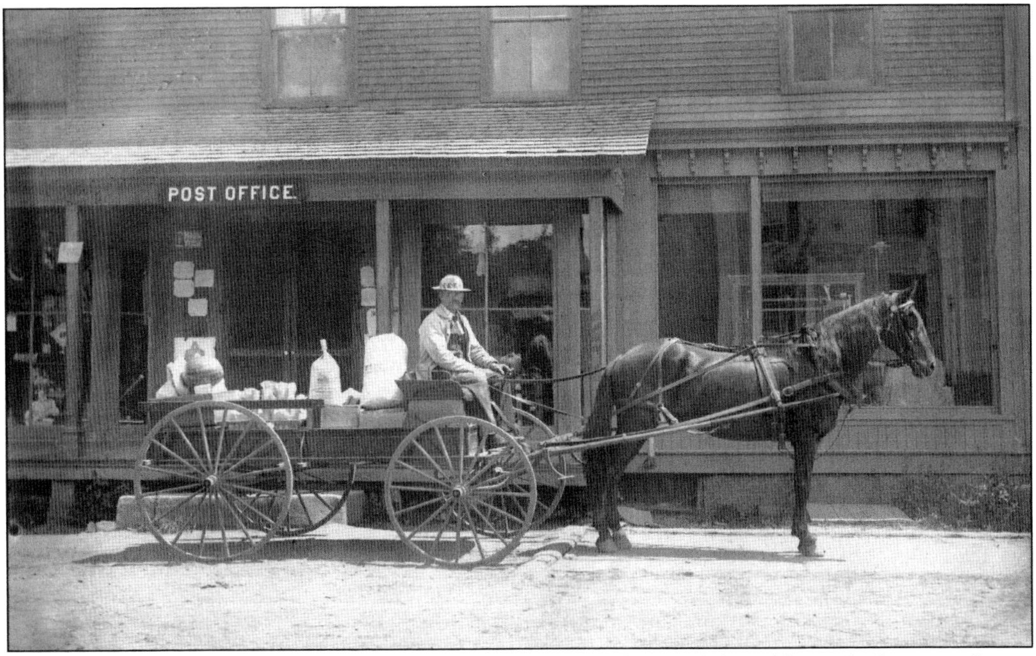

In 1900, Harvey Cheney is ready to deliver groceries in front of the old Lynde Store and post office. The store was torn down in the early 1930s.

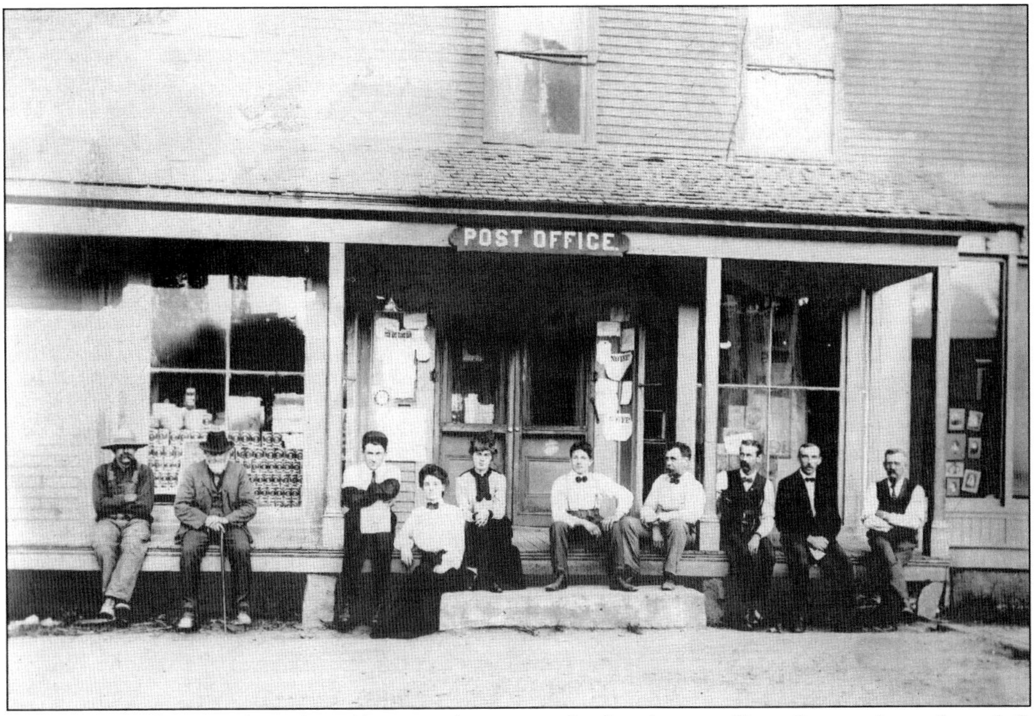

A favorite gathering place for village residents was the local post office. Pictured are, from left to right, M. Staples, Liberty Jeffords, Lester O. Morgan, Sadie McKee, Bertha L. Seaver, Frank Downs, Sherman Winchester, Henry Pole, George Edson (owner), and Harvey Cheney. (Courtesy of Bertha Morgan.)

Fern Angus Recor (1891) worked in the Williamstown Post Office for George Wilber. In 1912, she married Harry M. Lasell; they had seven children. The post office was a busy place to work, and time was of the essence; note the two windup clocks on the back shelf.

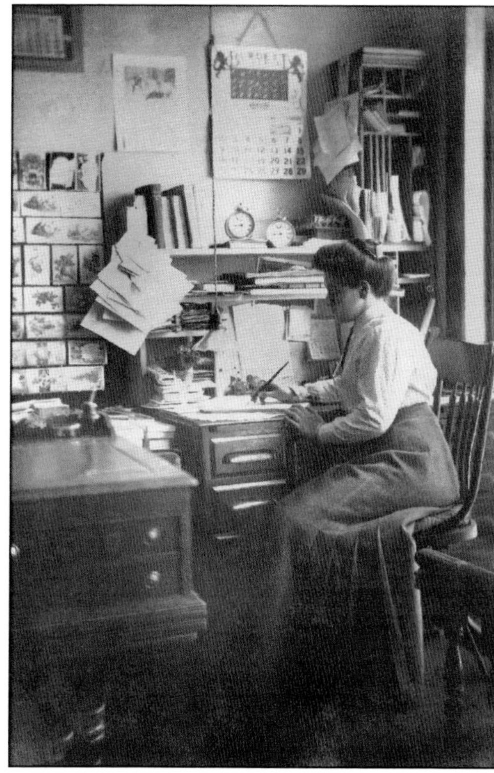

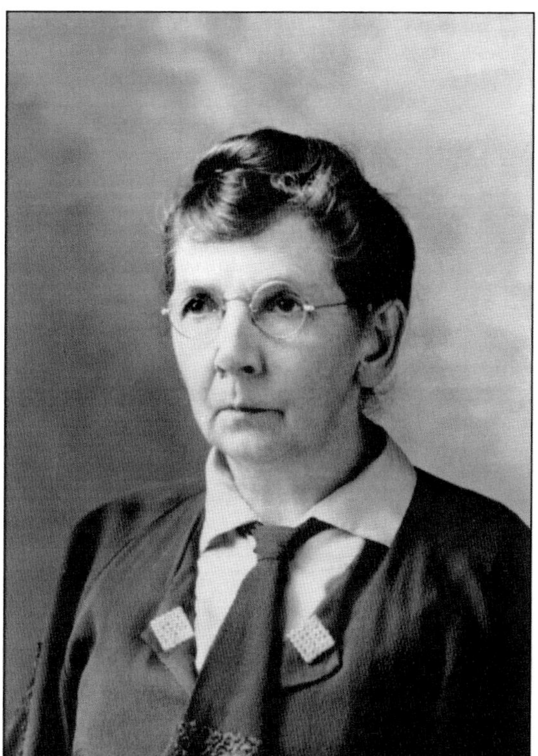

Belle H. Covell was a teacher, church officer, and post office worker. She worked in the post office for 20 years, of which she was postmistress 13 years. Spare clerks Evelyn M. Covell and Gertrude Jeffords also assisted in the work of the post office. In 1937, Belle Covell was the first representative from Williamstown to serve in the Vermont legislature. (Courtesy of Evelyn M. Covell.)

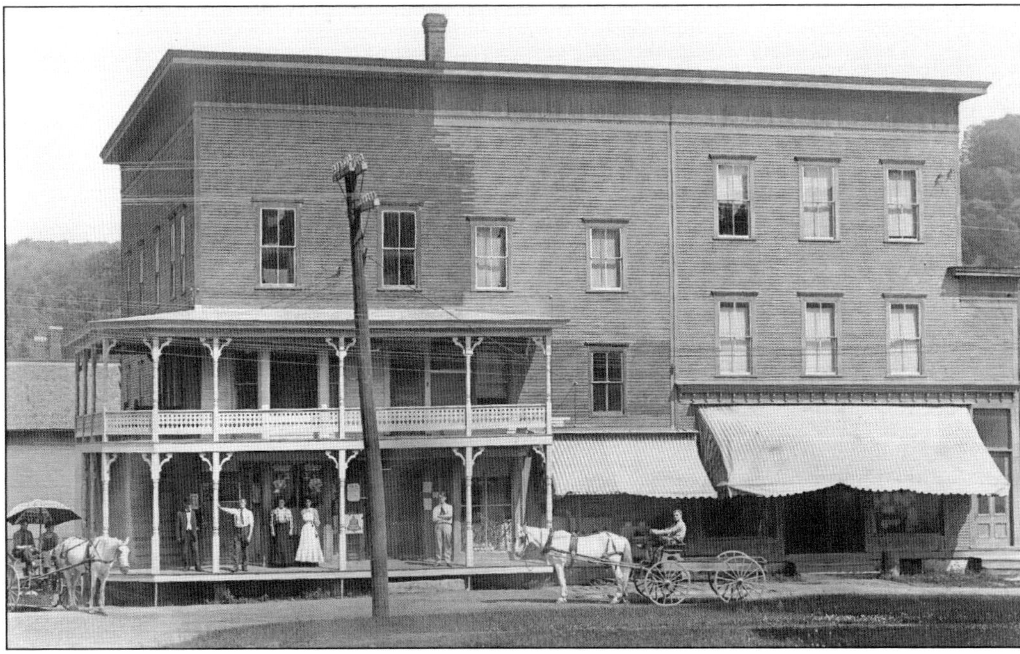

The building shown here, located in the historic district of Main Street, is the Ainsworth Store. It has had an active history. The Ainsworth Store later became the James K. Lynde Store. In 1992, it was the site of Stein's Filling Station, and it became the Depot and Main Citgo station in 2002.

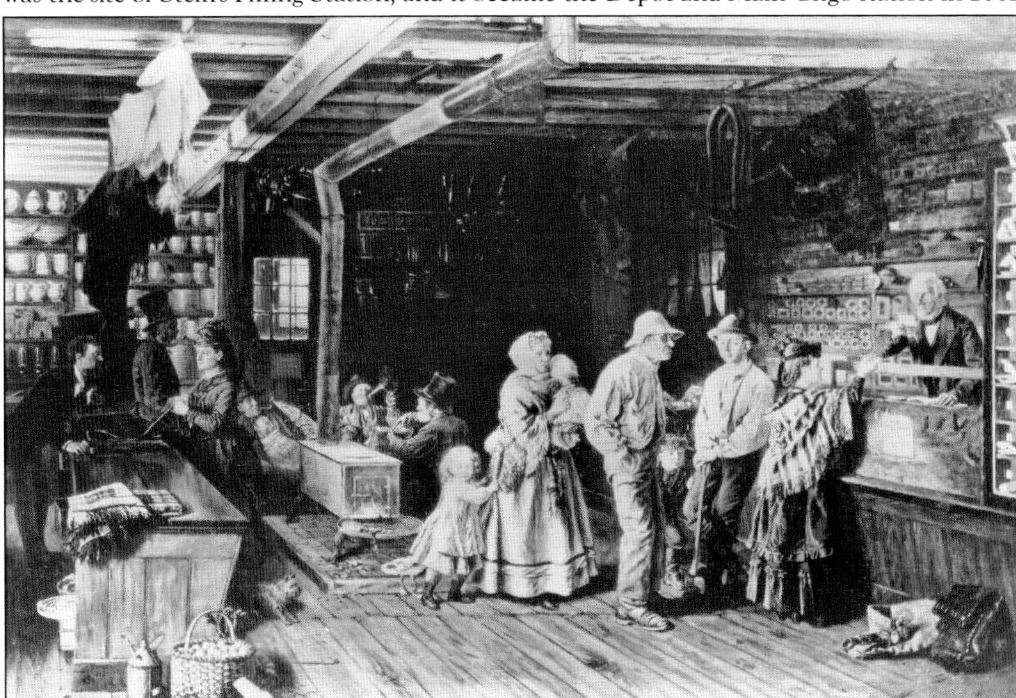

This mid-1800s drawing by Thomas Waterman Wood of Montpelier shows the interior of the Ainsworth Store. Note the little dog on the floor and the men playing cards and smoking around the potbelly stove in the background. (Courtesy of Bertha Morgan.)

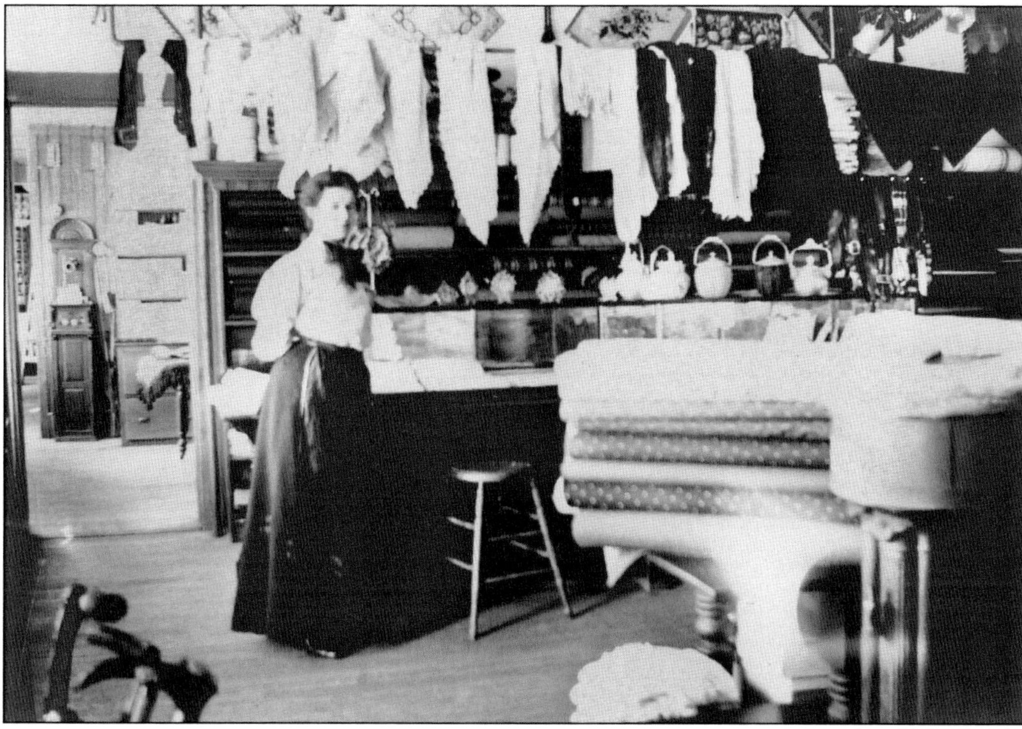

Pictured here in 1900 is the inside of the dry goods department store of J.K. Lynde, where Mrs. Glenn McAllister is the clerk on duty. Note the bolts of cloth, teapots, and the variety of clothing displayed above her. (Courtesy of Bertha Morgan.)

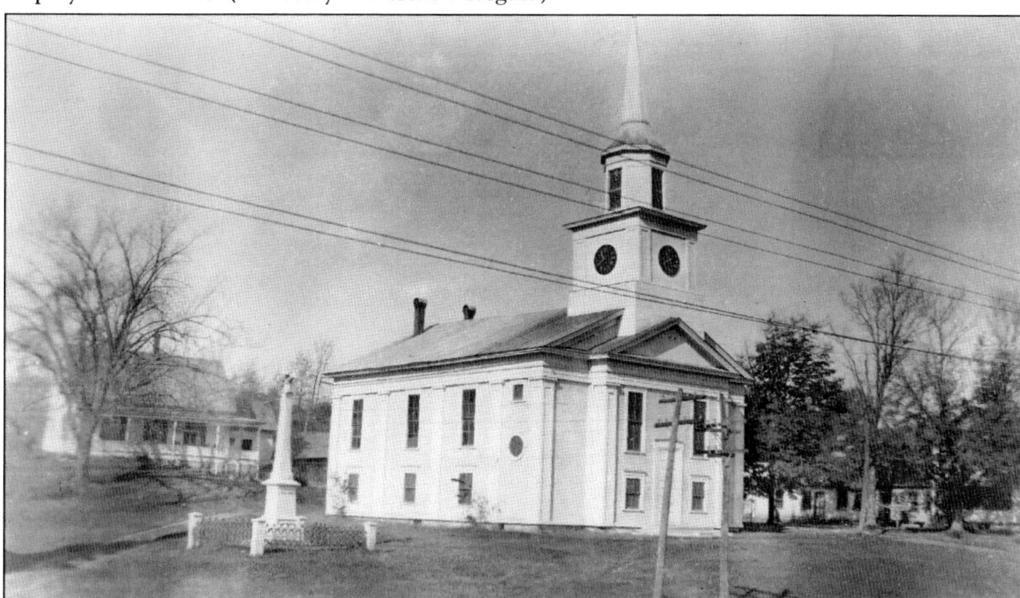

In 1869, the Civil War Soldiers Monument was erected on the south lawn of the Congregational church. It is topped by an eagle with outspread wings and surrounded by a cast-iron fence with granite corner posts. The 25-foot-tall white marble monument with a granite base was erected in remembrance of Williamstown's heroes who lost their lives. (Courtesy of Ruth Whitney.)

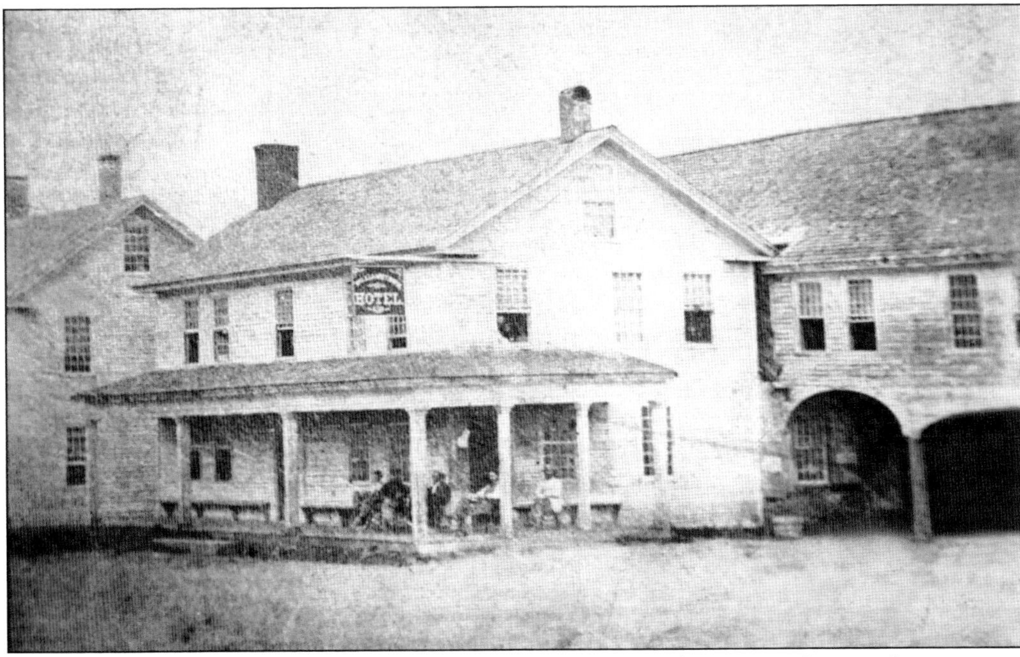

On the site of what was known as the old Hibbard house, David Watson, who was the proprietor for over 50 years, built the first hotel in Williamstown. It burned in 1874. According to the *Orange County Gazette*, Watson also built the first tannery in town. He married Anna Elliot and reared a family of 12 children. (Courtesy of Ruth Whitney.)

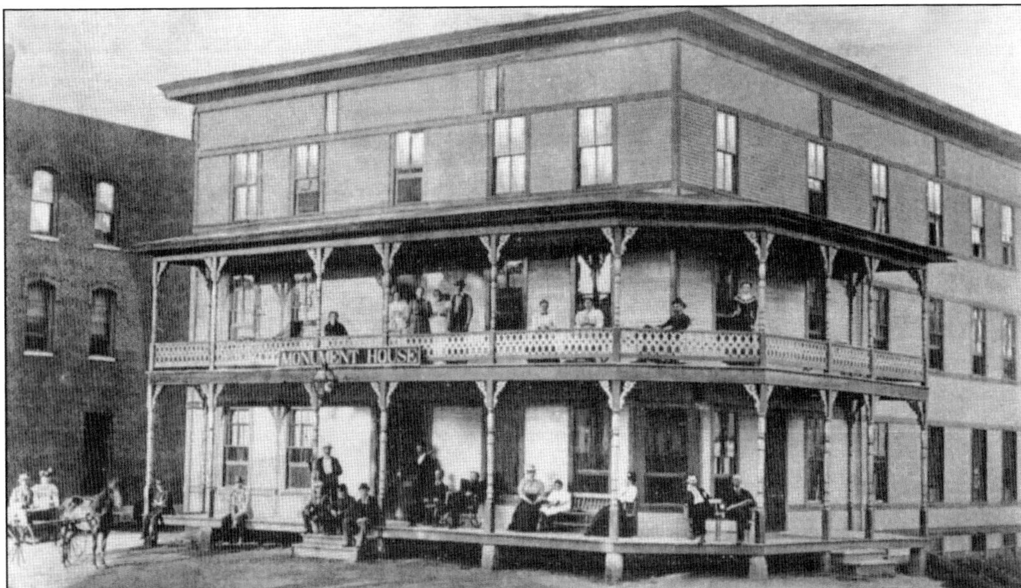

A *Williamstown Herald* special edition reported in 1892 that a kind and pleasant man named A.S. Winchester leased the Monument House of the Williamstown Granite Company. The reverse of this Monument House postcard shows C.H. Corliss was the proprietor. The Monument House offered guest rooms for the weary traveler and tourists for $2. The house was equipped with modern conveniences of the times like steam heat, running water, and electric lights.

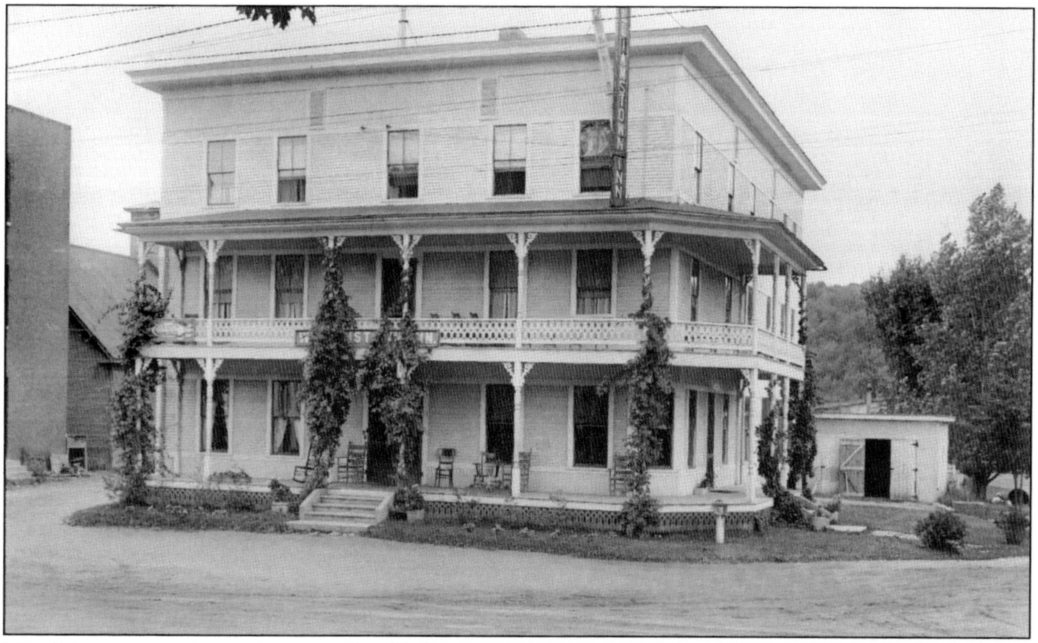

The Monument House became the Williamstown Inn, and in 1931 it became the Kings Tavern. The tavern offered a place to relax on the porch while watching life go by on the street. Visitors could have a bite to eat with a glass of imported ale. (Photograph by Eastern Illustrating; courtesy of Bertha Morgan.)

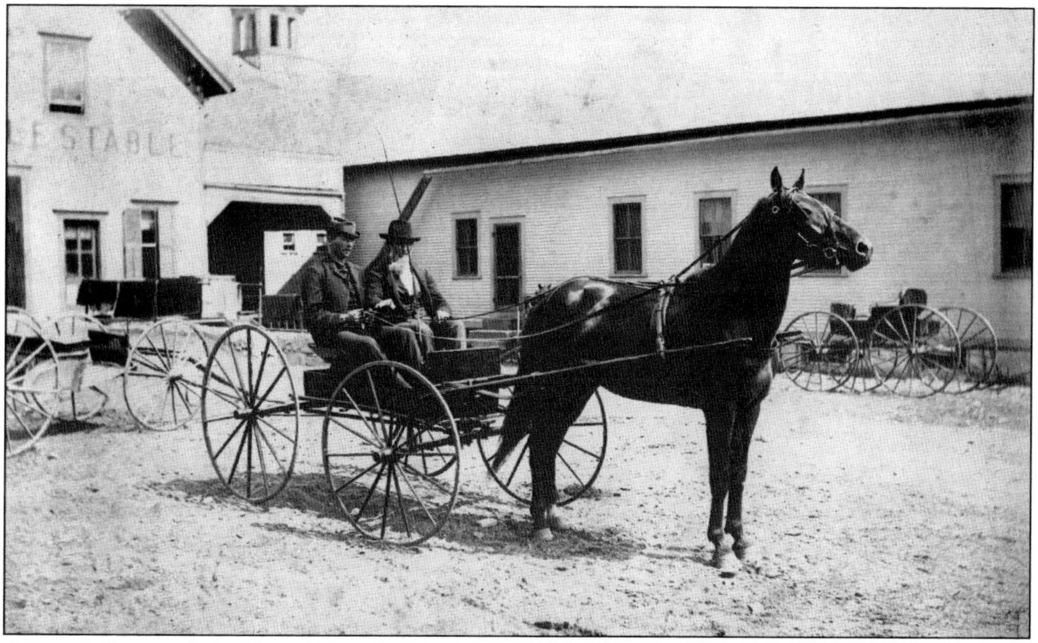

Albert Whitcomb (left) and Enoch Martin are pulled by a proud, well-muscled Morgan horse in front of the livery stables in the Village. Livery stables were an integral part of a successful downtown when the horse was the main means of travel. Weary travelers could leave their horses at the stables, and if a resident did not have a horse, they could rent one along with a buggy, sled, or wagon.

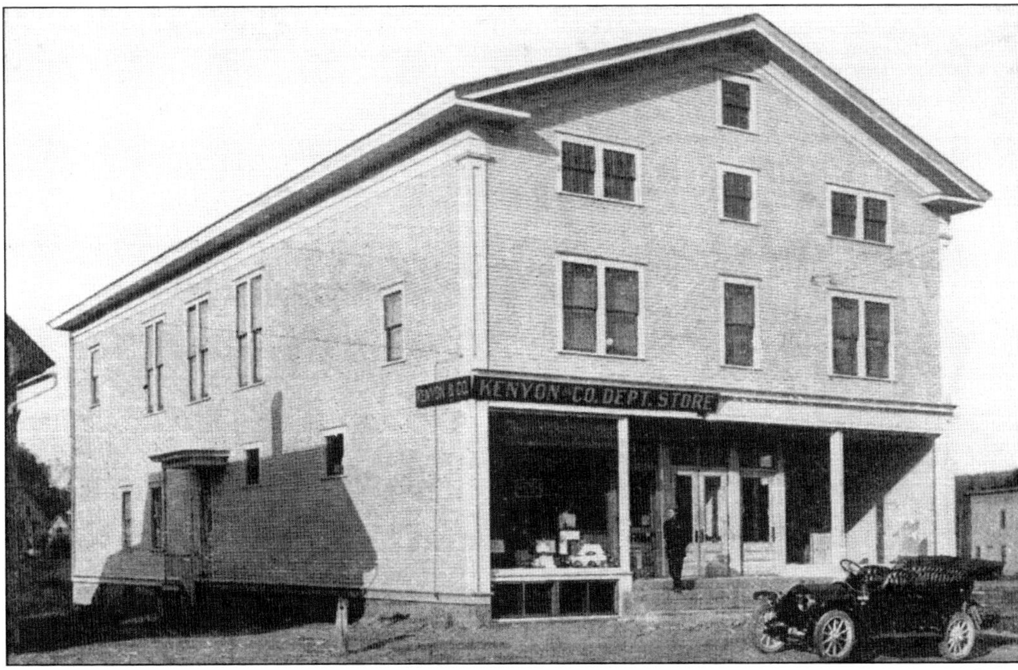

This postcard shows a man walking into the C.N. Kenyon & Company Department Store located in the Grange Building in 1912. Note that the top is down on the Ford touring sedan. The automobile was advertised in the *Barre Daily Times* as the "Joan of Arc Machine" at a cost of $690. (Photograph by Robson & Addee Publishers.)

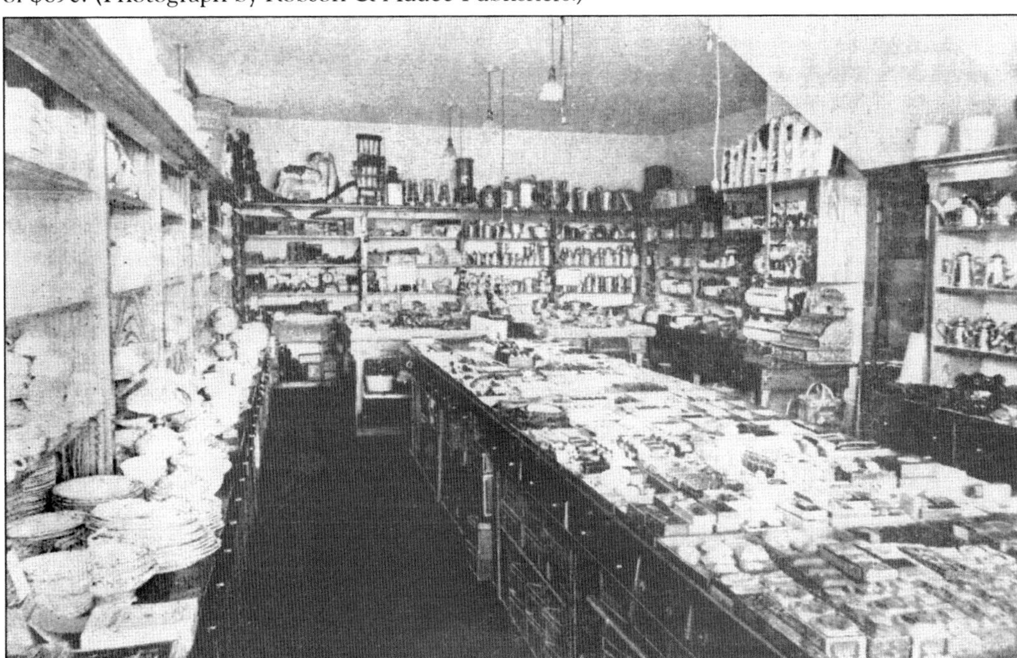

This postcard shows the interior of the C.N. Kenyon & Company Department Store in the 1900s stuffed to the brim with anything the customer could possibly need or desire. Note the hundreds of drawers in the display cases. (Courtesy of Bertha Morgan.)

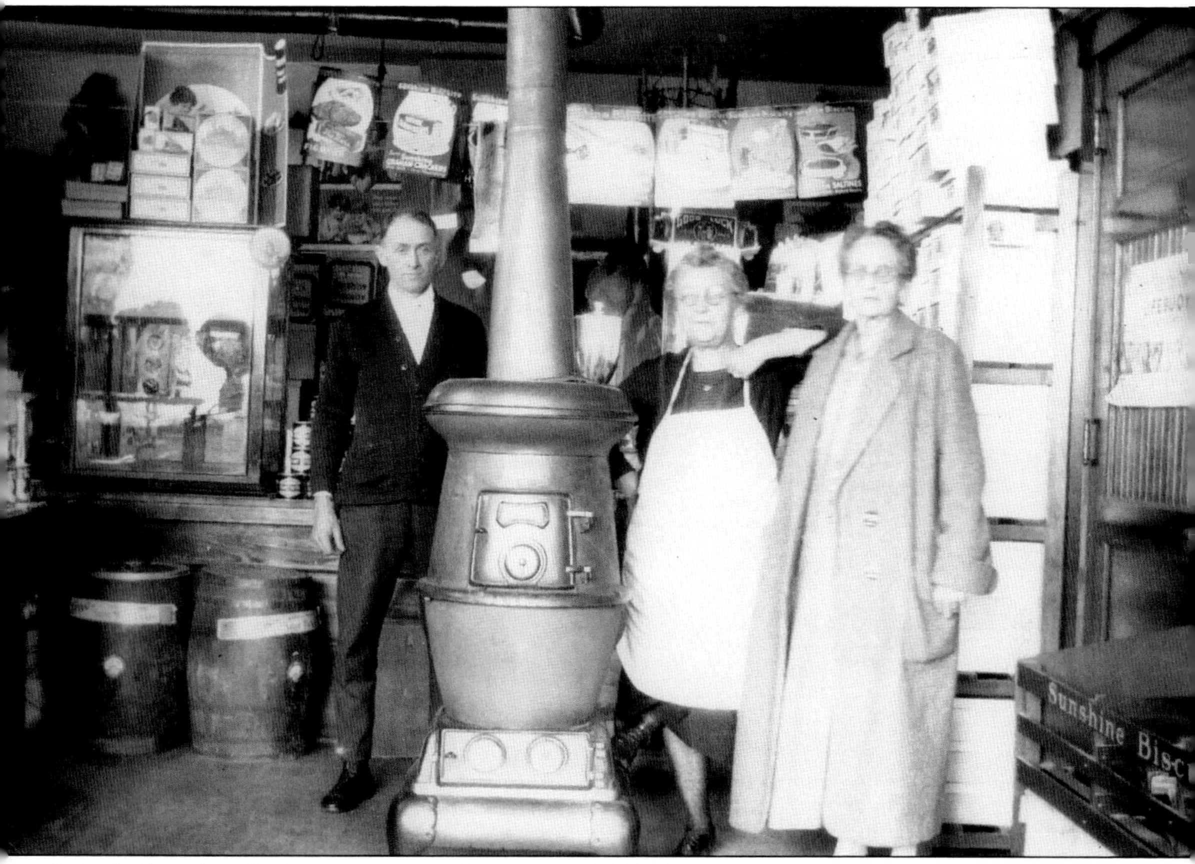

Jack (left) and Nellie Jamieson, with their cousin Nell Martin, are in their grocery store in the Grange Block. They sold the store to Dora Bruce in 1929. Note the box of Sunshine Biscuits in the front of the store and the pickle barrels on the floor behind Jack.

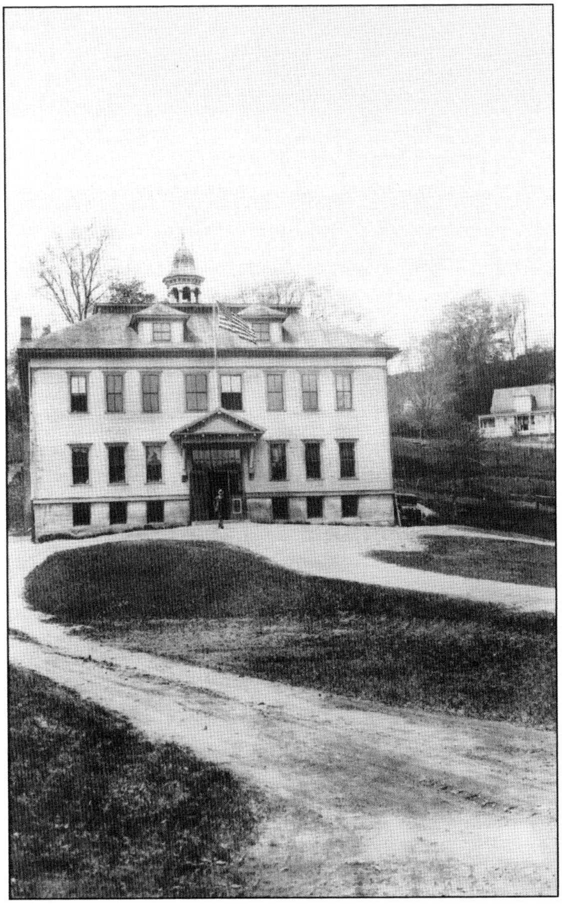

The *Orange County Gazette* sums up the village in 1896 as having an additional two general stores, a new and very fine hotel, a furniture store, jewelry store, tin shop and hardware store, two drugstores, a grocery, meat market, carriage and lumber sale agency, two blacksmith shops, a creamery, millinery store, repair shop, three churches, about 100 dwellings, and an elegant graded school building named the Village School (pictured). (Courtesy of Harriet (Murray) Ashland.)

Etta Covell stands with her fifth- and sixth-grade students in front of the Village School in 1913–1914. They are, from left to right, (first row) Dorothy Chenoyeth, Verna Gale, Ruby Wilfore, Isobel Kynoch, Irene Wright, and Barbara Boucher; (second row) David Irons, Donald Erskine, Kenneth Call, Wayne Farnham, Robert Kynoch, unidentified, Stewart Lora Wilfore, and Evelyn Gilbert; (third row) Howell Seaver, Leon Wilfore, Hazel Erskine, Marion Martin, Maggie Stewart, and Evelyn Covell. (Courtesy of Bertha Morgan.)

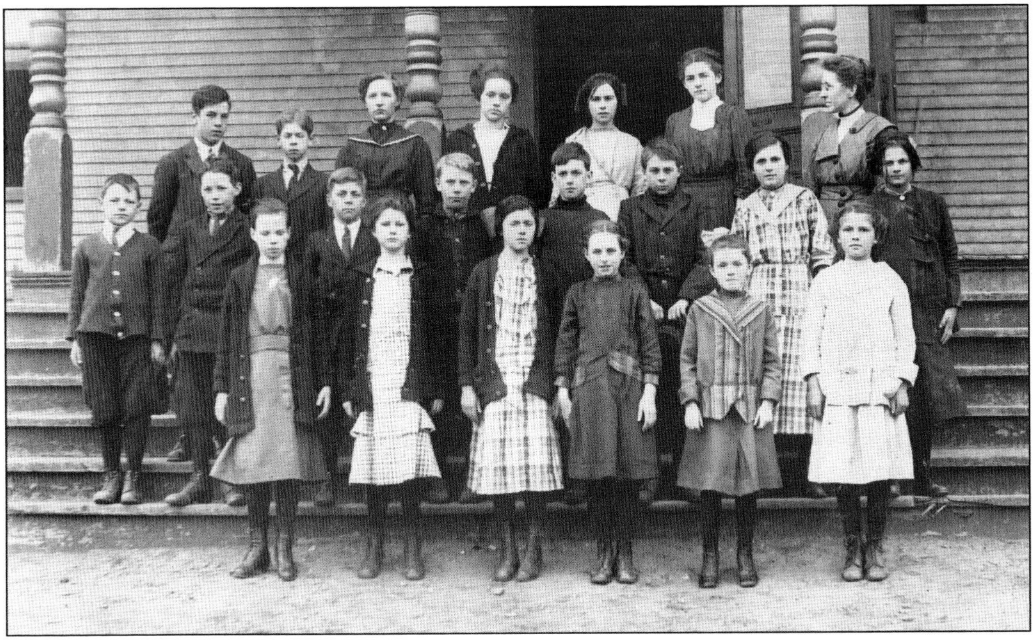

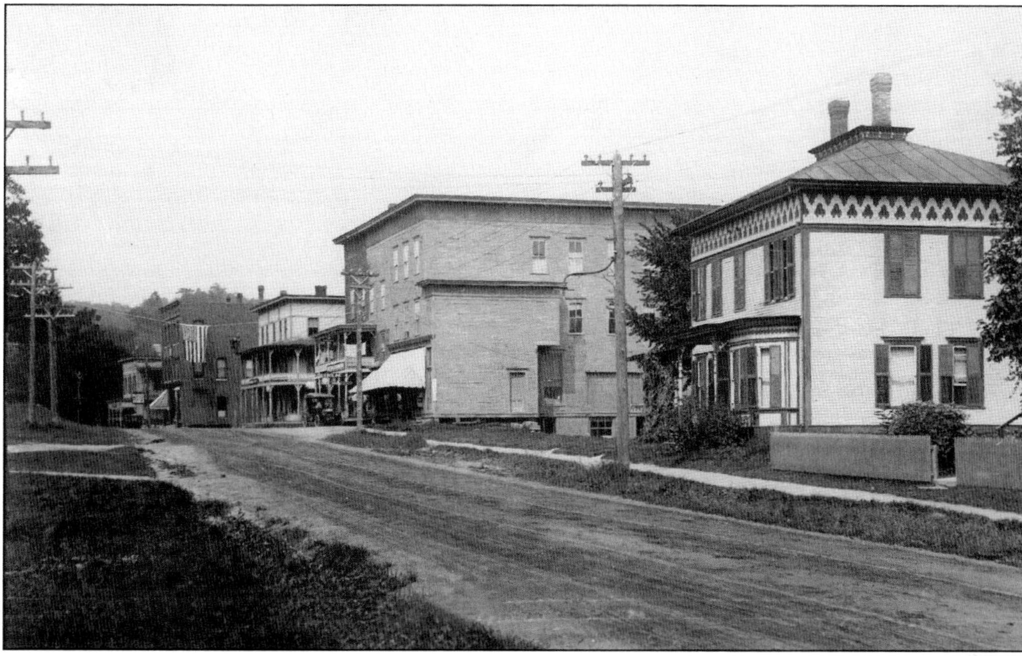

On February 6, 1917, Mary McAllister sent this postcard of Main Street to Lucy Whitney, who was in the local hospital. For many years, Whitney boarded girls from surrounding towns at her house during the school week, and they would return to their homes for the weekends. Neighborhood girls would go to her home for lunch every school day. (Courtesy of Irene Walbridge.)

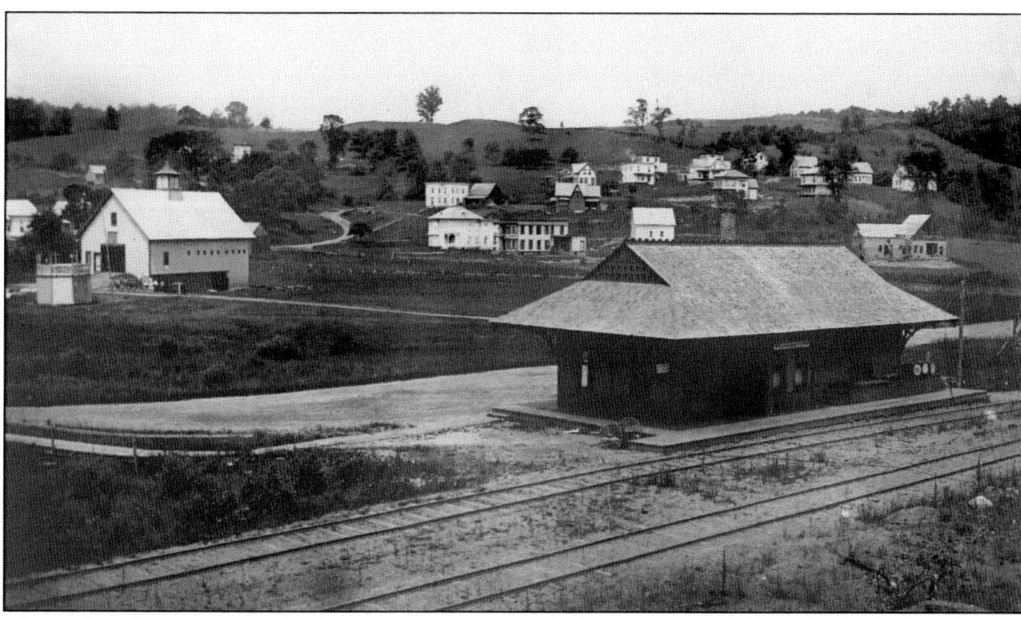

The railroad station was the hub of Williamstown, with three trains in and out each day. The economic life was closely associated with the development of the Central Vermont Railroad. (Courtesy of Martha Aldous.)

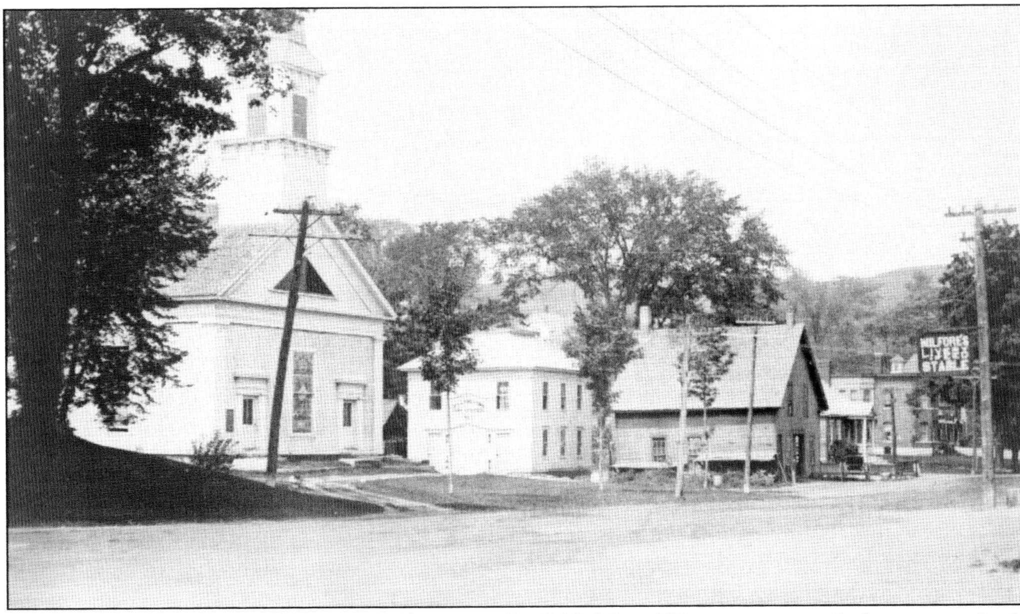

The fire district was formally organized in 1911. In 1915, Mary Waterman provided money to build the first Williamstown Firehouse. It was erected at the south end of the village, next to the Methodist church. The current fire station is located on Depot Street. (Courtesy of Bertha Morgan.)

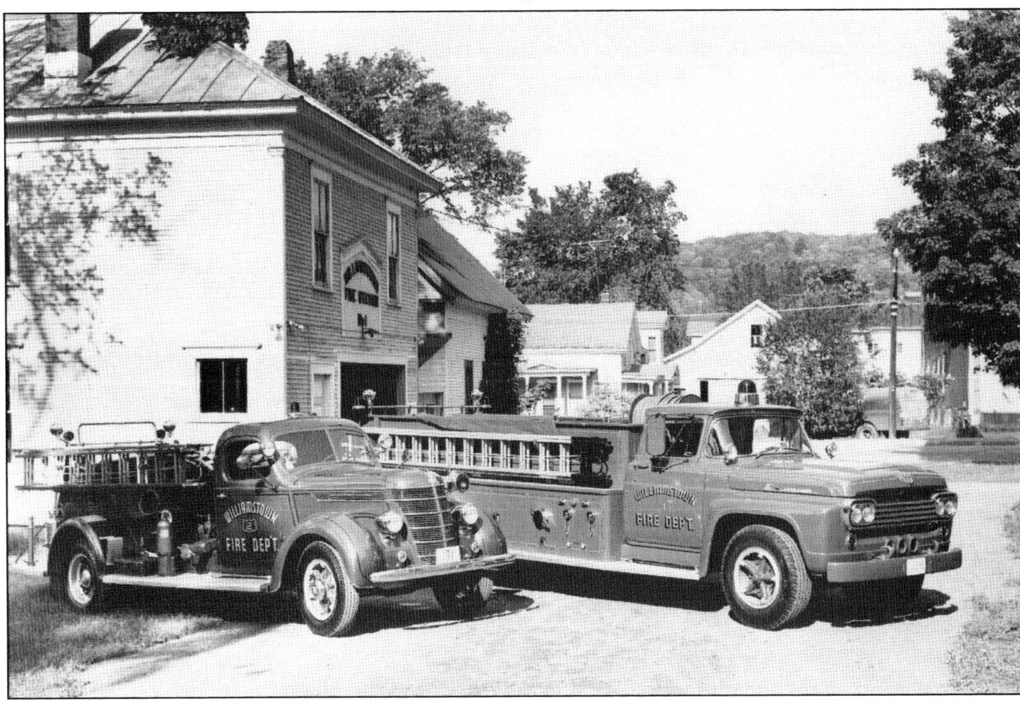

Soon after the Williamstown Firehouse was built, a horse-drawn water pump on wheels was purchased. The firefighters had to run on foot to the fire until the motorized firefighting vehicles were invented and the introduction of running boards and back steps were added for the men to ride on the vehicle; note the running boards on these fire trucks. (Photograph by MacIver Photos.)

Williamstown's natural environment is filled with marshes, wetlands, rivers, and ponds. A devastating flood hit central Vermont in 1927. The *Barre Daily Times* reported that the Green Mountain streams rose so rapidly that there was little time for warning. Sadly, Jennie Drury (pictured), of Williamstown, dropped dead as she watched floodwaters from a bursting dam.

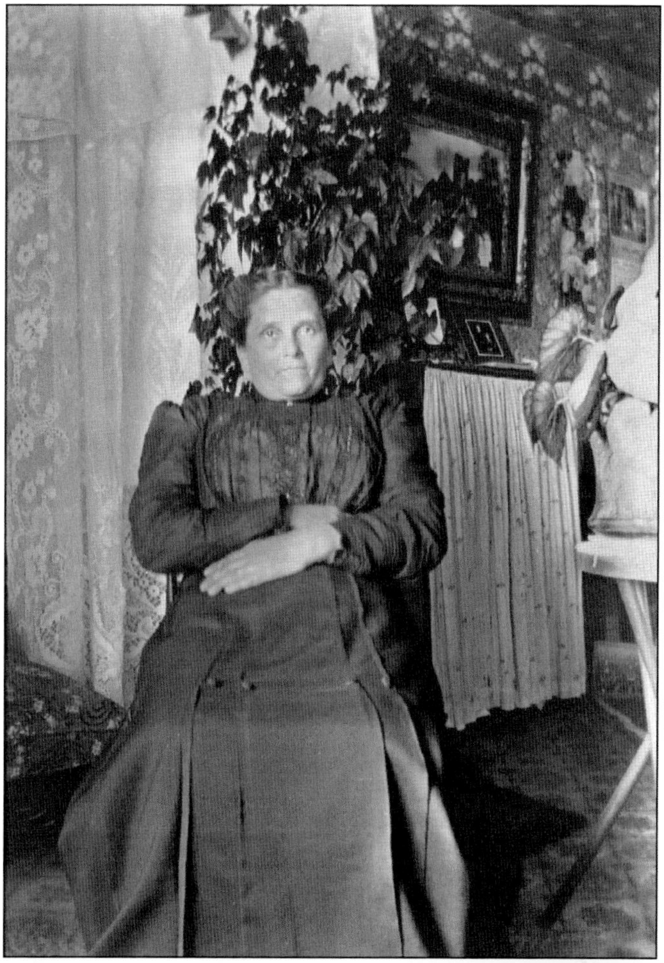

The 1927 flood damage is shown beside the garage on Brook and Main Streets. Blanche Martin's house is the center house. The combination of the 1927 flood damage and the Depression made it difficult for Williamstown to recover economically. While better roads and transportation made life easier for individuals, the competition between towns increased, making life more difficult for the village businesses.

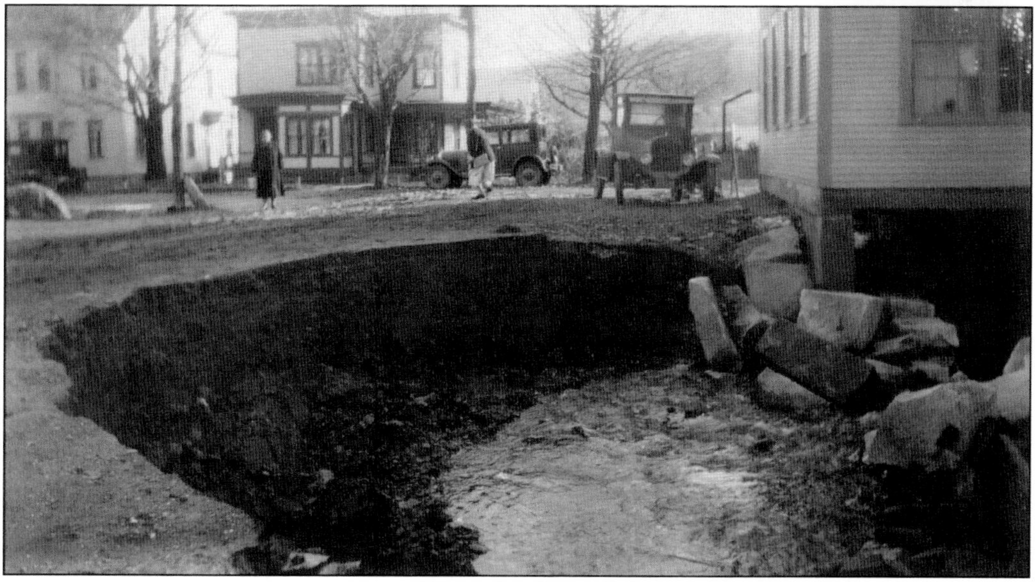

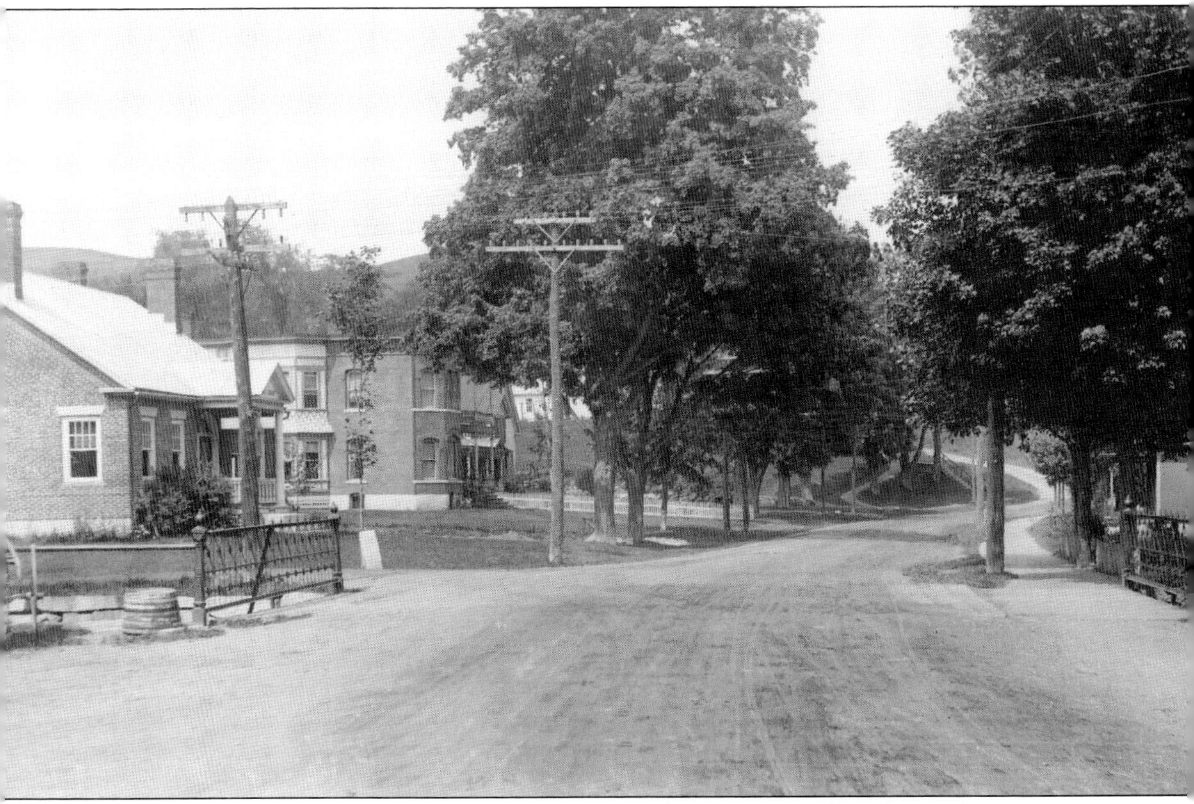

This postcard shows Main Street at the corner of Routes 14 and 64. Note the iron gates on each side of the culvert where the Stevens Branch River passes under the road. Many of the village roads and homes get flooded from time to time in the spring. (Photograph by Eastern Illustrating Company.)

Three

Travel and Transportation

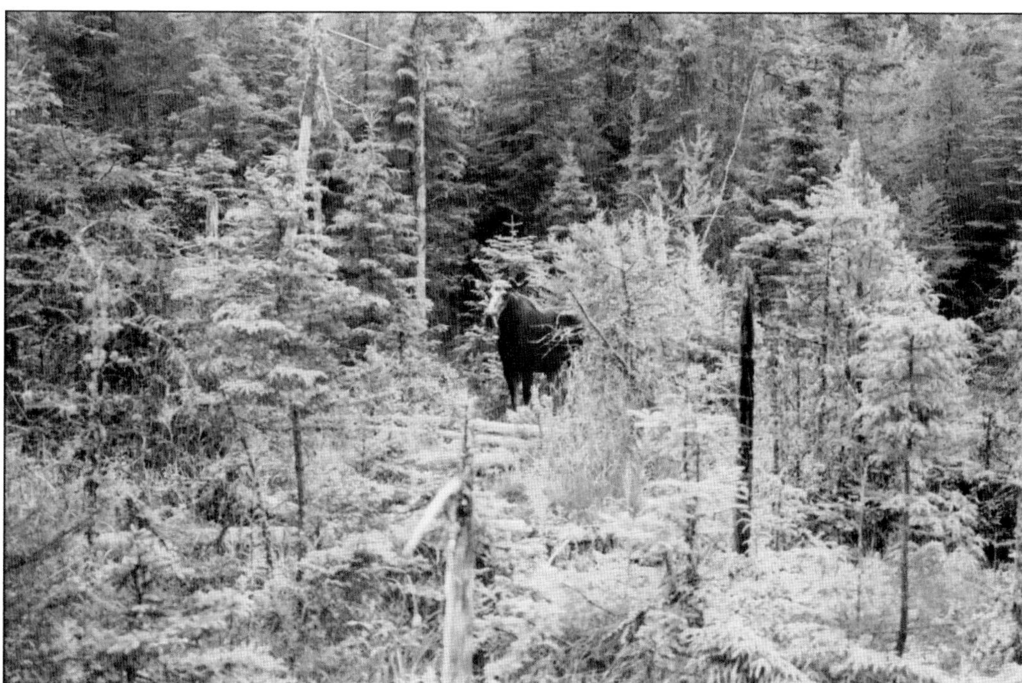

When this area was first settled, there were no roads. The Vermont Historical Society states that often the pioneers followed watercourses or paths beaten down by large animals through the wilderness. This image shows what the natural and untamed land may have looked like in the past. The moose at center is a native to Vermont. (Courtesy of Doreen Chambers.)

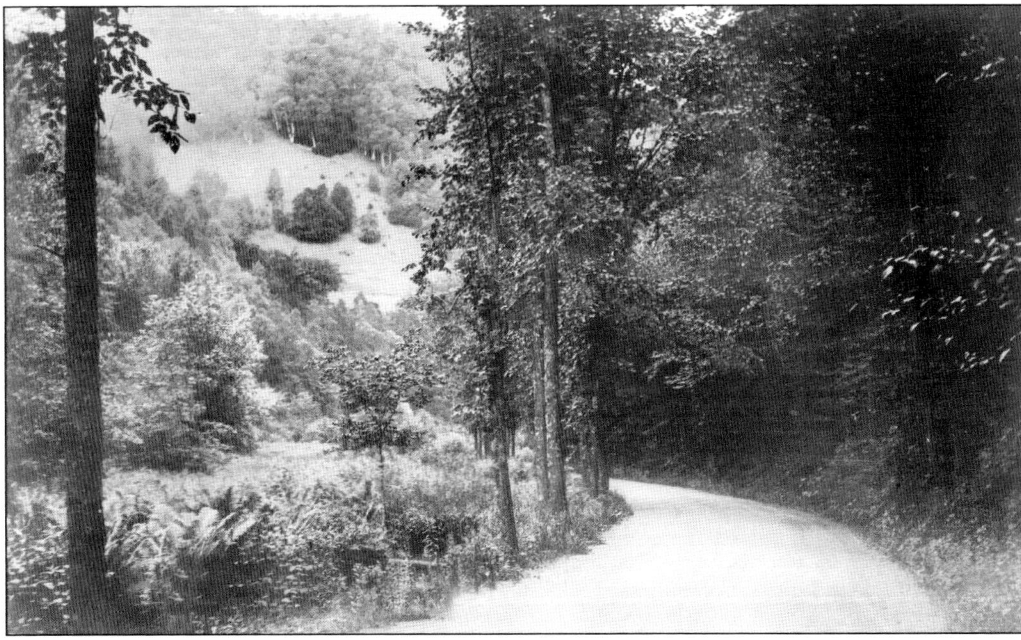

Aaron Martin was one of the pioneers who came to Williamstown in 1796. The Martins had a family of 15 children. Two of Martin's teenagers (a boy and a girl) were assigned the task of driving cattle from Connecticut. They were told to follow the marked trees and head north from South Royalton to Williamstown. When they came upon a section of the trail that forked, they had a disagreement and split up, each traveling in a different direction.

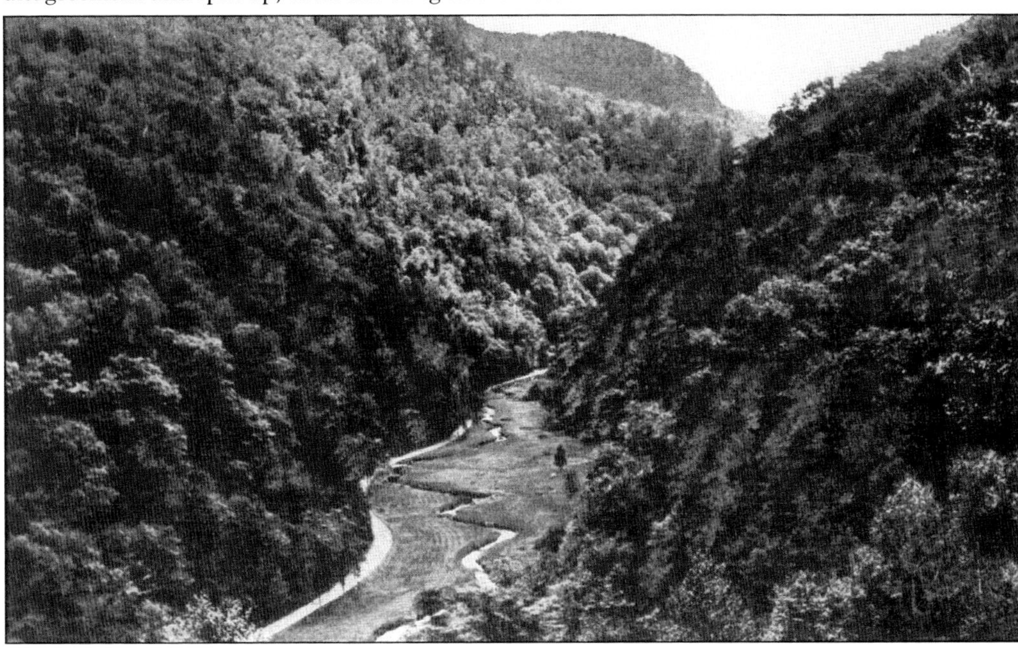

Aaron Martin's teenage girl Betsey ended up spending a night alone in the gulf. Following a blazed path, the boy herded the cattle down a mountain pasture, which ended north of the Gulf Road. The two teenagers unexpectedly found each other and traveled together to their new home in Williamstown together. (Photograph by Green Mountain Card Company.)

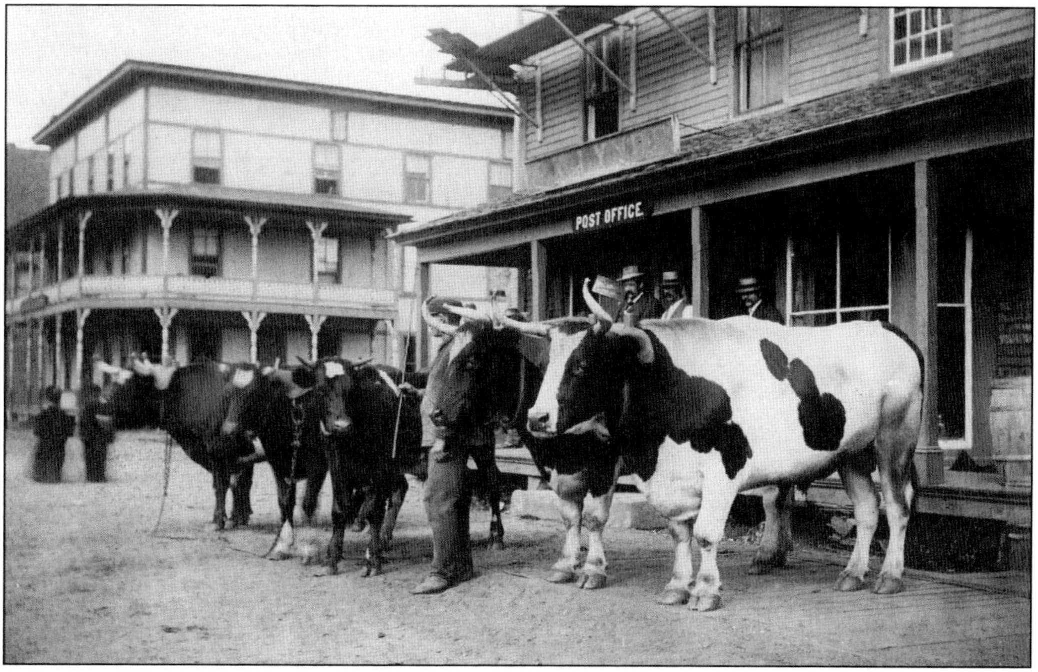

Oxen owned by H.H. Martin are lined up in front of the Lynde Store and post office. In the mid- to late 1700s, the original blazed paths were widened to sufficiently accommodate horse- and ox-drawn carts. Roads in Williamstown were originally named for the families who lived on them, like Bador, Hebert, Isabelle, and Seaver Roads.

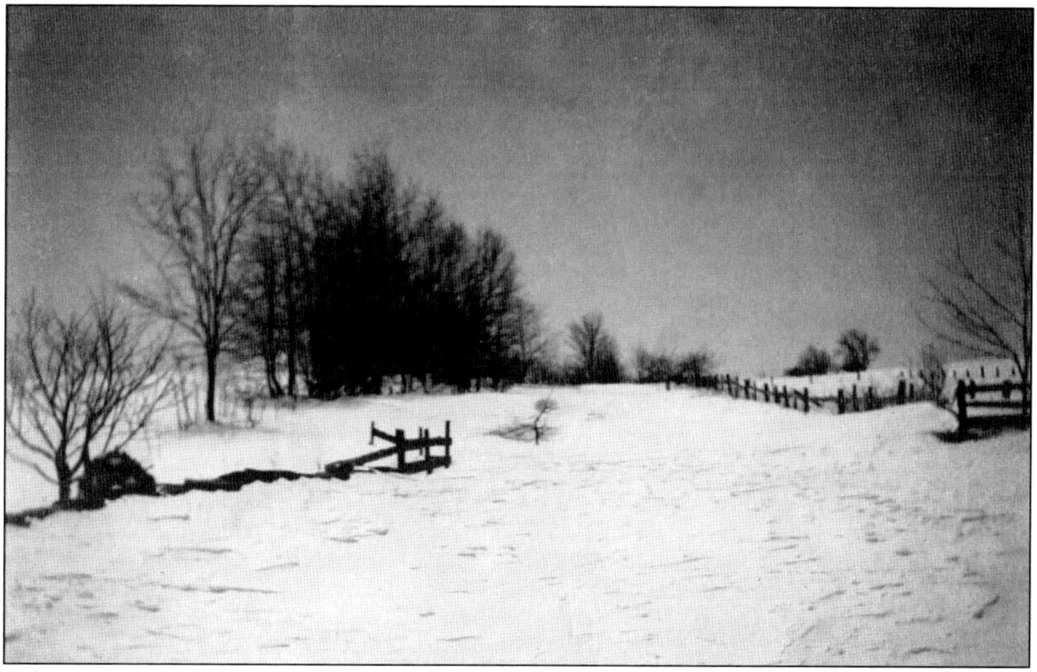

A lonely winter road shows what most rural back roads looked like after a heavy snowfall in Williamstown. Most roads were not used in the winter; many people just used horse-drawn sleighs. Many roads were also not used during mud season.

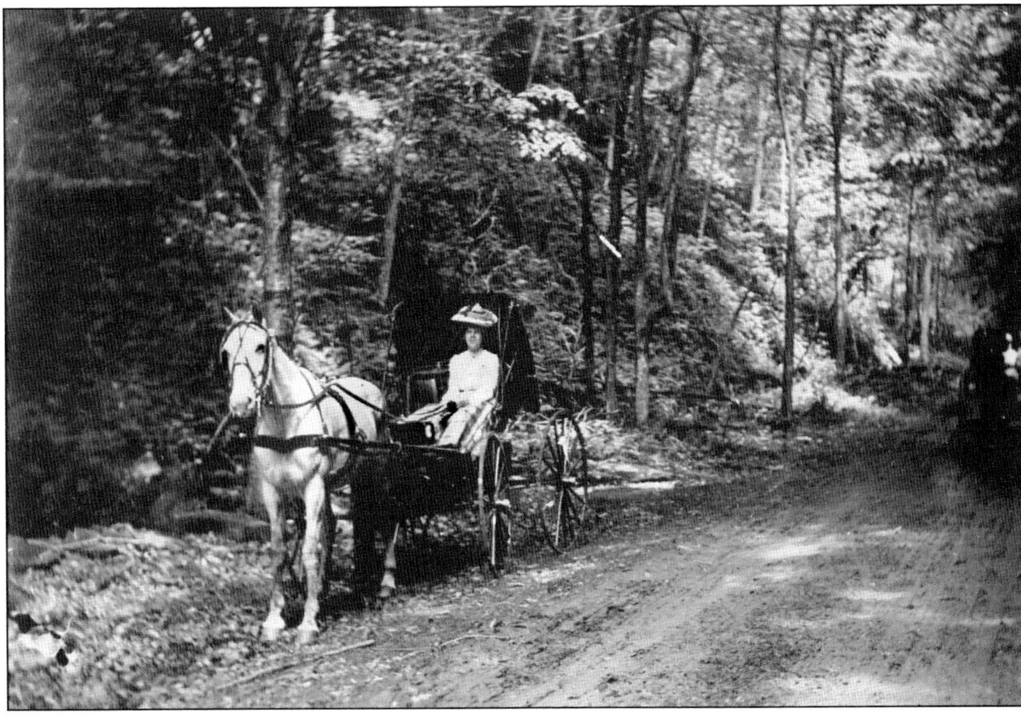

Summer was the time to get out of the house and ride around town. Shown here are two women traveling by horse-drawn buggy into town through the Williamstown Gulf. A playful dog romps alongside the buggy in back. It would take over an hour to get to Barre from Williamstown in a horse-drawn buggy; it made sense that the village provided all the necessities of life.

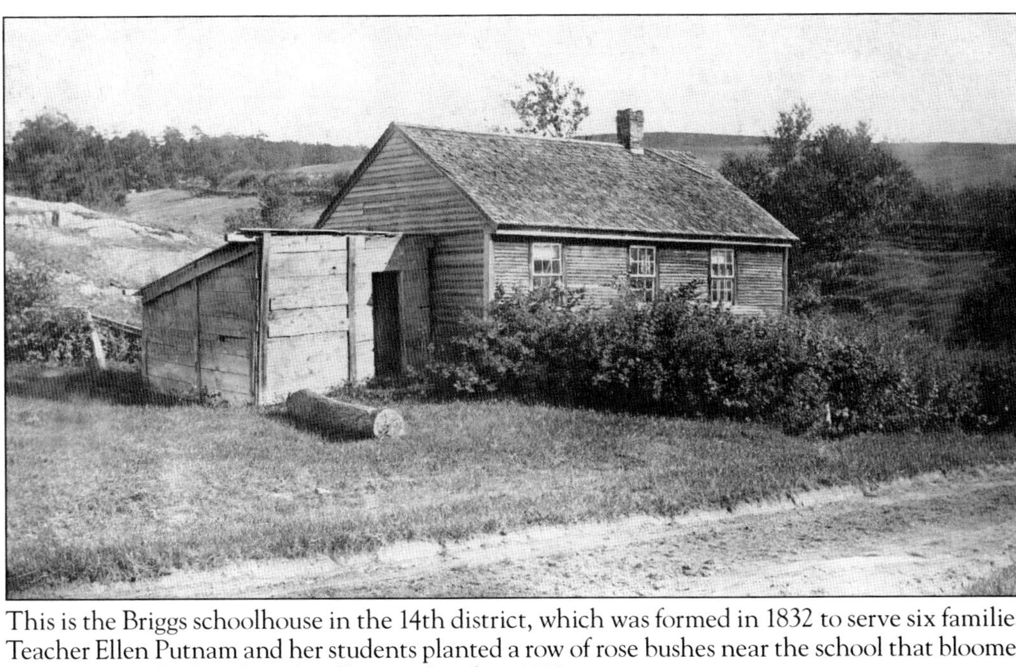

This is the Briggs schoolhouse in the 14th district, which was formed in 1832 to serve six families. Teacher Ellen Putnam and her students planted a row of rose bushes near the school that bloomed and spread well after the schoolhouse closed in 1893.

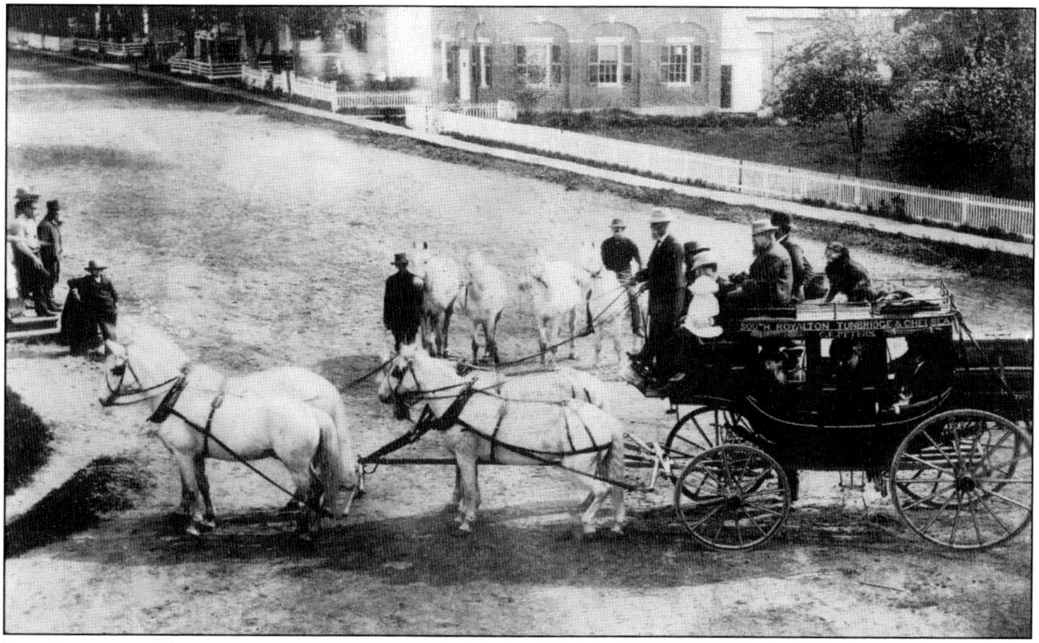

Roads were still quite primitive even into the early 1800s when the Williamstown Gulf road became a stagecoach route. There were two competing stagecoach businesses that traveled through the gulf, one from Montpelier and the other from Barre. The six- or eight-horse teams made regular trips and were on the road all the time. The coaches carried rum, mail, and other important cargo. This 1884 photograph shows the Chelsea–South Royalton stage coach in front of the Orange County Hotel in Chelsea. The driver was Charles E. Peters of Chelsea. (Courtesy of Ruth Whitney.)

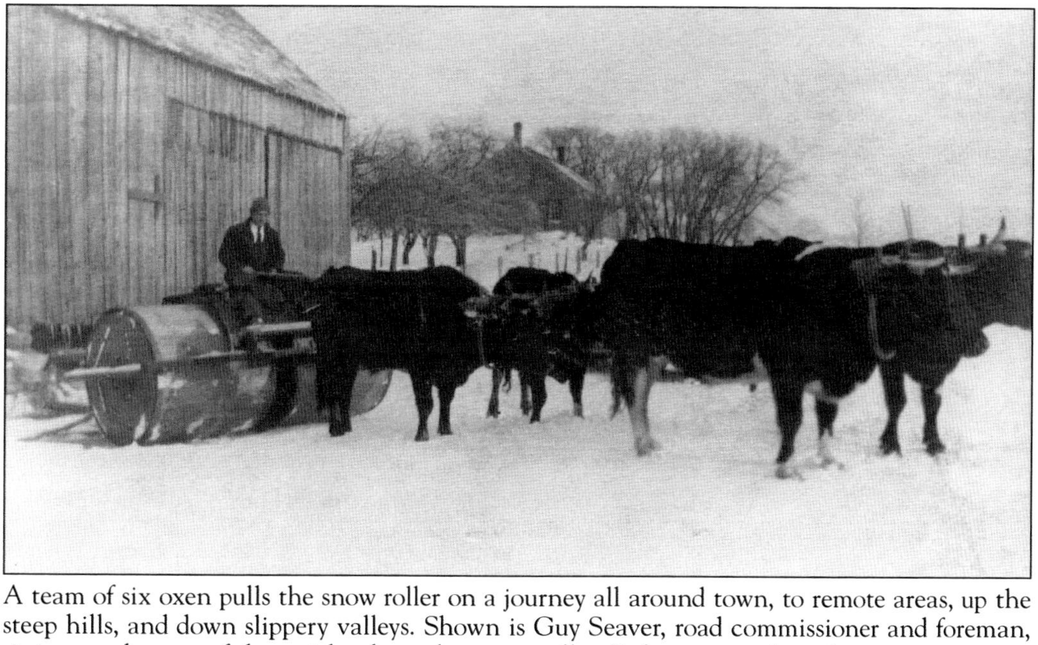

A team of six oxen pulls the snow roller on a journey all around town, to remote areas, up the steep hills, and down slippery valleys. Shown is Guy Seaver, road commissioner and foreman, sitting on the seat of the weighted wooden snow roller. Before cars and trucks were a common sight on the roads, winter roads were made passable by these snow rollers.

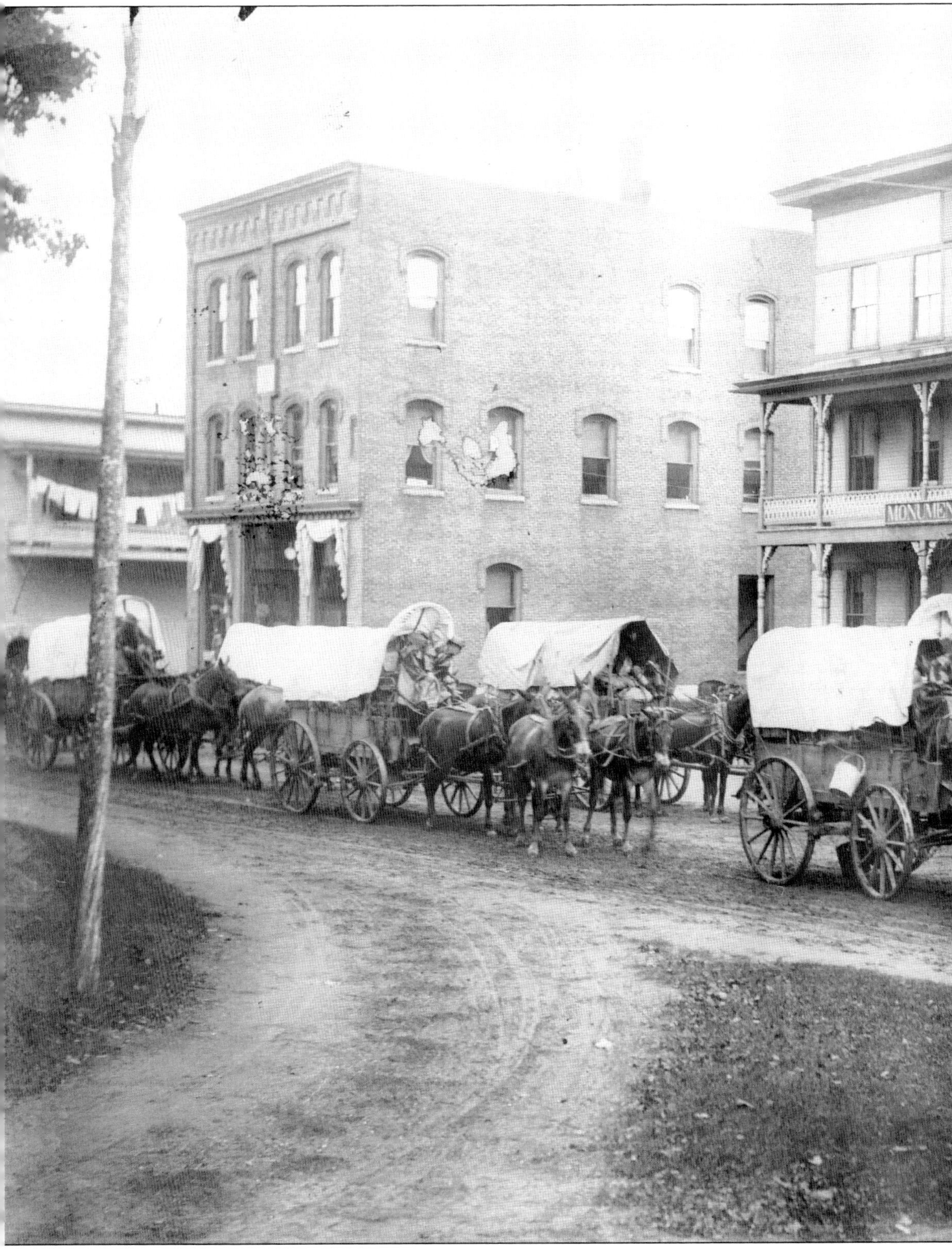
MONUMEN

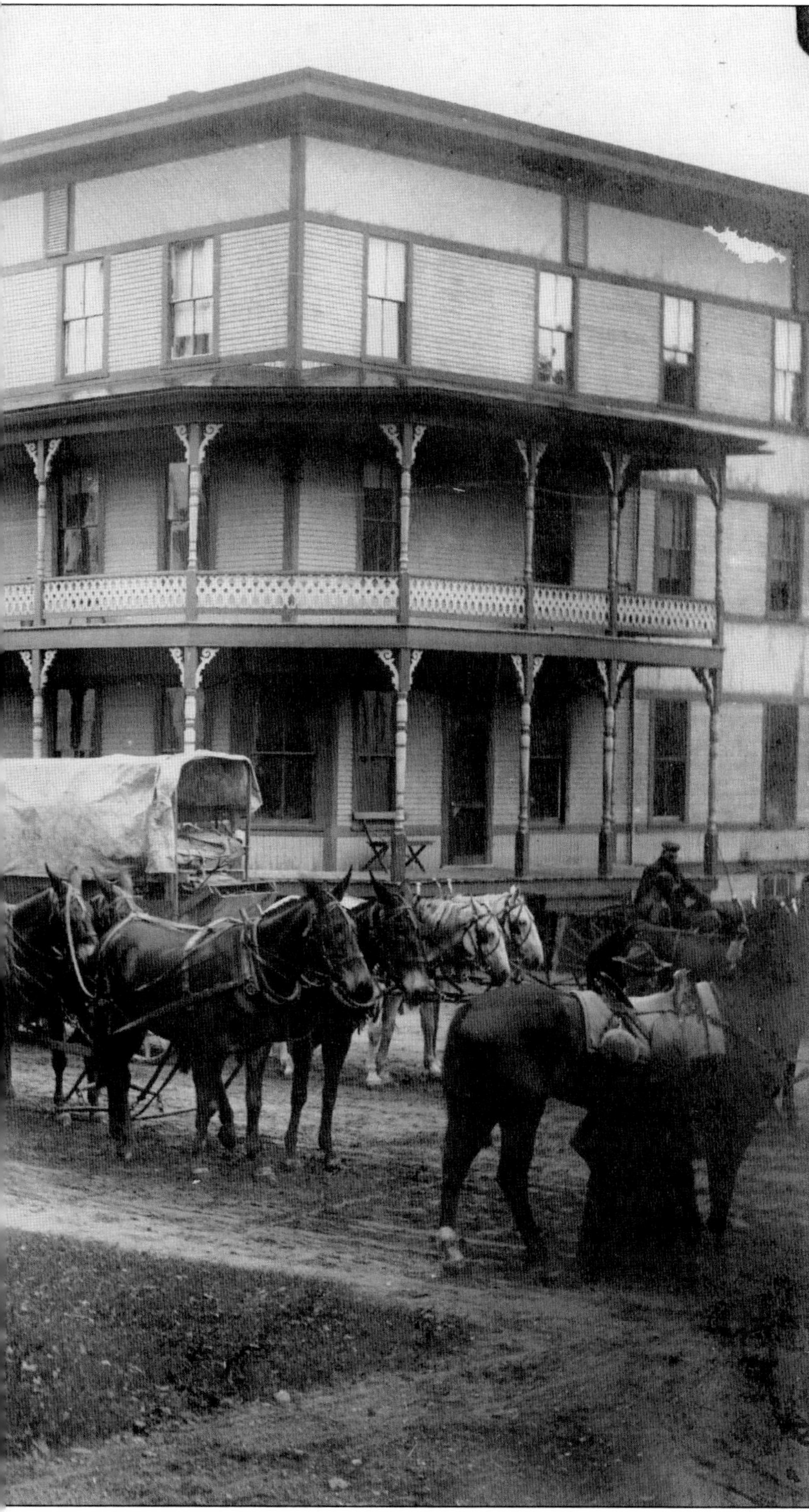

The "battery" is shown passing through Williamstown in the early 1900s on its way to Portland, Maine, possibly headed to Fort McKinley. The covered wagons stopped briefly in front of Main Street's Monument House. Note the variety of mules pulling the covered wagons. The major fuel at forts was coal, and a system of loading, transporting, and storing the fuel was developed, usually relying on mule-drawn wagons.

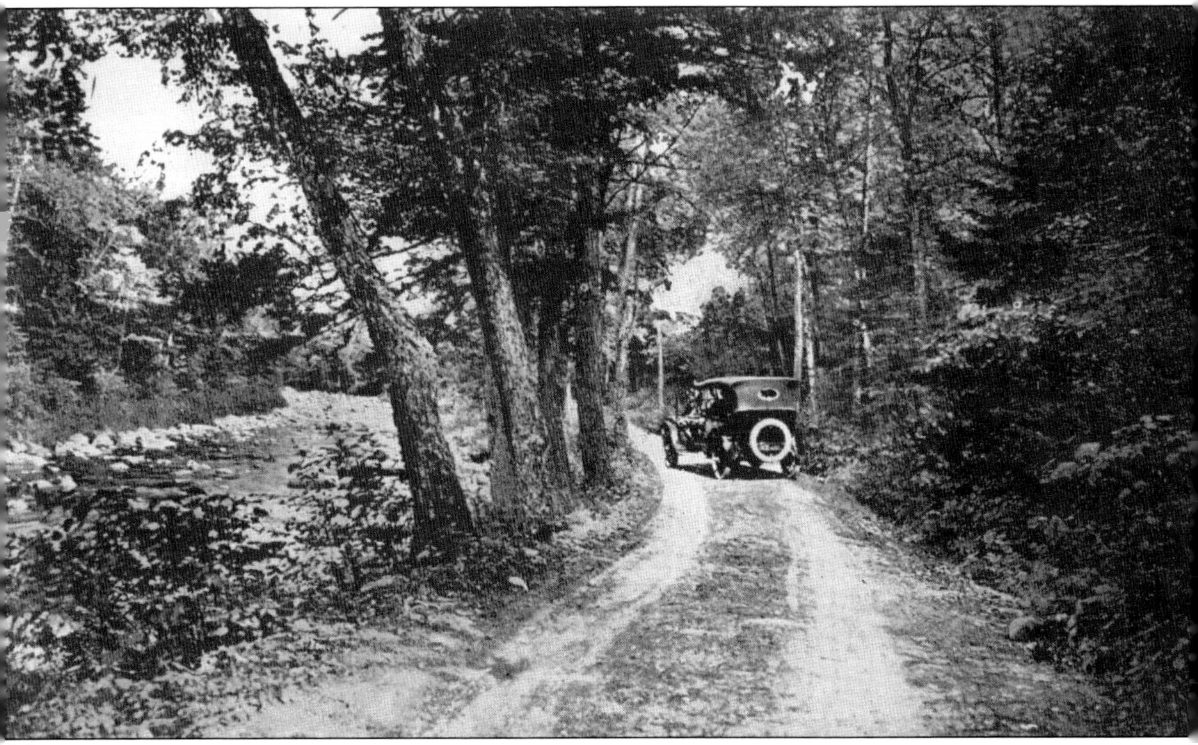

Early on, Williamstown did not have enough money to build new roads. The *1912 Encyclopedia, Vermont Biography* reports that in 1799, "Elijah Paine generously invested his own private money into building the Paine Turnpike. In Williamstown, it ran along the established public highway. Paine erected three turnpike gates for the collection of tolls, which amounted to 5¢ for every man with a horse and up to a high of 31¢ for a four-wheeled pleasure carriage drawn by two horses." The tolls helped to defray the cost and ongoing maintenance. The "horseless carriage" did not come until the late 1800s. (Photograph by Landscapes.)

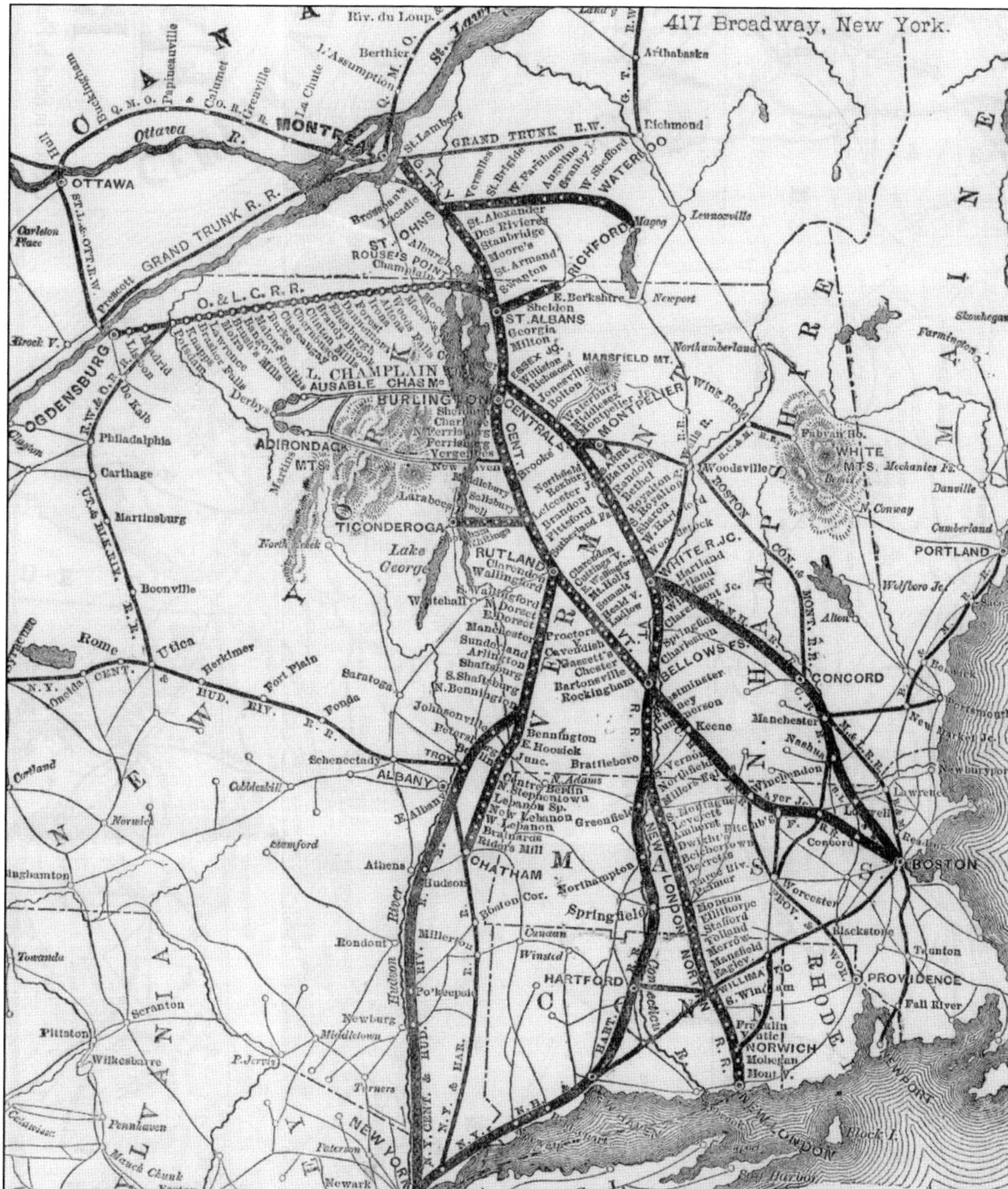

The Central Vermont Railroad decided to extend its Montpelier and White River Junction line from Barre to Williamstown. This 1879 map shows the railroad stretching all the way from Canada to New York. The *1845 Report of the Survey of the Gulf Route from Berlin via Montpelier to Royalton*, states "the Williamstown Gulf route is a favorable one for construction of the railroad. The whole distance is in a beautiful, rich, and highly cultured country; there is scarcely any other section of Vermont of superior fertility."

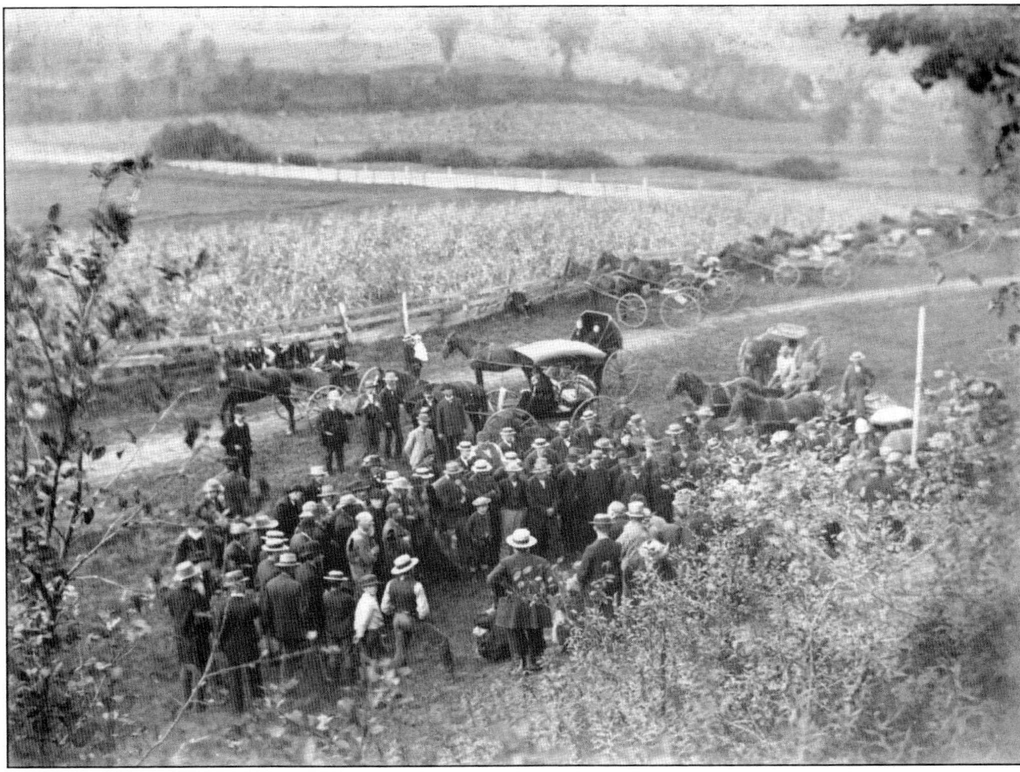

Shown here is a ground breaking celebration for the Williamstown Branch Railroad line in 1887. Initial plans had the main line running through Montpelier and the Williamstown Gulf. Due to the political will of Charles Paine (son of Elijah Paine), a Northfield man, the new route through Northfield was chosen instead of the route through Williamstown; Williamstown ended up with just a branch and switching station. Note Enoch Howe's cornfield in the background, now Seaver Community ball field.

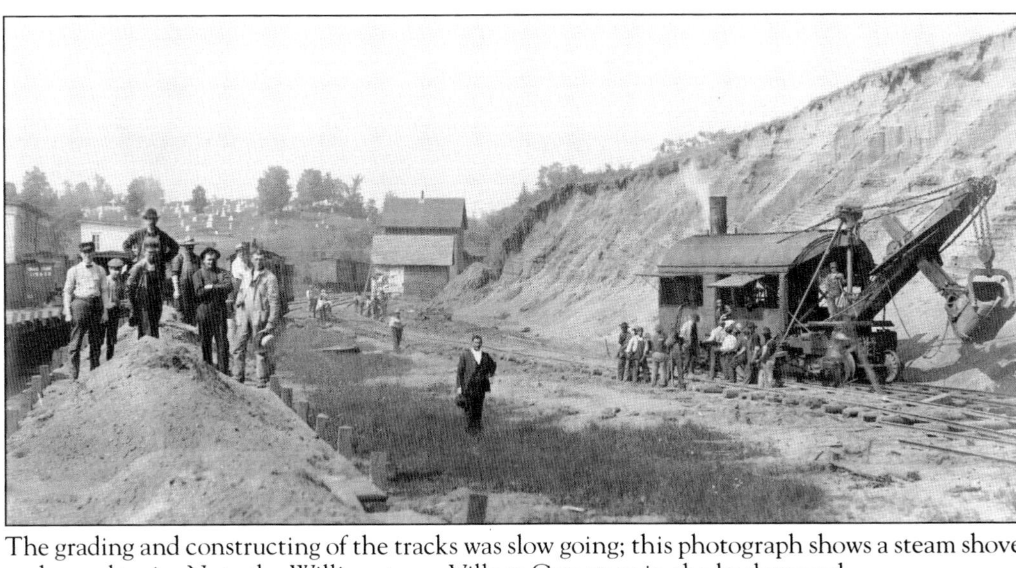

The grading and constructing of the tracks was slow going; this photograph shows a steam shovel and gravel train. Note the Williamstown Village Cemetery in the background.

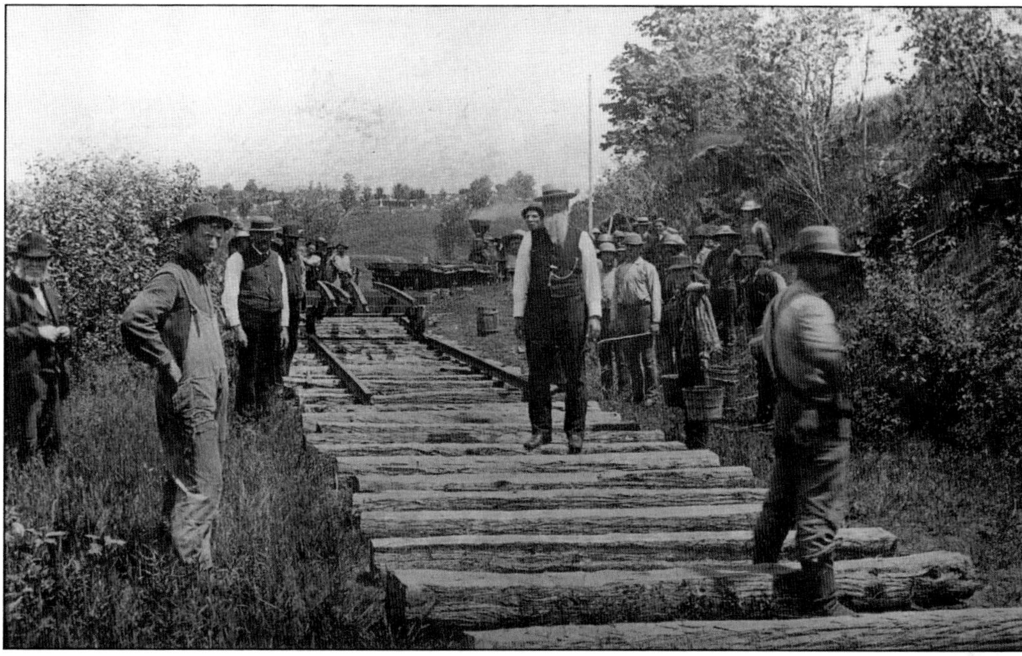

These workmen are constructing the railroad with timber beams in 1887–1888. Rails were produced in fixed lengths and needed to be joined end-to-end to make a continuous surface on which trains could run. According to the *1845 Report Survey of the Gulf Route*, "A single tract with trail is eighteen feet long, weighing fifty-six pounds, per linear yard, with cast iron joints." (Courtesy of Ruth Whitney.)

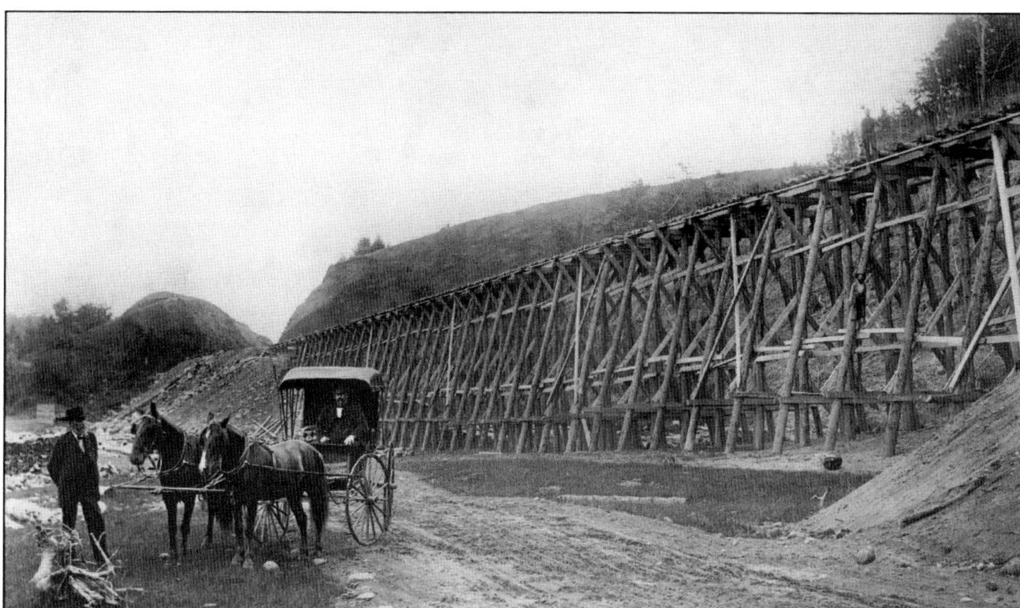

Timbers are erected to form a trestle over a depression to support the railroad and get the train to its destination. Note the man standing on top of the trestle and a second man standing on the side of the trestle.

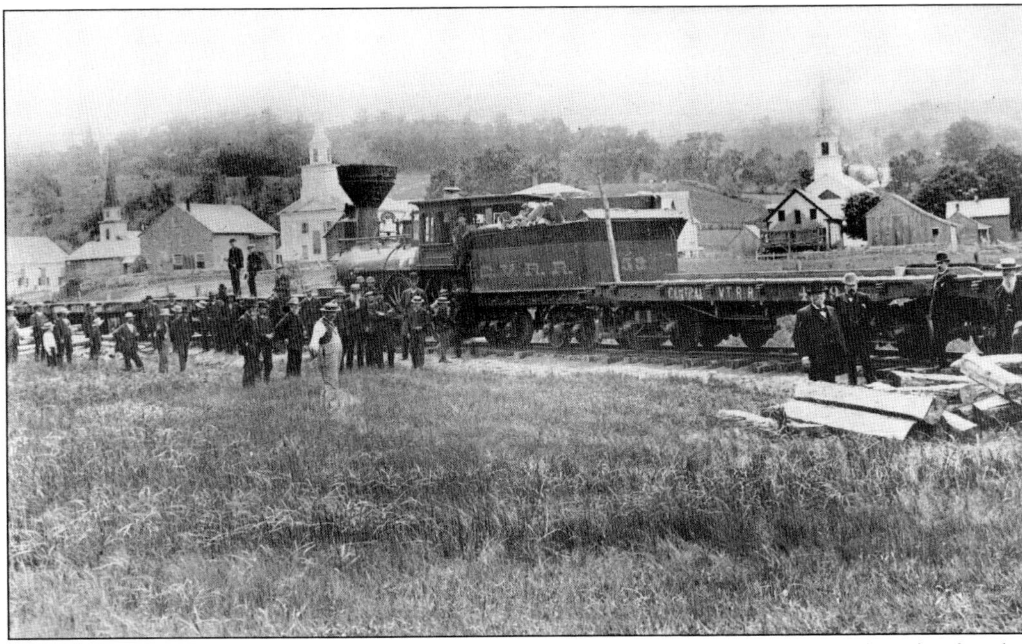

In 1888, the first Central Vermont Railroad train came into Williamstown. Note the pile of timber beams. The photograph shows workers lined up in front of the bell-stacked, wood-burning freight train. According to *The Williamstown Branch: Impersonal Memories of a Vermont Boyhood* by R.L Duffus, "Conductor Jim Kennealy would steam up the engine and apprentice Mr. Webb (known as "Old Man Webb") would open the throttle to move the train." (Courtesy of Ruth Whitney.)

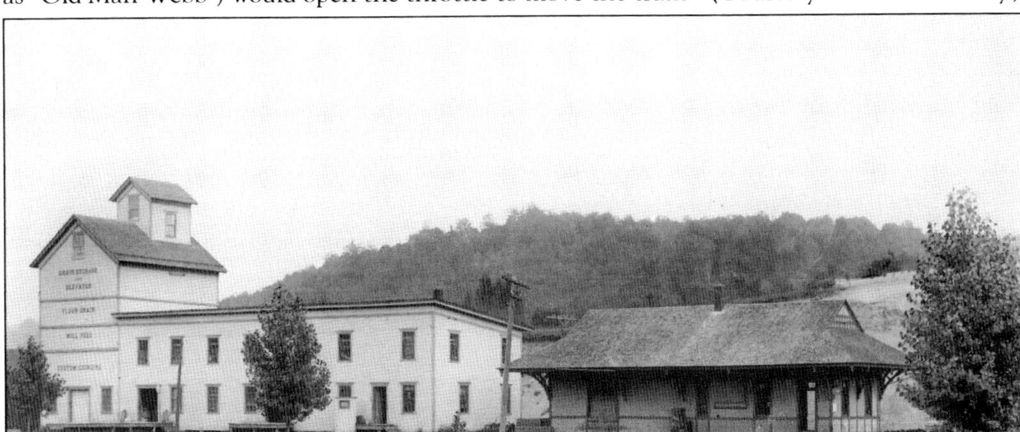

It was helpful to have a railroad near a business; this photograph shows the feed store next to the railroad station. The coming of the railroad had a great impact on Williamstown because the quarries and other businesses could now more easily move their granite, lumber, wool, and other goods to market. (Photograph by Studio of Eastern Illustrating; courtesy of Ruth Whitney.)

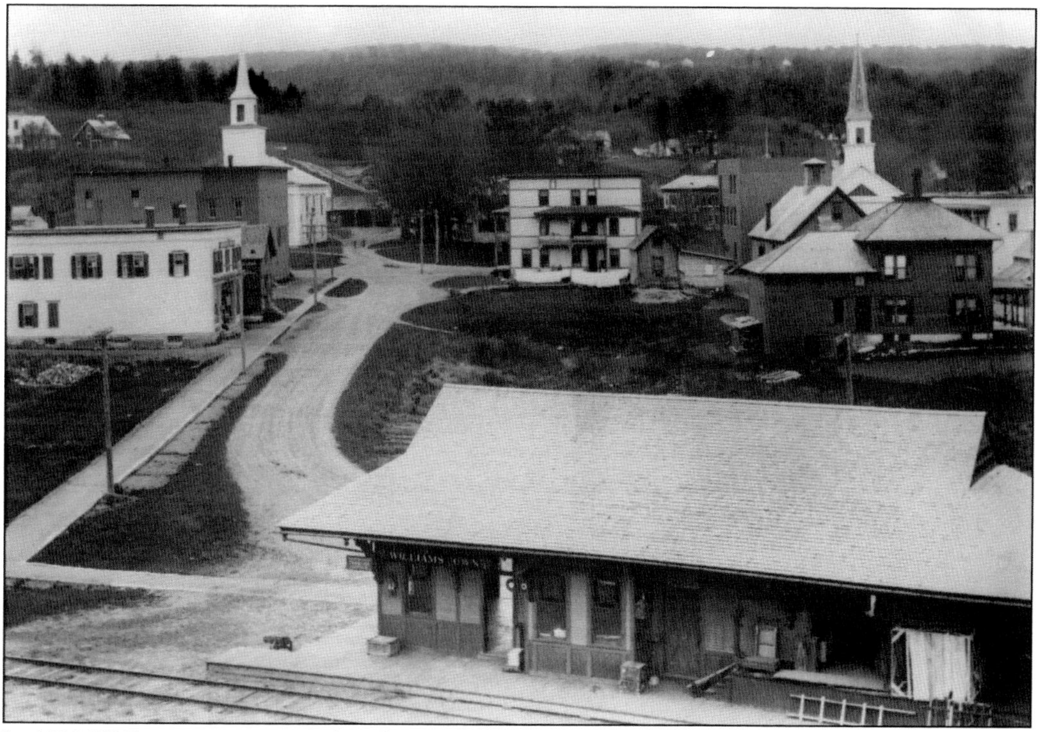

In 1889, Williamstown received its depot; inside the depot were the stationmaster's office, waiting room, and booking office.

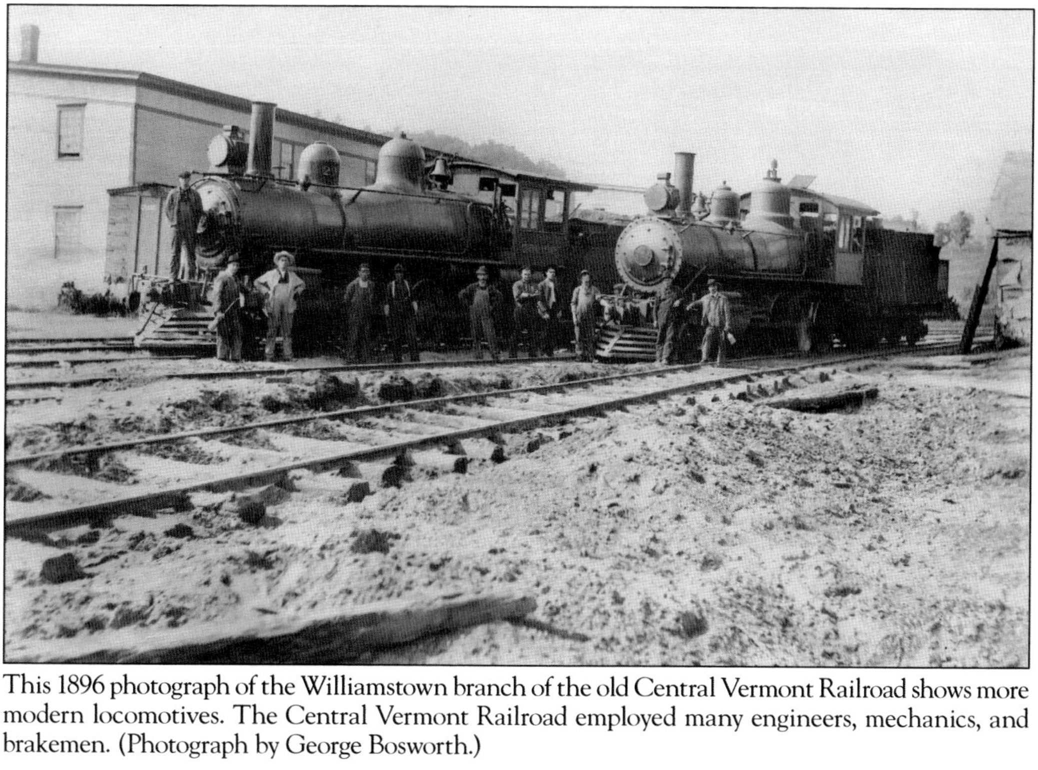

This 1896 photograph of the Williamstown branch of the old Central Vermont Railroad shows more modern locomotives. The Central Vermont Railroad employed many engineers, mechanics, and brakemen. (Photograph by George Bosworth.)

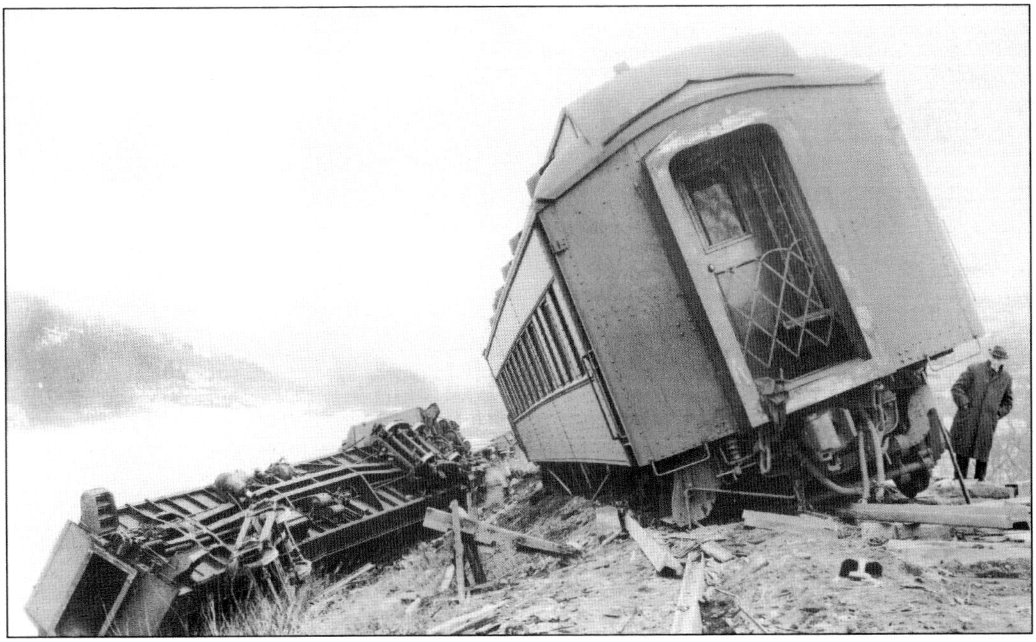

Williamstown also had the benefit of a passenger train station in the early 1900s. On August 26, 1907, train No. 203 of the Central Vermont Railroad had an accident on Dodge Bridge in Williamstown.

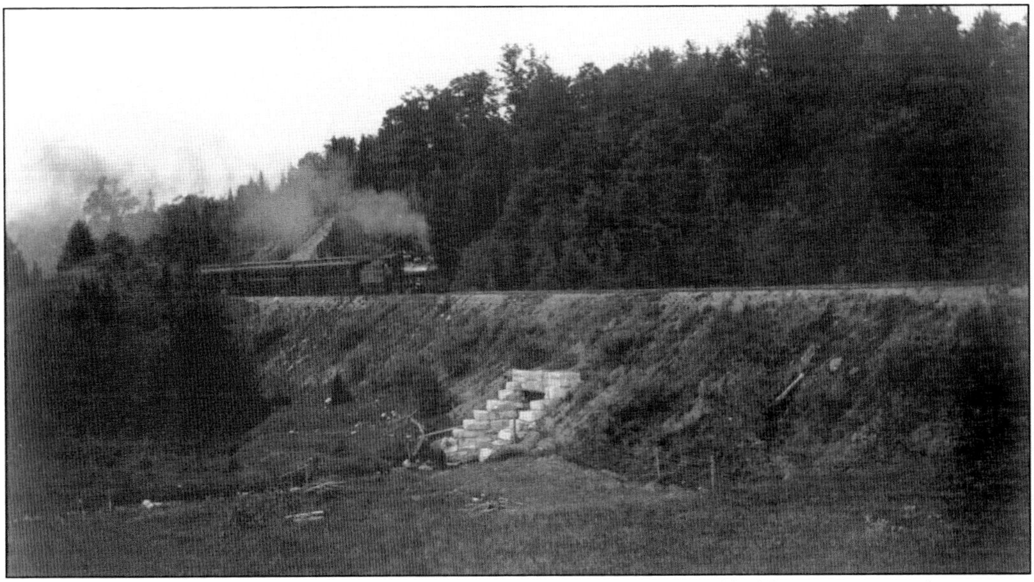

The Williamstown "Cannon Ball" speeds along the track propelled by a mammoth engine, belching clouds of black smoke along its path.

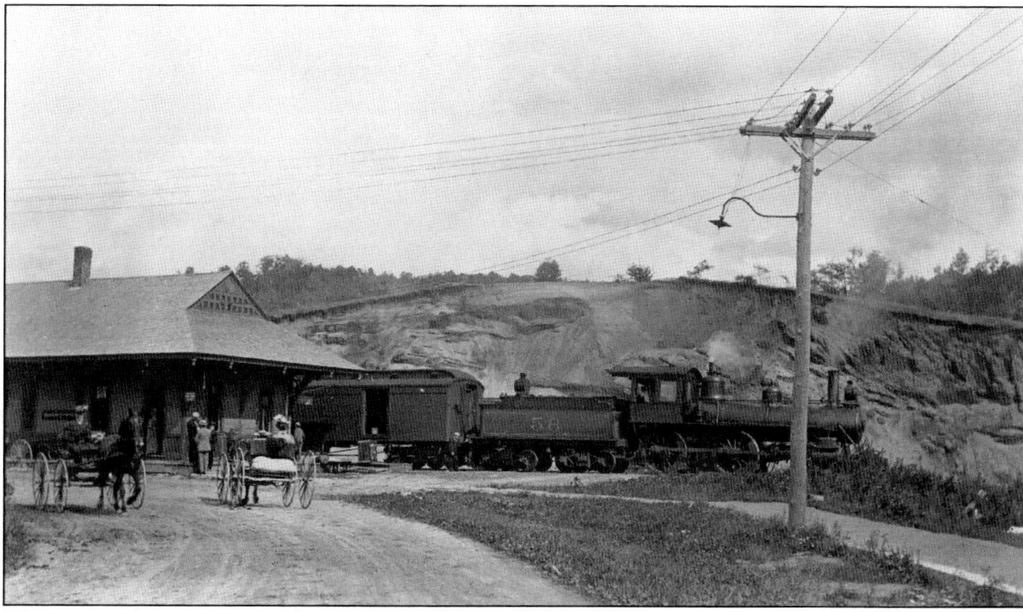

There were long pauses at depots for refueling. In 1926, when this photograph was taken, horses were still a primary means of transportation and were used for shopping around town and to meet the trains.

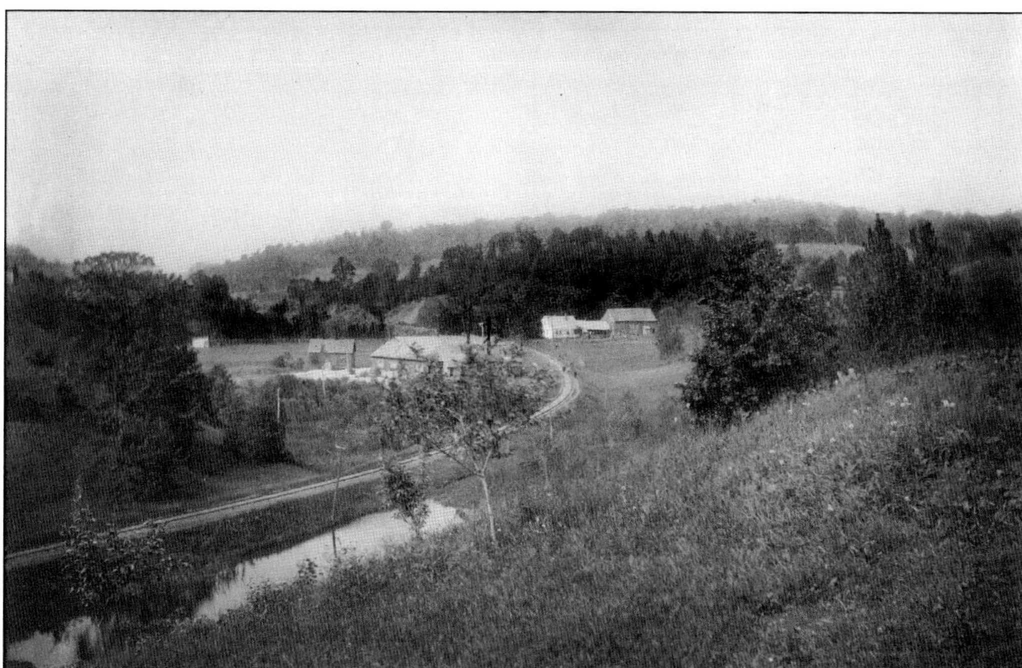

During the great flood of 1927, the water washed out the railroad tracks. Note the railroad's proximity to the river. The *Barre Daily Times* noted that reconstruction began in 1929. The first train after the flood was a single, self-propelled electro-gasoline combination car.

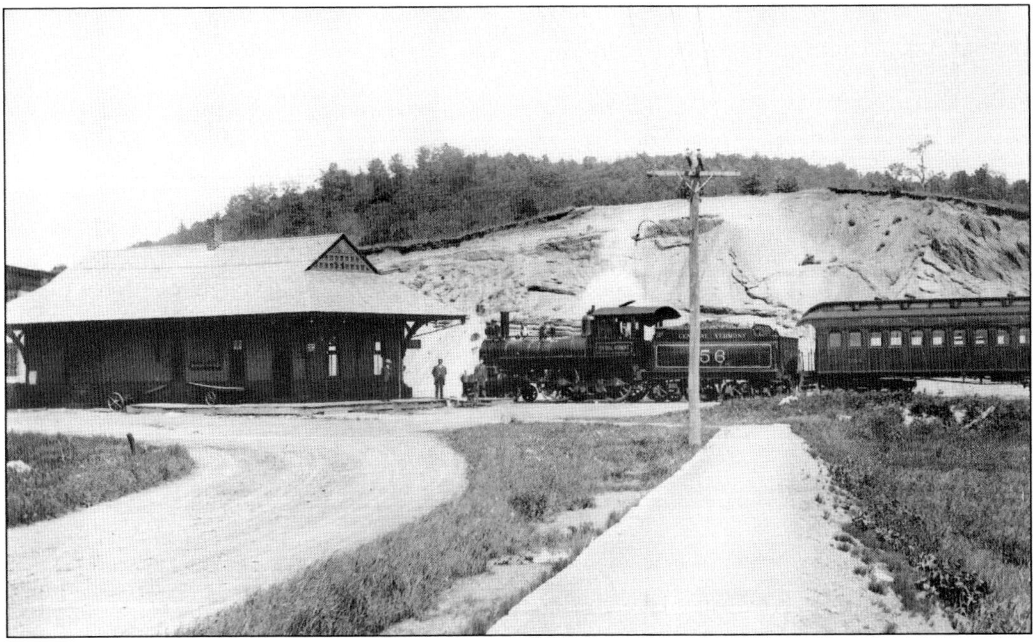

The clip-clop of horses' hooves could still be heard along Depot Road until the mid-1939, when the iron horse took its last ride. The Williamstown Branch Railroad lasted 50 years. This photograph shows the last train that came to Williamstown on September 15, 1938.

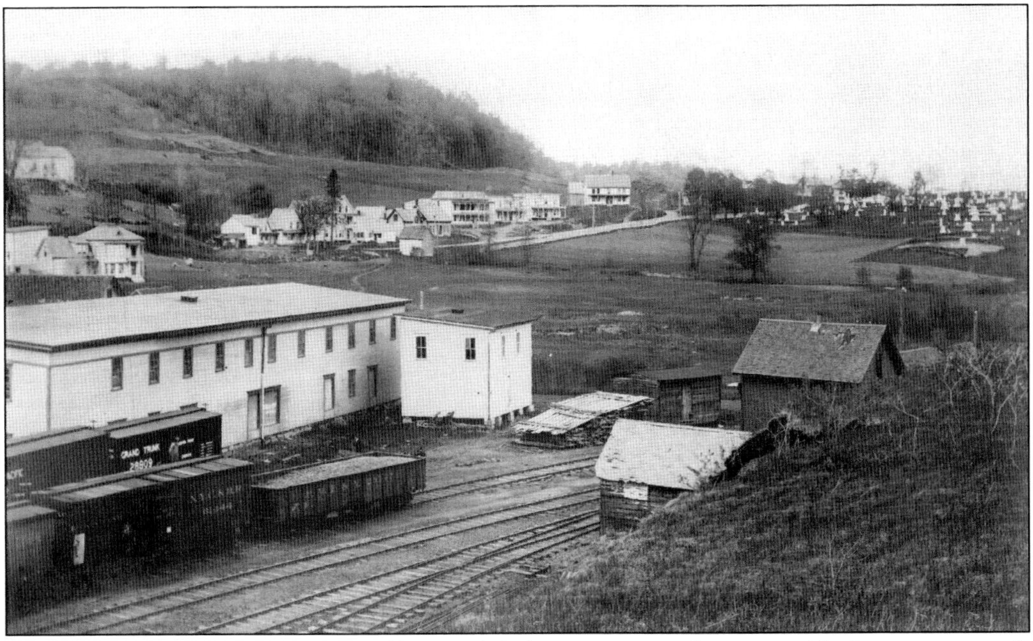

The railroad enriched and enhanced human life; however, once the cars and highways improved, railroad profits significantly declined. Shown here is the back of the feed store and train tracks with idle boxcars. The boxcars had been used to carry freight like grain, granite, lumber, and many other items. Note the village cemetery in the background.

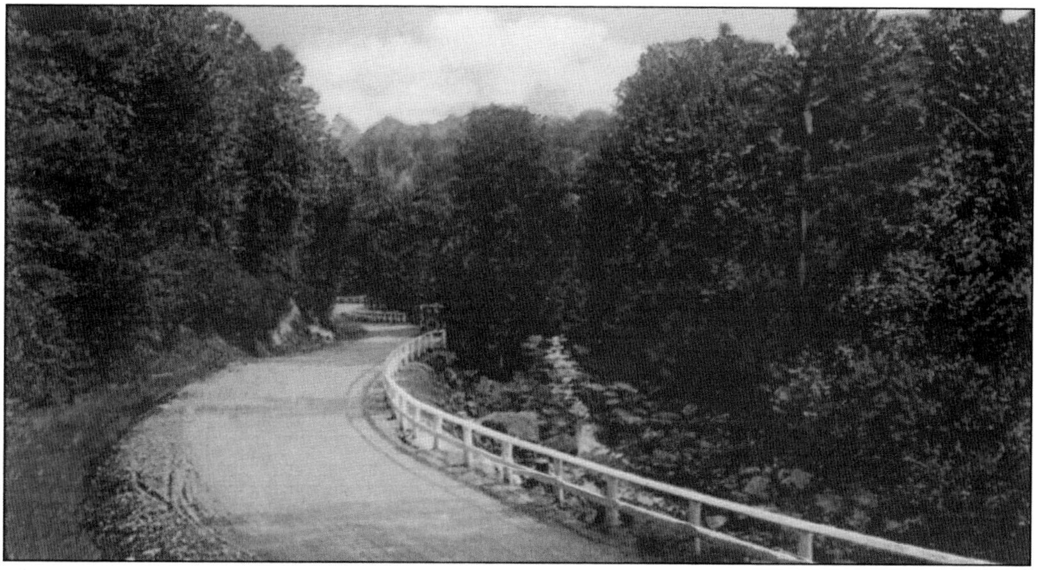

This postcard shows Route 14 just south of the village where it heads into the Williamstown Gulf. Roadmen in the spring would have to plow dirt roads and regravel them, pull cars out of the deep mud, repair the roads, and straighten the guardrail. On the other end of the gulf, the town road commissioner may have had to dodge Canada geese chicks playing in the road. (Photograph by Landscapes.)

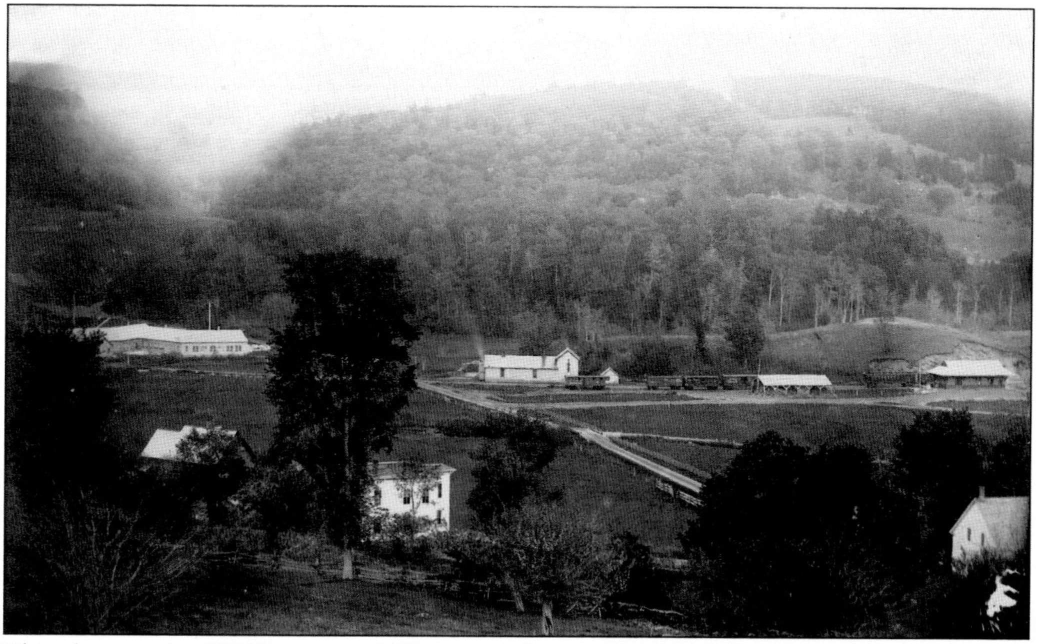

This photograph of Williamstown Village was taken in the 1890s. (Courtesy of Ruth Whitney.)

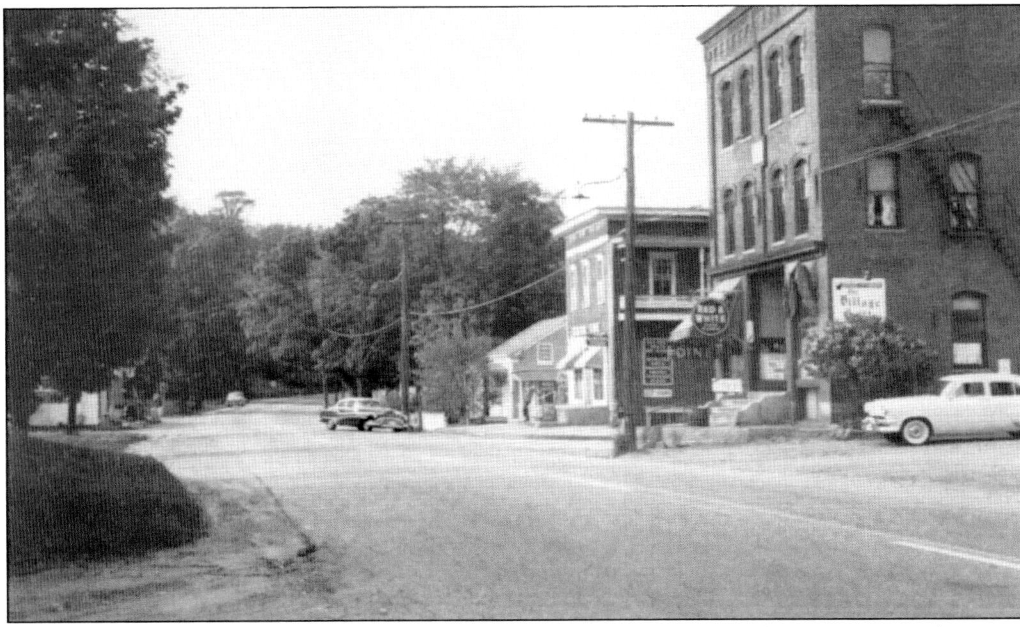

In the mid-1900s, Main Street in the village was paved to accommodate cars. Note the paved road with the line down the middle. Also note the two-door car parked on the side of the store near the electric poles. With the advent of the automobile, the demand for carriages, harnesses, and livery stables decreased. This photograph is dated 1954.

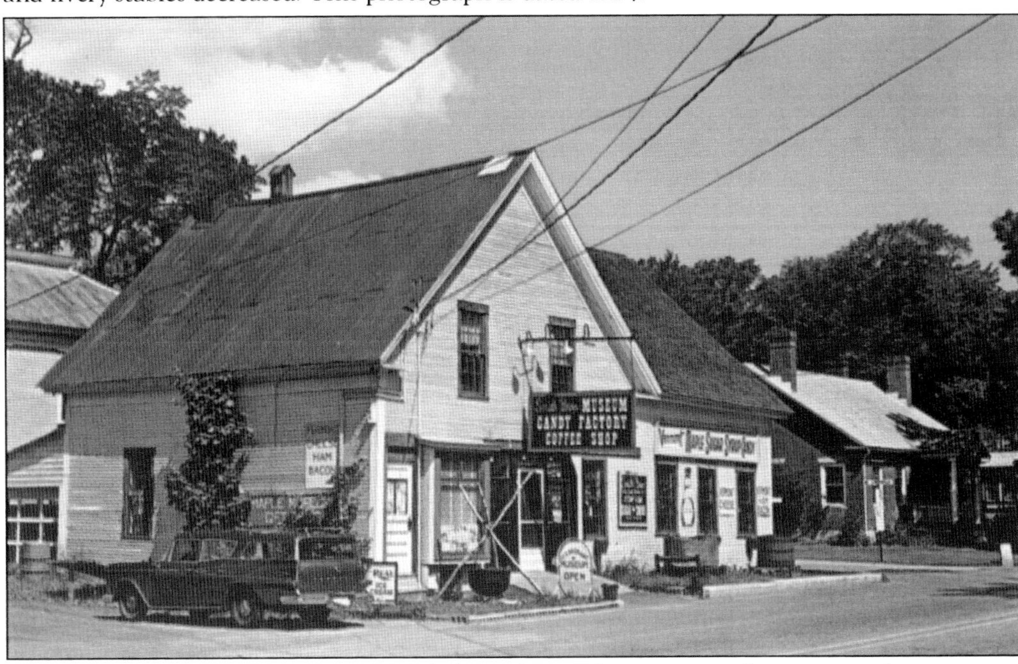

The automobile opened up more possibilities for residents to travel to surrounding towns to purchase a greater variety of goods. This postcard shows a 1956 four-door station wagon parked on the side of the Smith brothers' Museum Candy Factory and Coffee shop on Main Street in Williamstown, where visitors could get a sweet taste of Vermont agriculture—maple syrup products. (Photograph by Don Sieburg; courtesy of Martha Aldous.)

Four

Houses and Housing Style

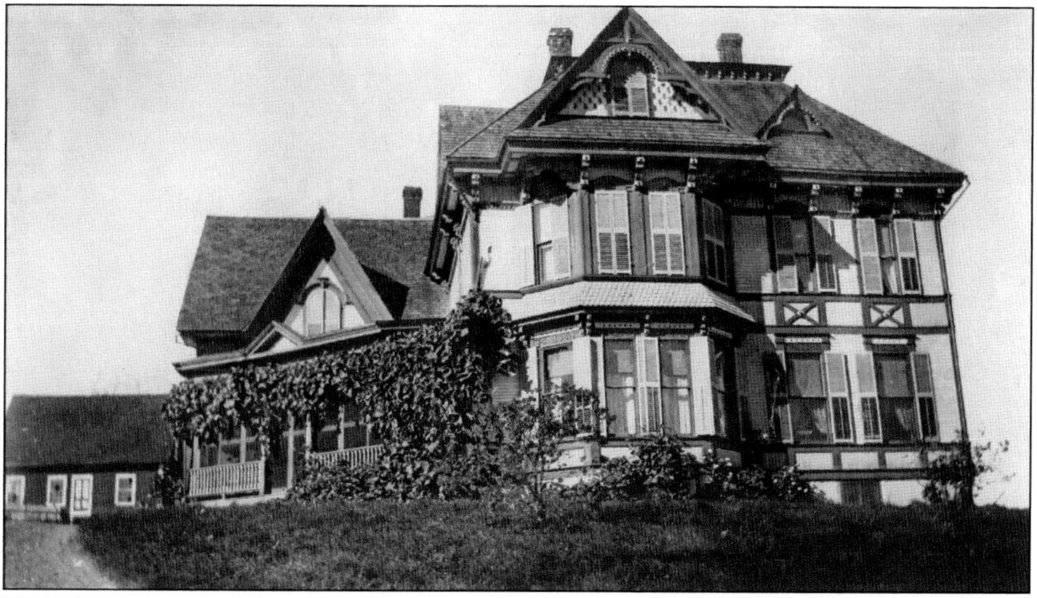

With the expansion of the railroads, people came from far away, like Italy and Scotland, bringing their building traditions with them. The *State of Vermont Historic Sites and Structures Survey* reports that "some building styles in Williamstown are loosely modeled on a few architectural traditions, such as pre-railroad Folk houses, Colonial, early Classical Revival, Italian, and Victorian." The large traditional farmhouses can be seen throughout Williamstown. Pictured here is the house of George Lynde, son of Cornelius Lynde, on Hebert Road.

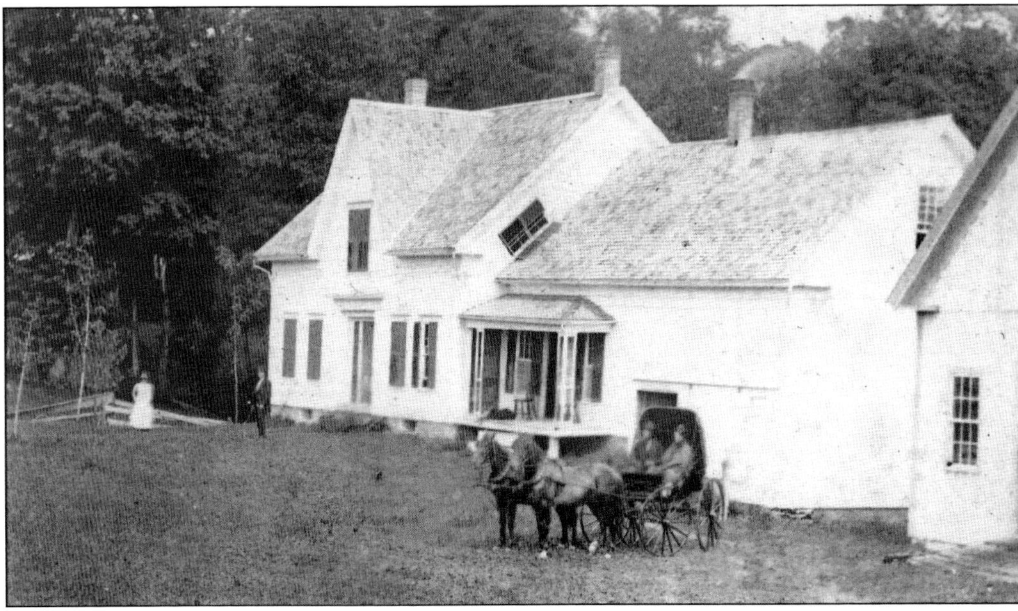

Shown here is the Hawley Gale farm built in the mid-1800s in the Lynde District. It was the home of Norman and Annie (Matheson) Murray in the mid-1900s. Like most farmhouses, it had an apple orchard in the back of the house, a maple sugar house, and barns for a variety of animals. (Photograph by C. Goodrich.)

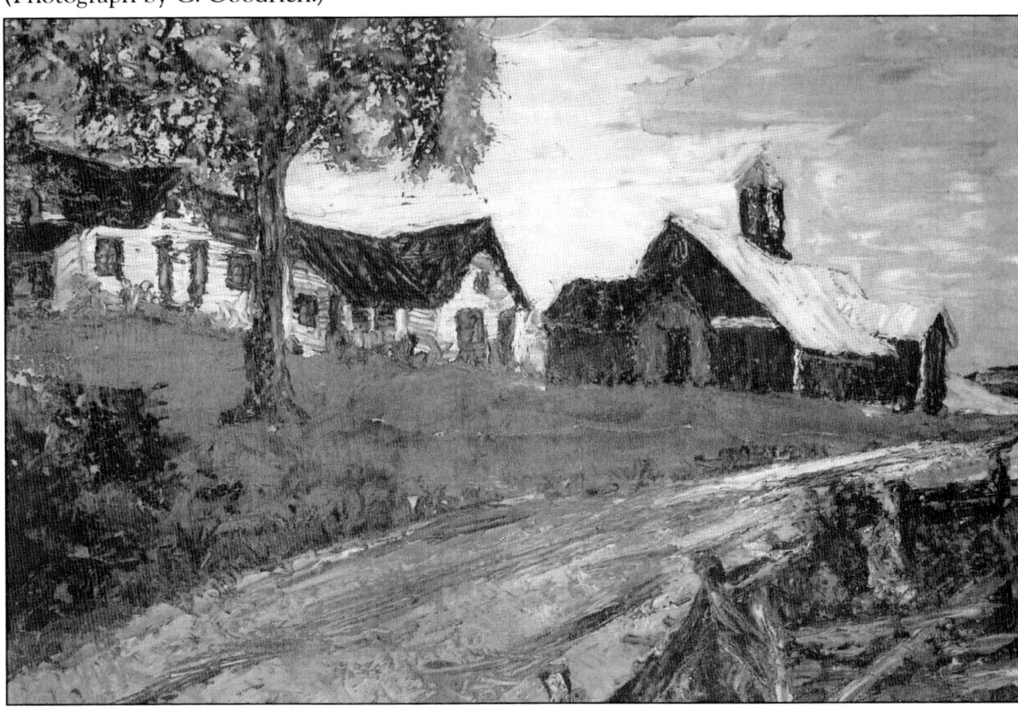

In 1943, Theodore Hengstenberg did this oil painting of the Hawley Gale farmhouse where his grandparents Norman and Annie Murray lived. Their oldest child, Ruth, married Theodore Hengstenberg. Their son Teddy was taking an art class in school, and his cousin Doug, a talented artist, came to visit his relatives in Vermont. (Courtesy of Teddy Hengstenberg.)

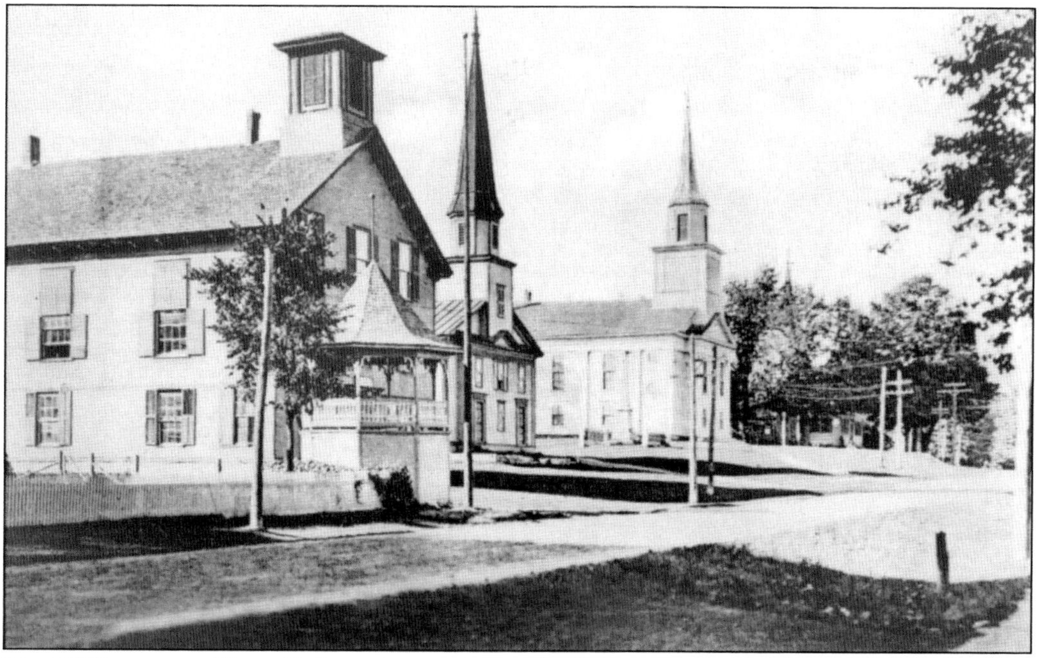

The Williamstown Town Hall, with a gazebo on the front lawn, was built in 1857. The building is in the Williamstown Village Historic District. The *Vermont Historic Sites and Structures Survey* reports "the roof has a cupola and ridge chimney. The entrance is located in the center gable end. Simple brackets support classically detailed cornice and pediment return."

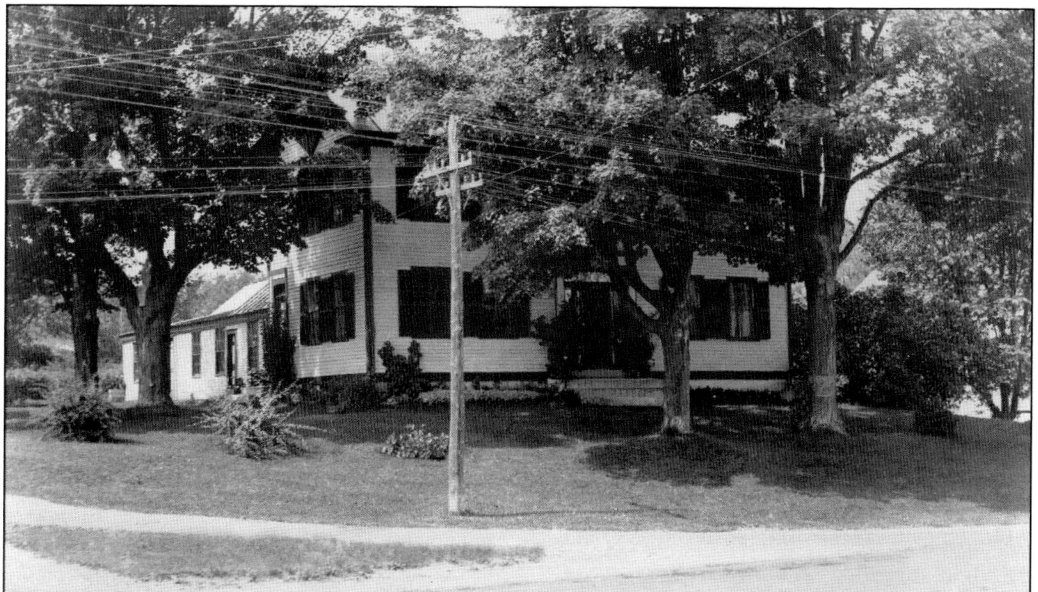

Pictured is the Robinsons' house, commonly known as the Walbridge House, on Main Street in the Williamstown Village Historic District. This is a pre-1820 Federal-style house, built by Darius Pride; it served as the Methodist parsonage from 1860 to 1890. The house has two stories, plus an attic, five-by-three-foot bays, and a post and beam frame. Inside the front entrance is a circular stairway with very fine, round balusters and a handrail with a slender newel post.

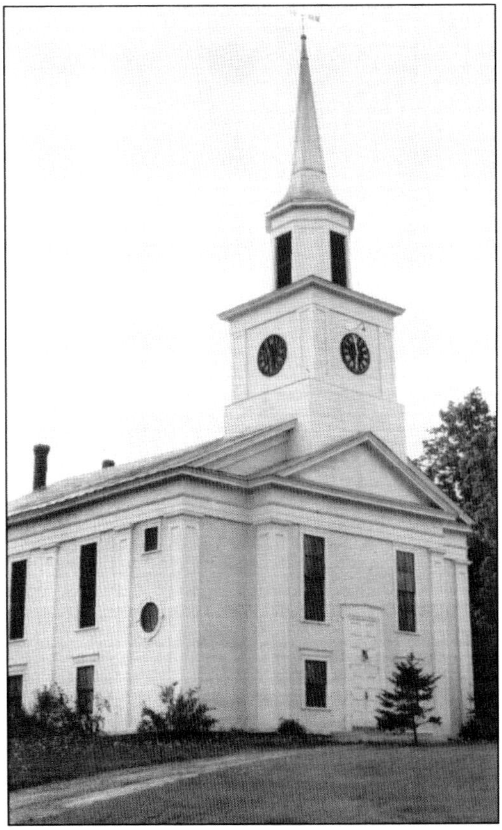

The Congregational church is in the Greek Revival style, with a gable roof and projecting pavilion with steeple. This land was deeded to the town by Perely Howe, who stipulated that this structure remain maintained according to the tradition of Greek Revival. A new church was built in 1851–1852, styled in the 1825 style (not Greek Revival). It was restored to better reflect the traditional style. In 1920, the clock on the 1890 steeple was added.

In 1895, George Bosworth, a Barre photographer, took this picture of nine partially identified builders holding a variety of tools used to build and spackle the inside walls of the Congregational church while it was being remodeled. From left to right are (first row) Jerry Hutchinson and two unidentified; (second row) Jessie Aubin, Paul Wilfore, Lewis Dragon, Charlie Williams, Oliver Dickenson, unidentified.

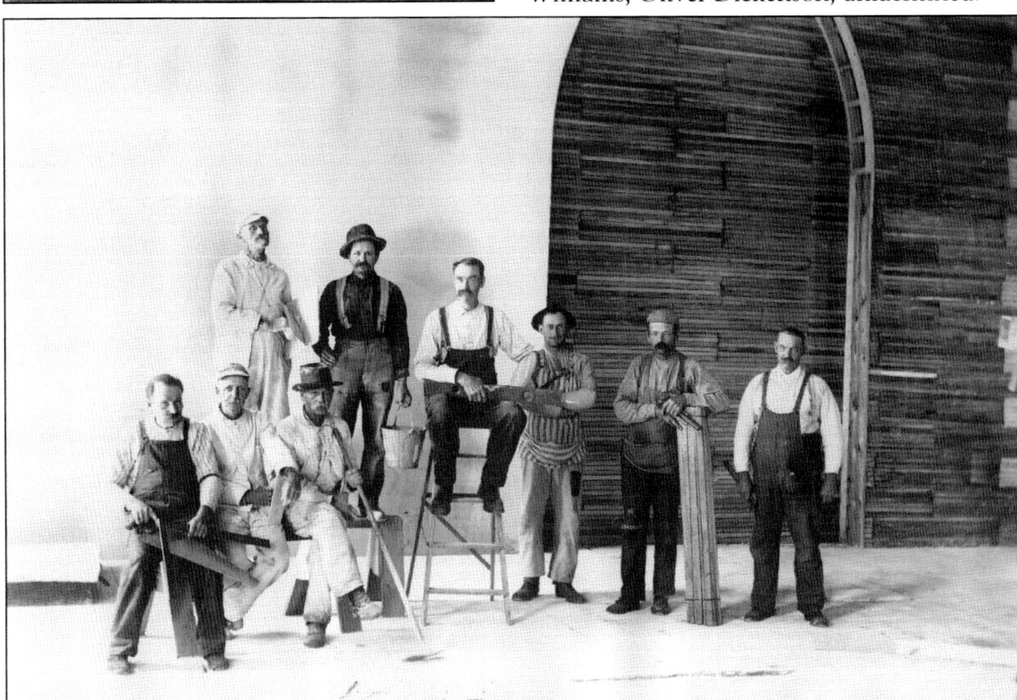

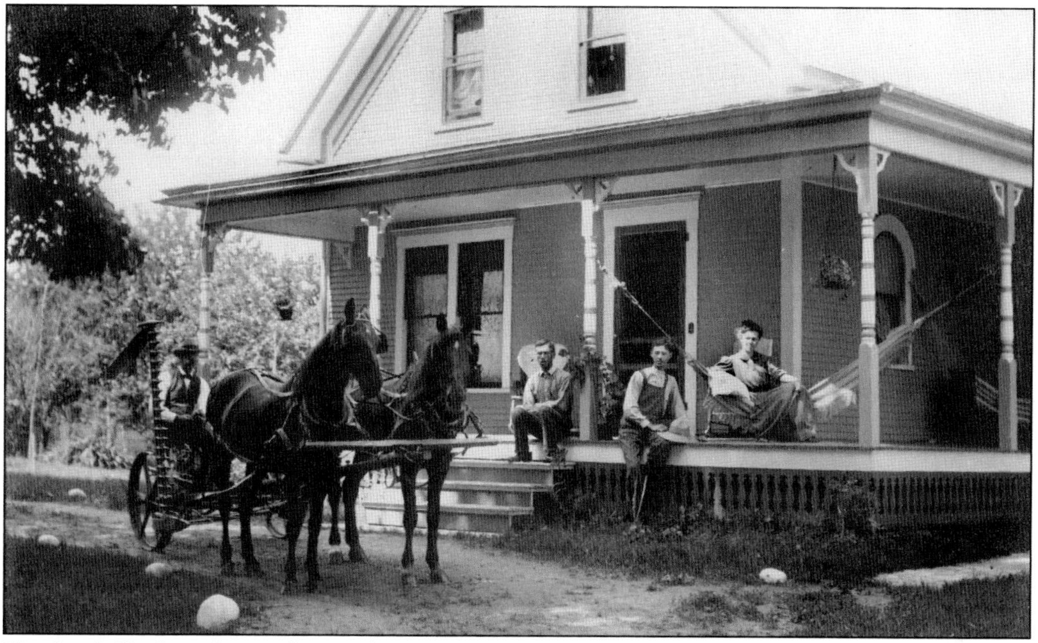

Hayden Jeffords is shown driving his mowing machine in 1910. His three children, from left to right, Percy, Richard, and Nina, are on the porch. Hayden Jeffords built the house in 1909. The carpenter was Jerry M. Hutchinson. Note the curved window and the wraparound porch.

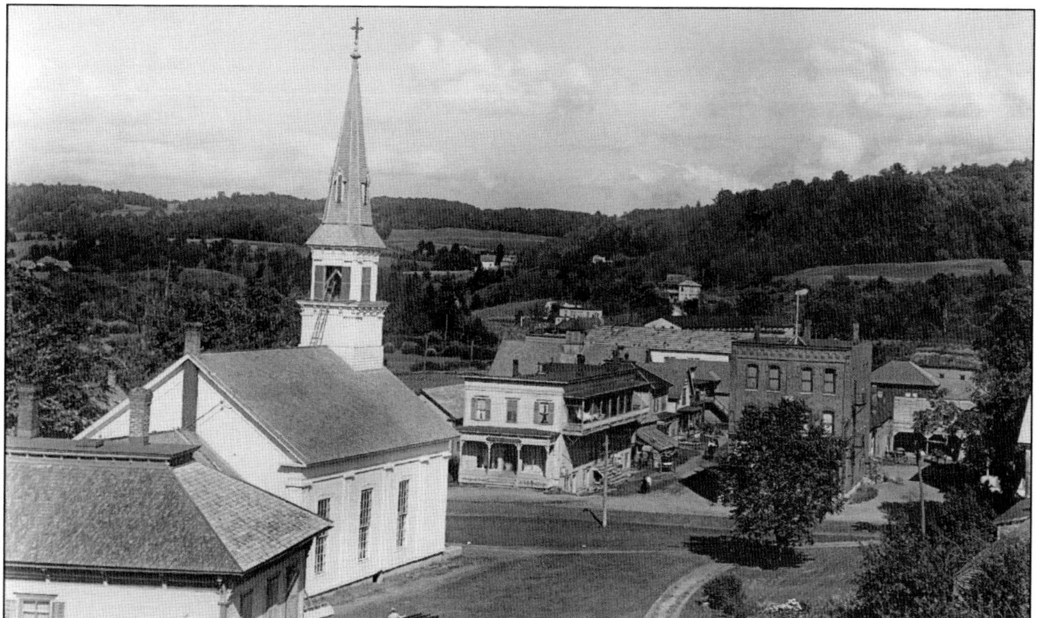

Pictured here is the Methodist church, which was built in the Federal style. Classical details include engaged pilasters defining four side bays and visually supporting fully articulated entablature. The building has a classically detailed gable front. Queen Anne, Italianate, and high-Victorian Gothic styles with shingles, paired brackets, and beautiful stained glass pointed windows are also found. Note the ladder on the roof leaning into the 1895 steeple window and the man leaning over the water trough.

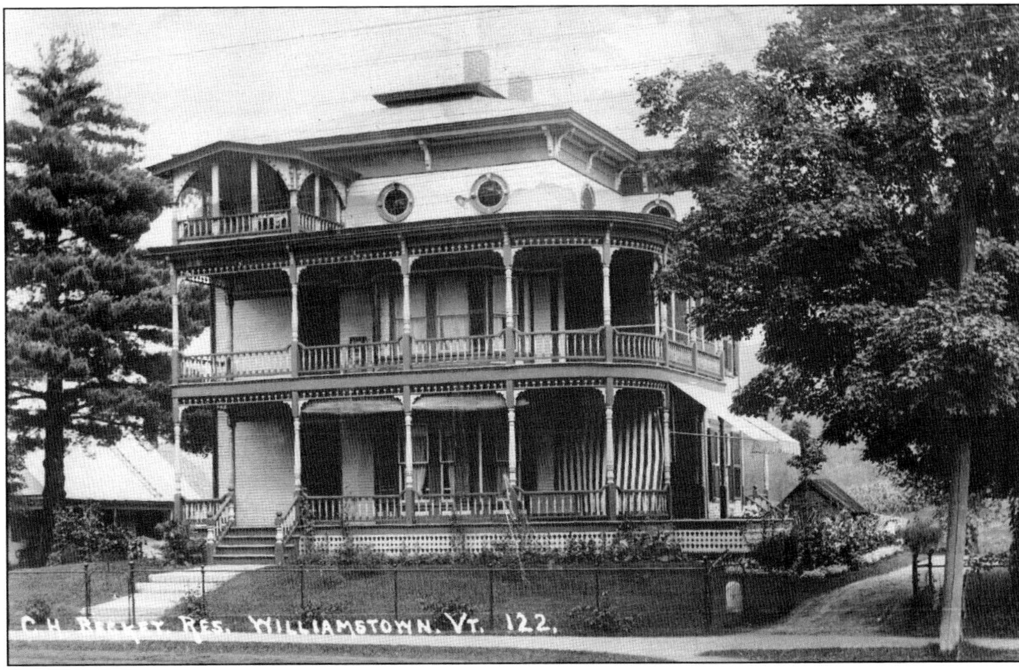

George and Belle Beckett's colorful Victorian house was built in 1898 on Main Street in the village. The porch was built to make a statement with its columns and elaborate pediments. The *Barre-Montpelier Times Argus* showcased the property in June 1992 as the Rosewood Inn and as being the only Vermont property featured in the book *America's Painted Ladies.* (Photograph by Studio of Eastern Illustrating.)

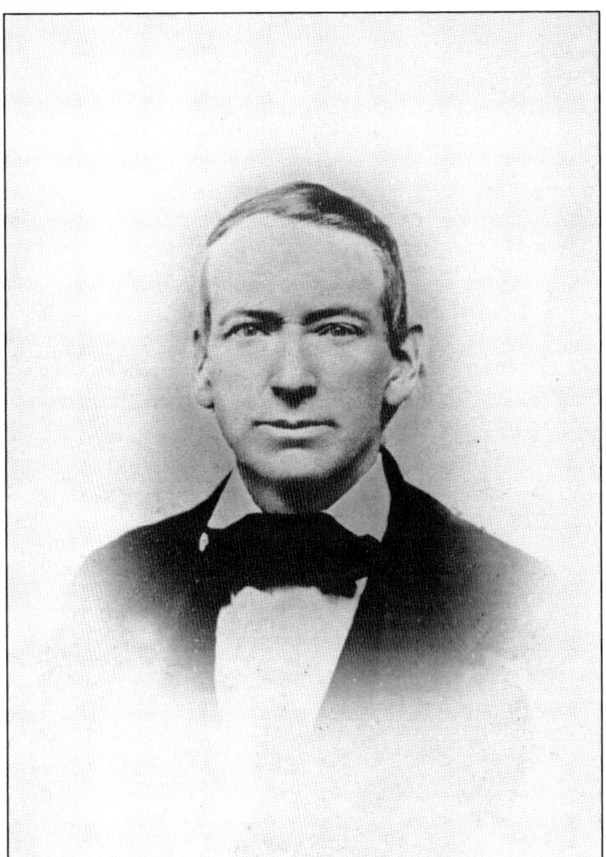

Pictured here is George Beckett, a well-known and respected man in town. Beckett held two town positions including town clerk and town treasurer. He was a deacon and treasurer of the Congregational church as well as a public notary. (Photograph by G.W. Dabis; courtesy of Irene Walbridge.)

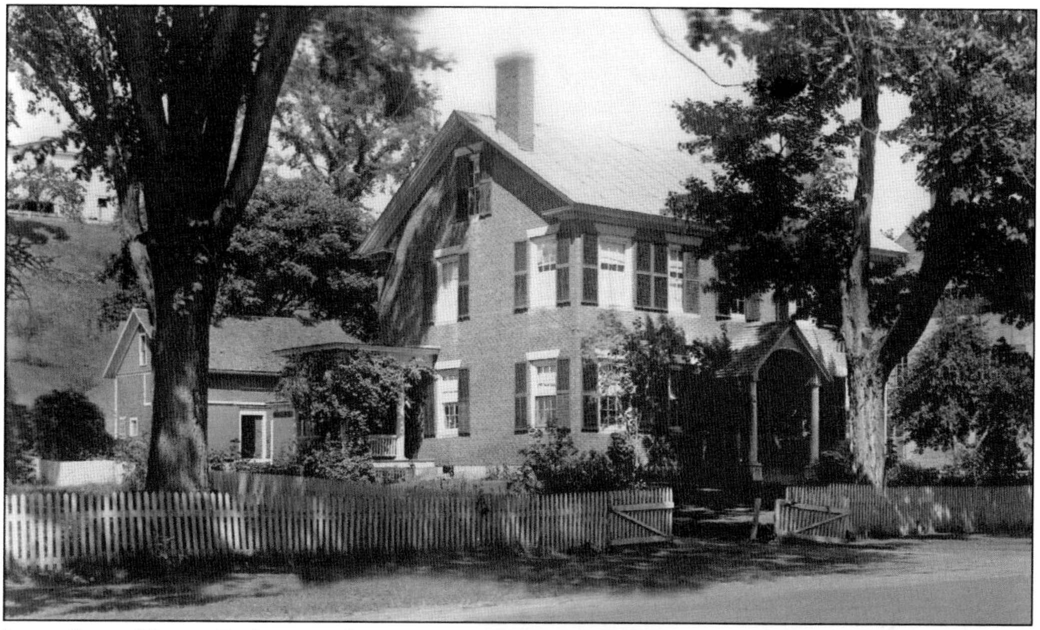

Laura L. and James E. Ainsworth owned this charming five-ranked Federal-style brick house. The two story house features a balanced symmetrical look, with the front door in the middle, and an even number of windows on either side. Federal-style houses also had a fan over the front door. Also note the double chimneys on both ends of the building. (Photograph by Eastern Illustrating Company.)

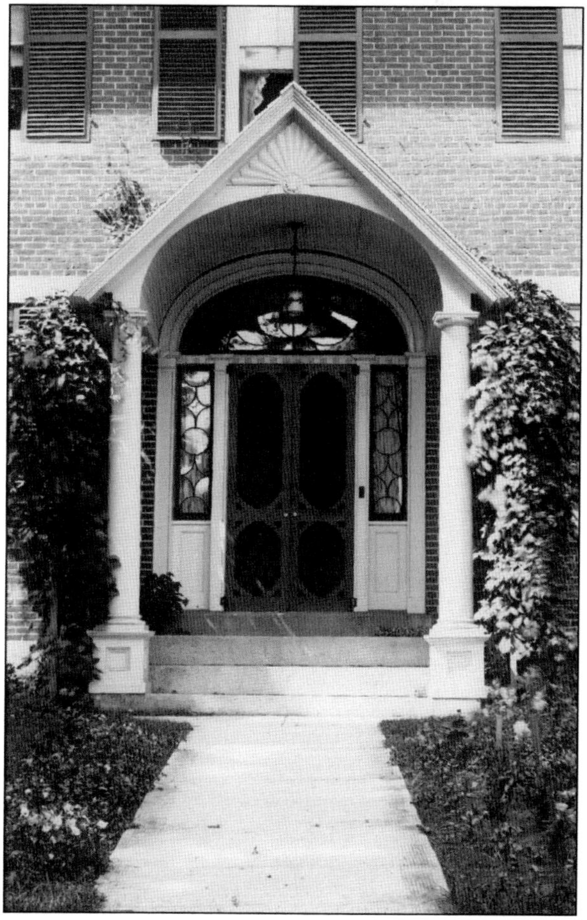

The front door of the Ainsworth house is shown on this postcard. Scrawled in longhand on the back is, "I like the door very much. How do you like it? Mrs. Laura Ainsworth." (Courtesy of Bertha Morgan.)

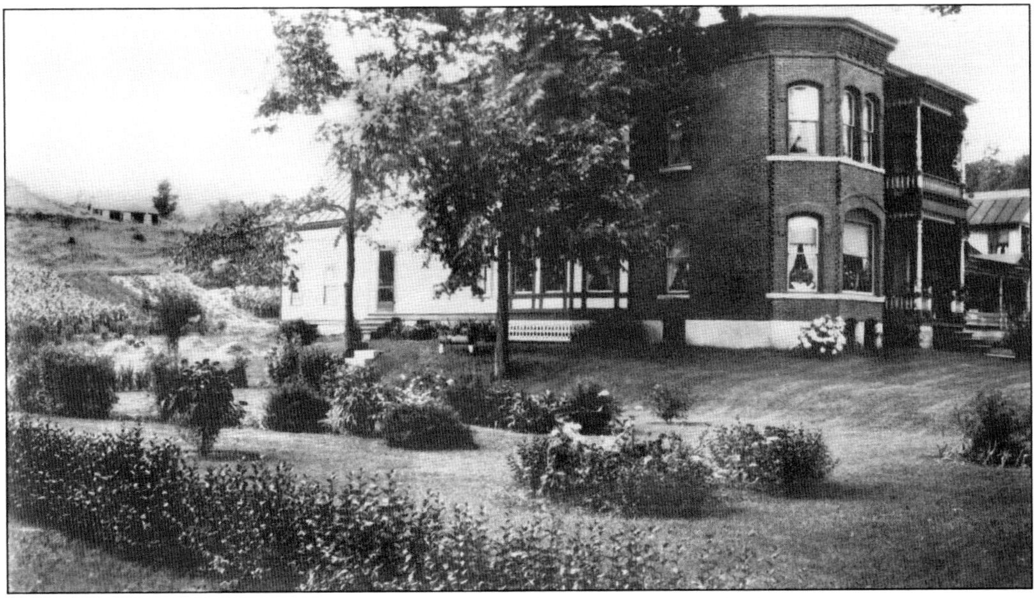

Williamstown Village is blessed with the beautiful brick house of Charles "Chas" and Leona Briggs. Following the Civil War, industrial and economic energy resulted in a variety of new architectural styles. Brick making also improved during this time, and bricks became easy to access and reasonably priced. Brick making was an important industry in the adjacent town of Northfield, and the railroad brought bricks into town from other states.

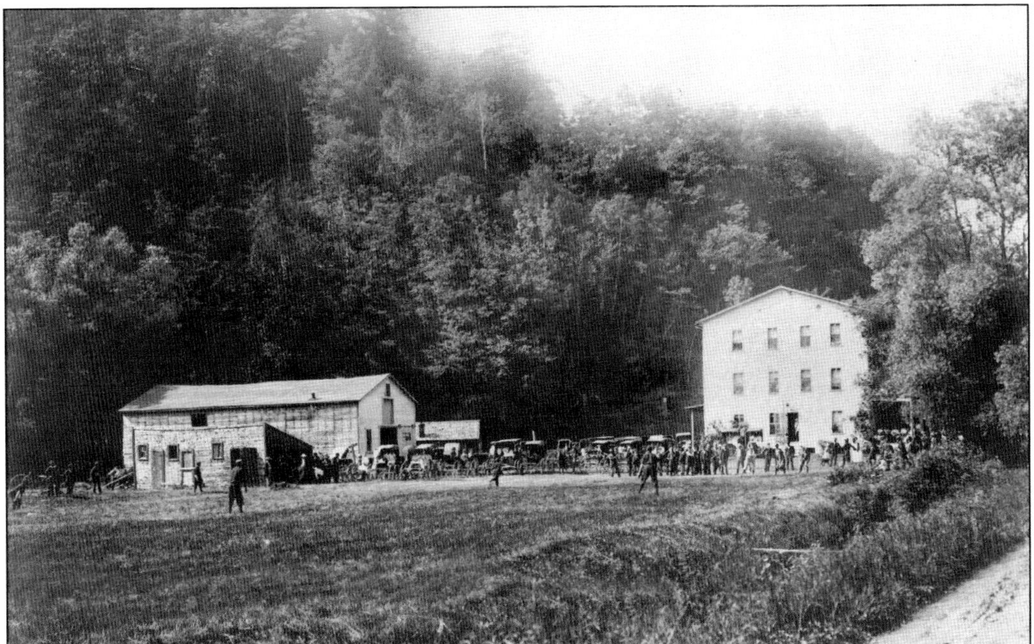

Shown here is the Gulf House located in the Williamstown Gulf. Men are playing baseball on the lawn during a Fourth of July celebration. The photograph was taken in the early 1900s.

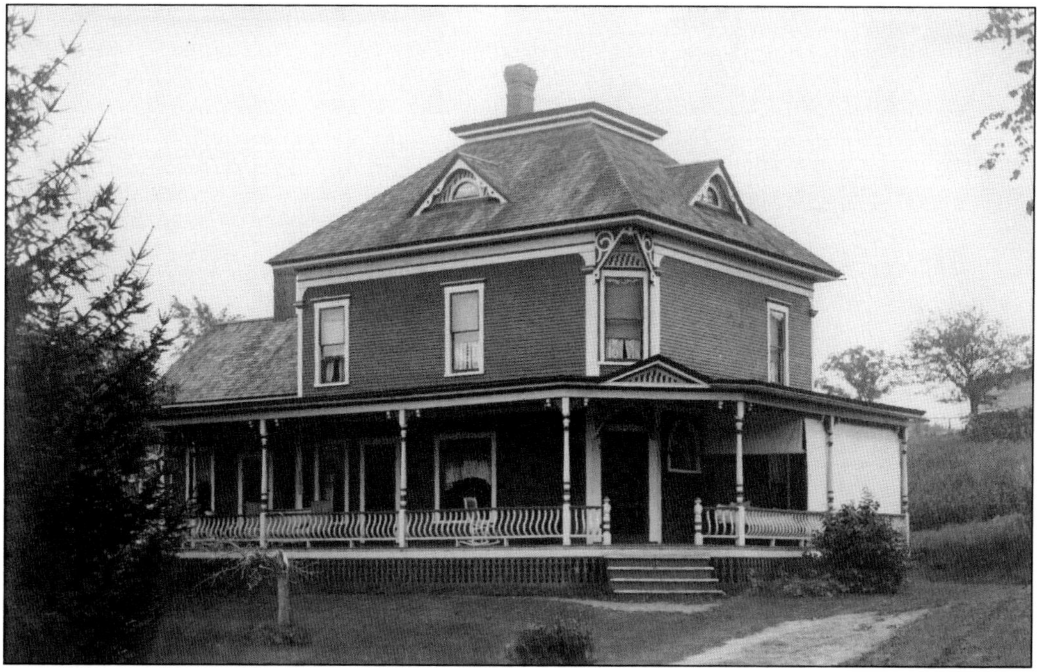

The W.V. Grearson house has a wraparound porch and central chimney. The windows show its beautiful decorative detail. Early houses were heated by wood and coal and lit by kerosene lamps. Water was either carried in from the back spring or there was a kitchen pump. Early houses had no indoor bathroom facilities; instead, individuals had to make use of an outhouse and used washtubs for bathing. (Photograph by Studio of Eastern Illustrating.)

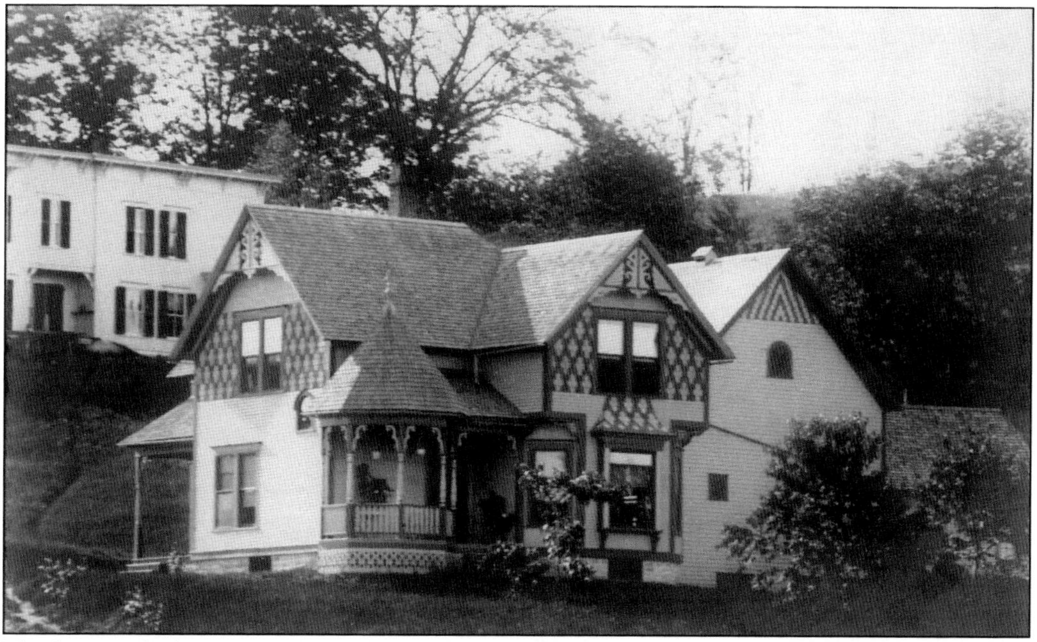

The house of John Dow is shown here; in the 1960s, it was the home of John White. The porch pavilion was a favorite during the Colonial Revival era. The band saw inspired carpenters to try new and creative ways of expression, as seen on the wall surface.

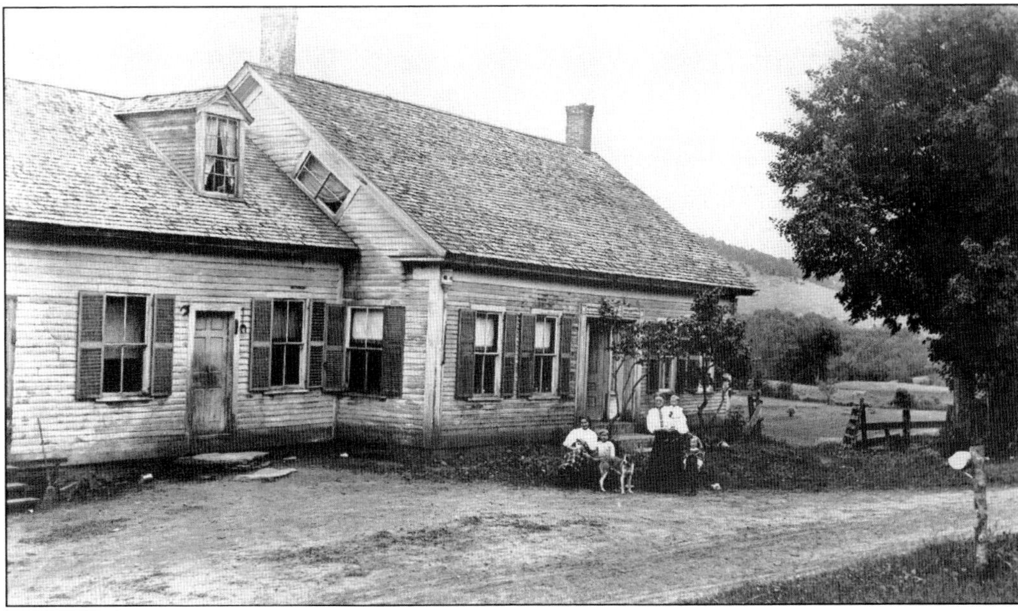

In 1803, Sam Adams owned this classic farmhouse. Most farmhouses were plainly painted white with red roofs. In 1858, E.H. Covell purchased this farmhouse.

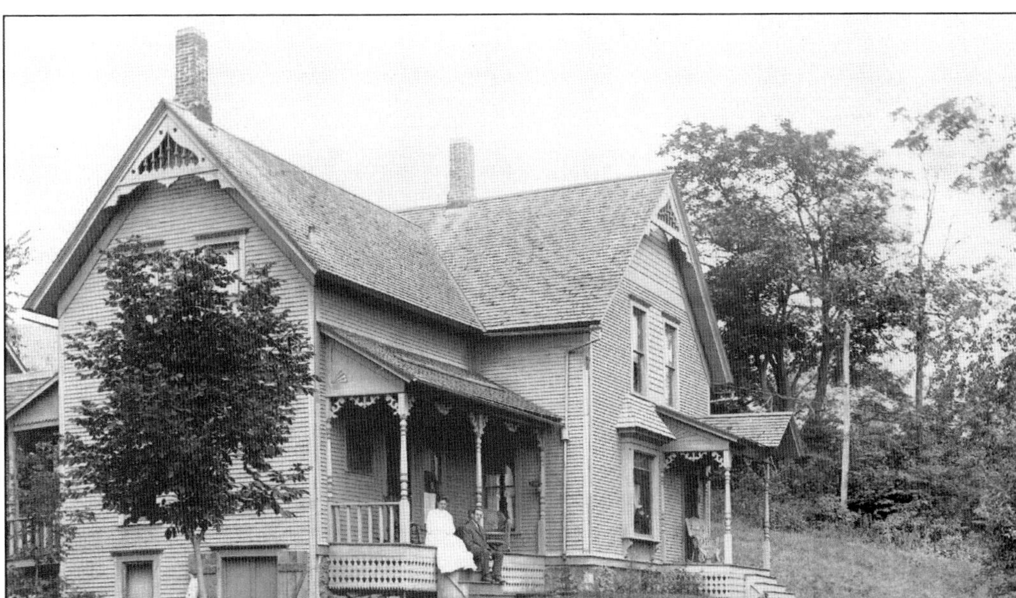

The house of Dr. Vern and Anna Edson is shown here; later on, Mr. and Mrs. Gauthier owned the house. It offers two or more porches for residents to sit outside, enjoy the beautiful view, and listen to the spring peepers singing in the fields.

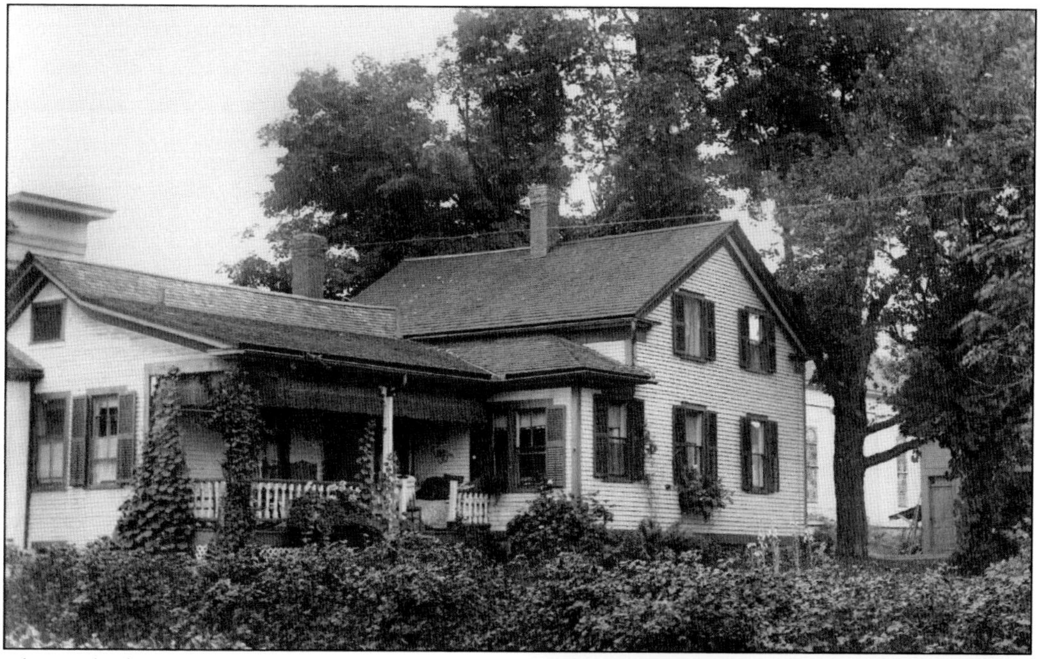

This is the home of Charles M. Seaver and Lissie (Work) Seaver on Main Street. Note the vines clinging to the front porch. Charles M. Seaver partnered with Lewis Mead Seaver in a grain and feed business.

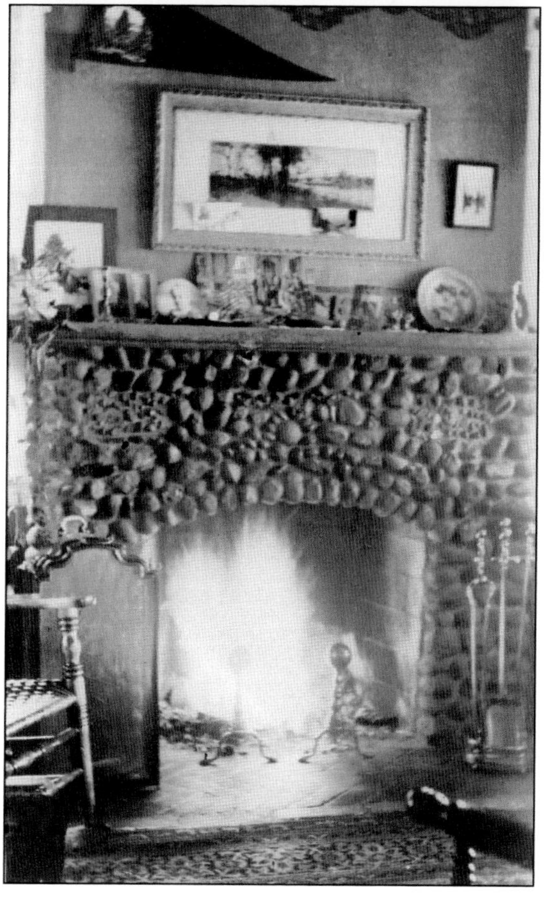

Early homes had very drafty walls, and most had many fireplaces. In the winter of 1900, when the snow was piled high outside, Charles and Lissie Seaver stayed warm and cozy inside the house near the often-replenished fire.

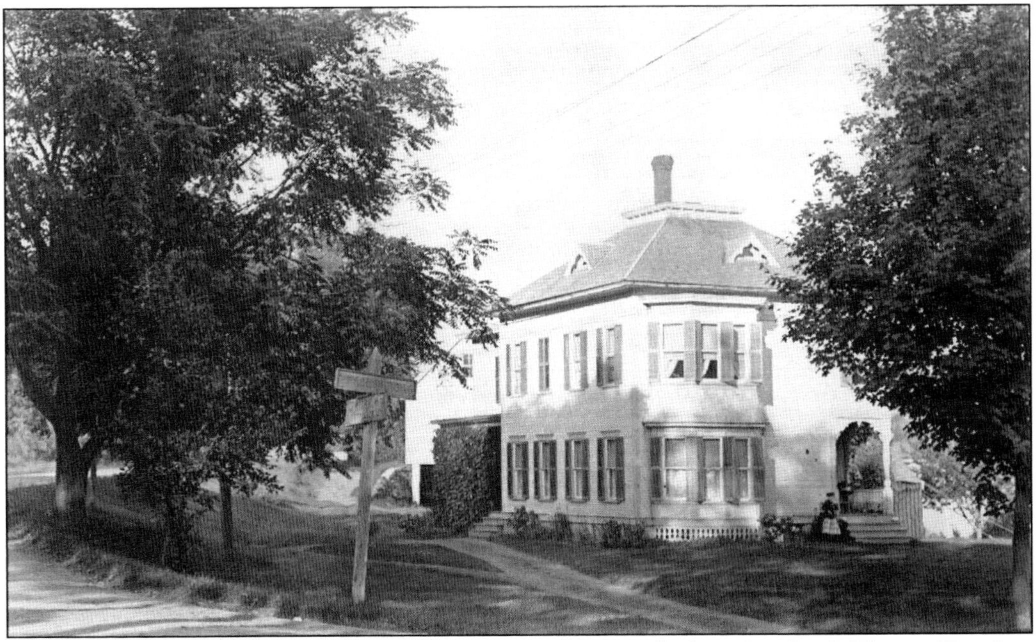

Early settler James Hopkins, who built this house, was originally from Scotland. The roof has four eyebrow dormers and a big central chimney, which served multiple fireplaces. Note the woman standing between the bay windows and porch. Inside the porch door, the house opened up to a very large hall that served as a great room.

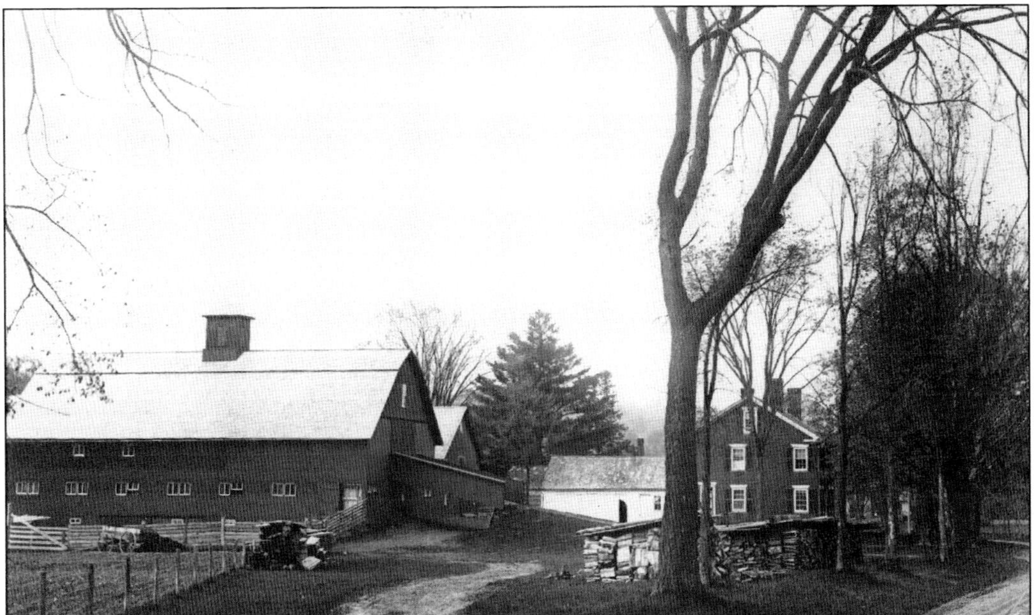

Pictured is the Chester Martin farm, later owned by W.Z. Pratt, Ruth Mould, and the Gardens; the barn burned in 1921.

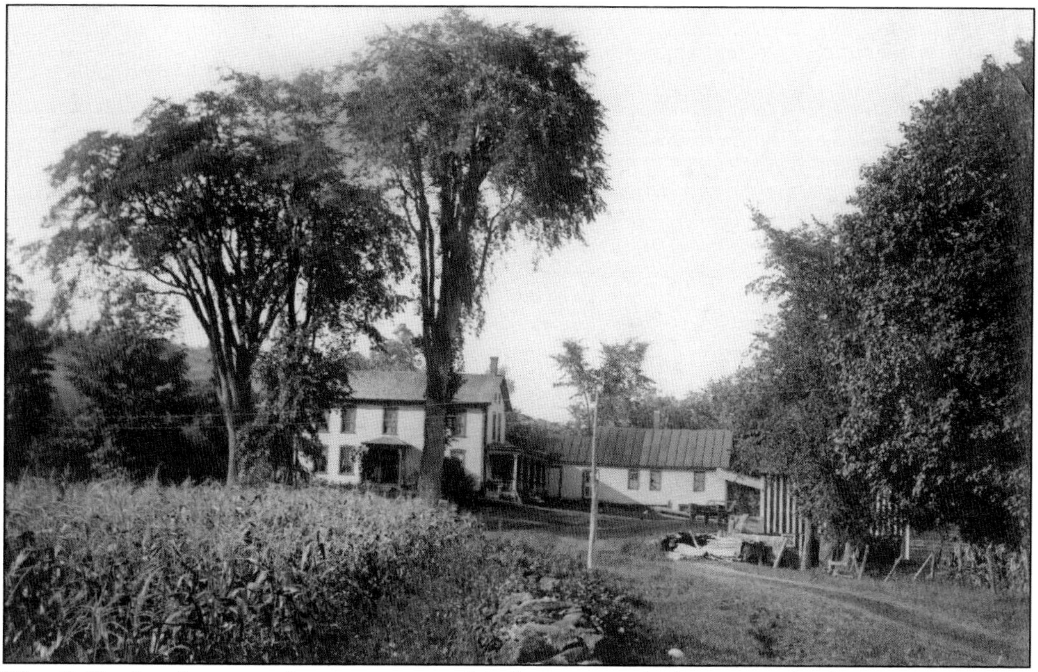

The Colby farmhouse and towering graceful elm trees with distinctive feather duster tops are shown here; tall corn grows in the front field.

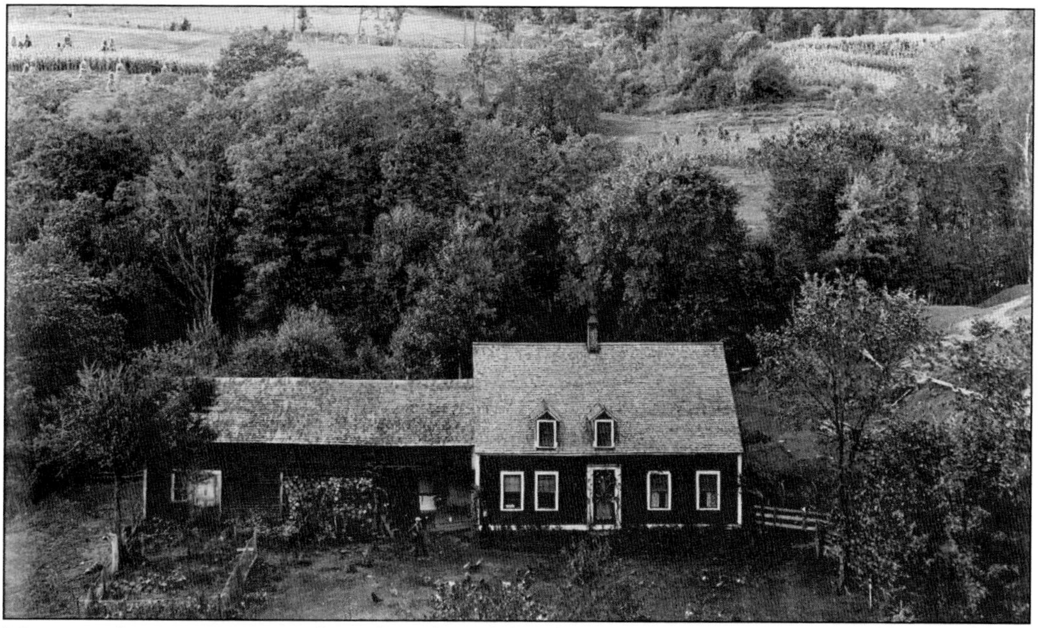

Many residents sent postcards to friends and family. This one reads, "Dear Aunt Lute I don't believe you will ever get down here to see what kind of place I am in so I am sending you this card. It is fine here in the summer. And I think it shall be alright this winter. I want to see you awfully and think I shall before time. With love to all - Nell." Nell stands near the left corner of the house.

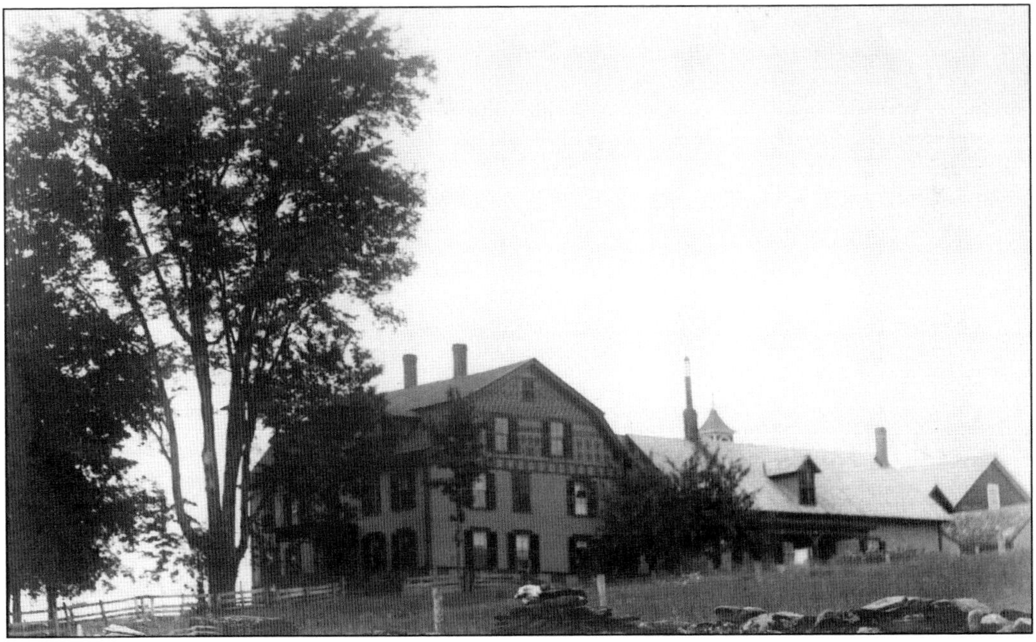

The rambling home of Charles and Lizzie (Work) Seaver is shown here. Note the barn and outbuildings attached to the house and the stone wall in the foreground. (Courtesy of Marjorie Call Mongto.)

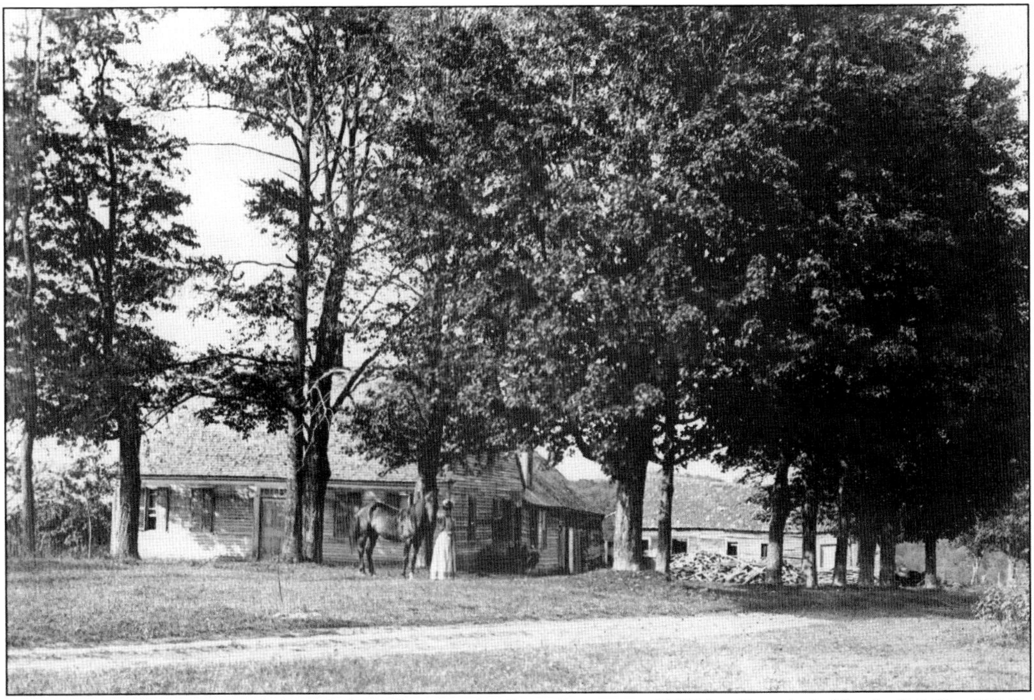

This farmhouse was built by Elisha Flint and taken down in 1907 by Frank Jeffords (1868–1934); he built a new house on the farm lot. Jeffords married May Pratt on May 1, 1891, and they farmed in Williamstown. Note the woodpile ready for stacking in the woodshed. Evenly spaced maple trees line the road.

Five

Industrial Development

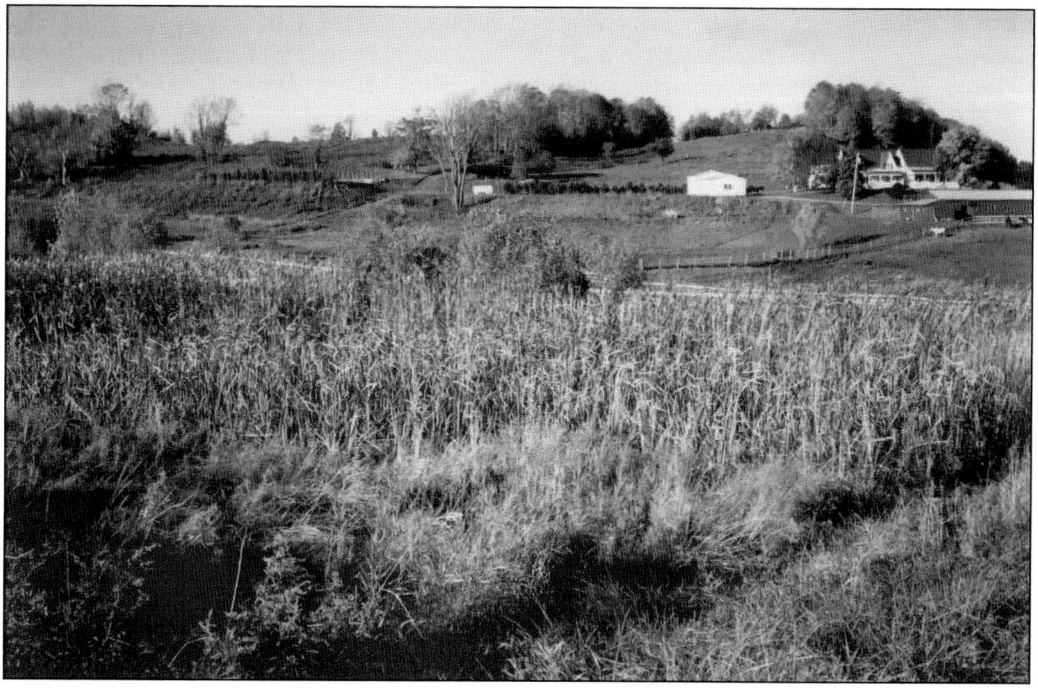

Thomas Davenport, credited with the invention of the electric motor, was born in a farmhouse on West Hill in Williamstown. In 1834, Davenport designed and built an electromagnetic motor, similar to today's DC motors. Although crude, Davenport's motor was the prototype for every electrical motor used in the world today. This picture shows the land where he lived as a child. The farmhouse was eventually torn down, and a new building was erected on the site.

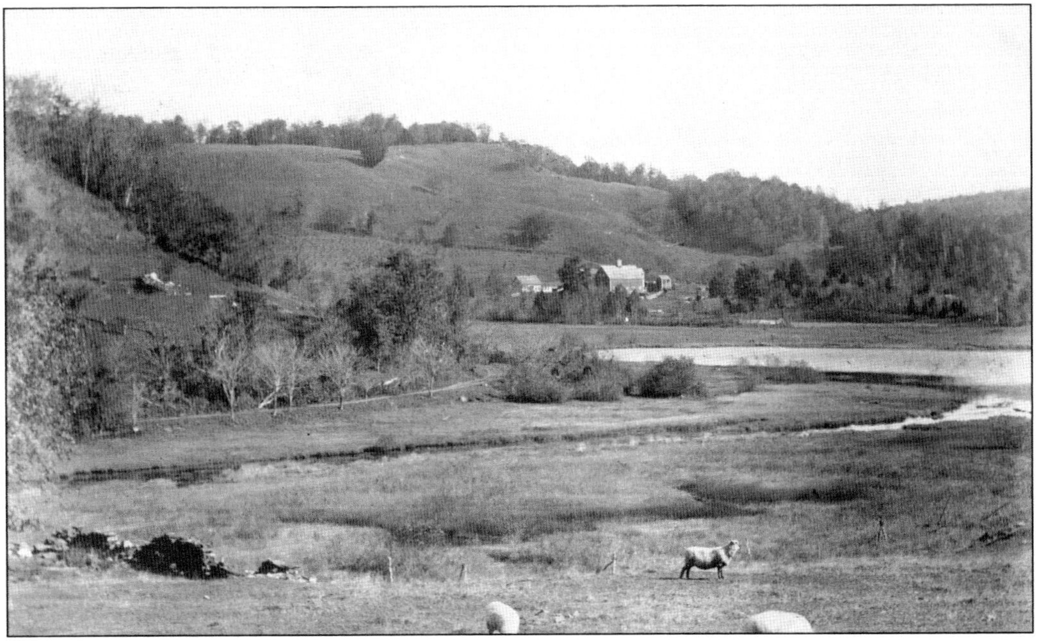

Early settler Elijah Paine was a scientific farmer owning many horses, cattle, pigs, and sheep. He worked from sunrise to sunset, eventually converting his rocky and barren hillside into very fertile fields. When Merino sheep were introduced to Vermont in 1812, Paine began breeding them and eventually had about 15,000. It was a lucrative business, as wool was used to make clothing and uniforms.

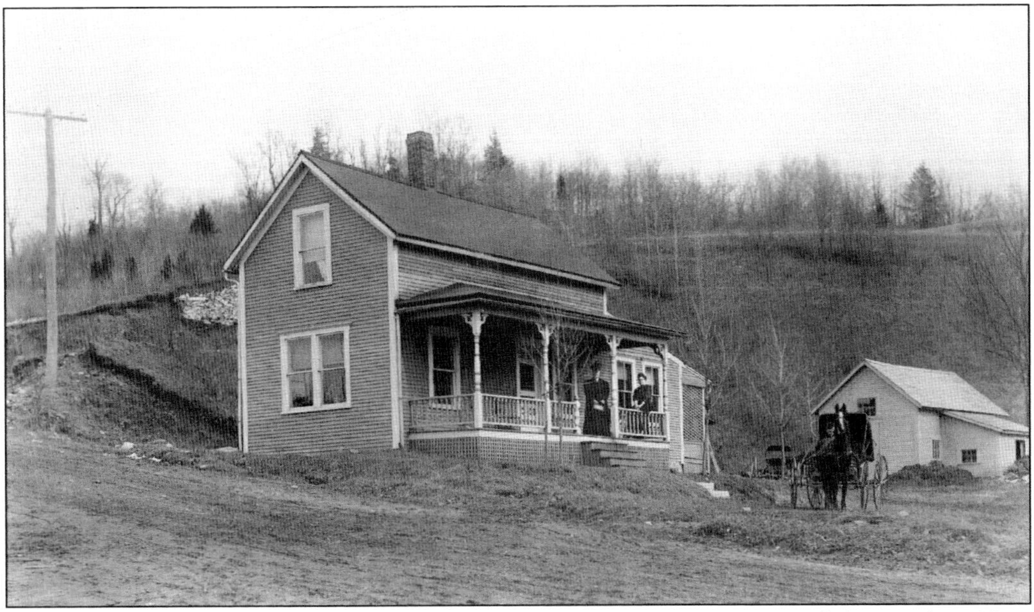

Dora Brockway (left) stands on the porch of her house on Quarry Street with her mother Alma Platt. Her father is riding in the horse-drawn carriage. The building was finally used as a creamery but was later torn down. A new house was built in its place that was occupied by Gordon Wilcox. Rural areas of Vermont did not start getting electricity until the early to mid-1900s. Note the electricity pole in back of the house.

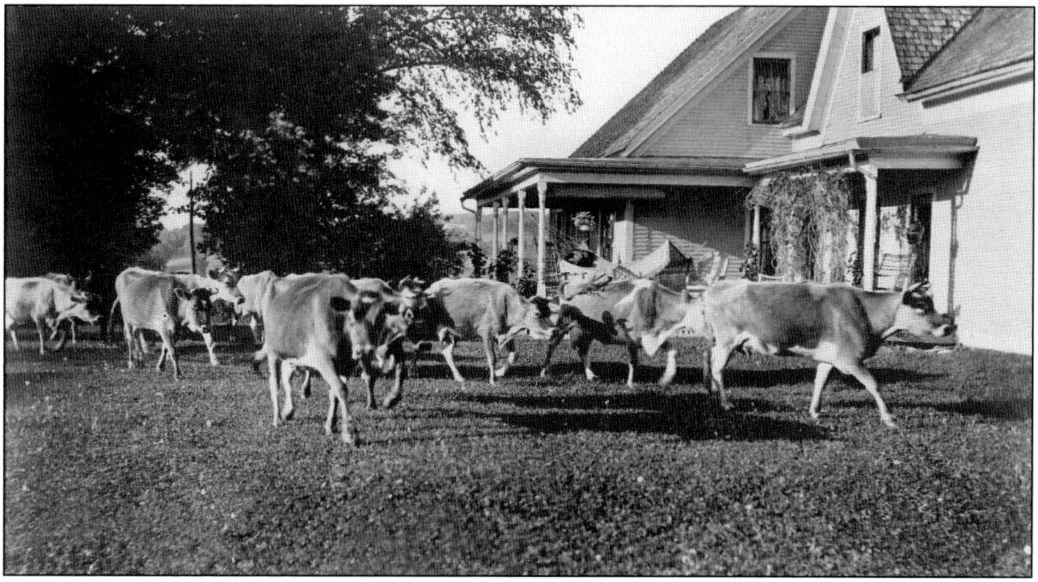

In the 1850s, the milking cow population increased while the Merino sheep population started to decrease. Farmers enjoyed the move from laborious tiny hand squeezes to sterilized powered milking machines. Other agricultural machines, like manure conveyors and tractors, helped farmers increase their businesses beyond their own family needs. Pictured here are cows on their way to the barn at milking time on Elenwood Farm.

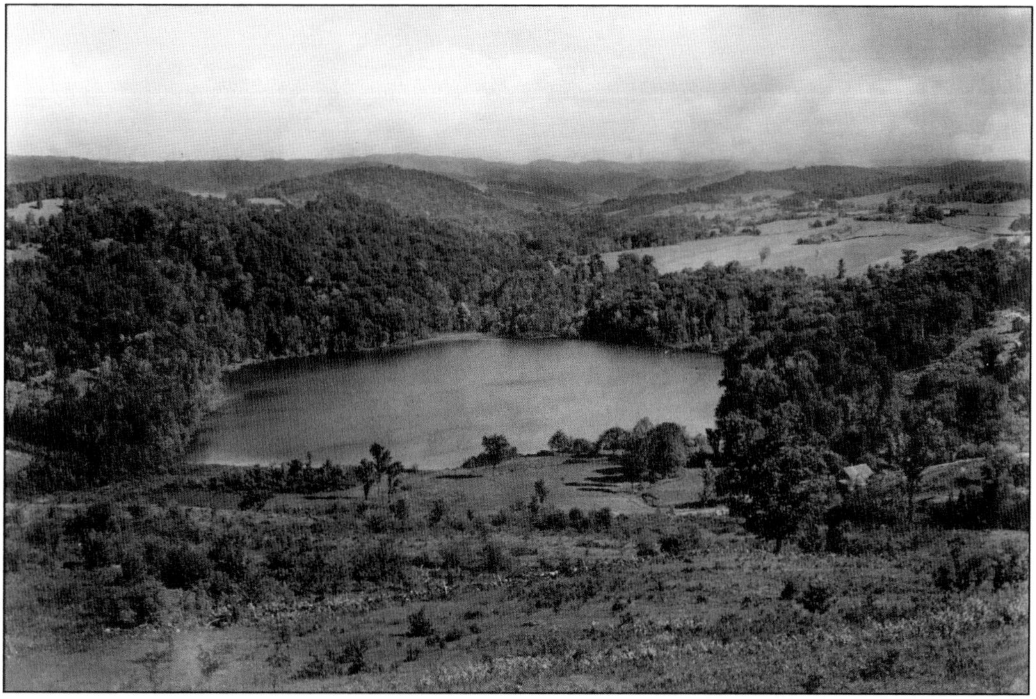

Williamstown is credited with having the first dial telephone system (with a switchboard) in the state of Vermont. Residents would pick up the telephone, and an operator would assist. The *Barre Daily Times* reported on January 27, 1930, that a telephone had been installed at James Lacillade's house on the Rood Pond Road and the ring was 1-22. Lacillade's land is pictured here.

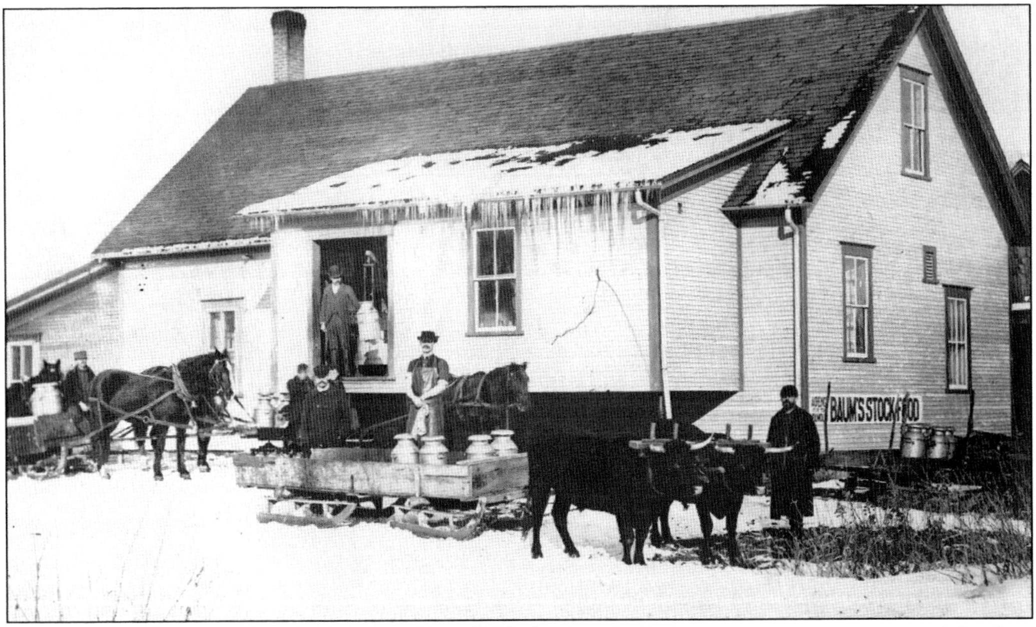

Pictured is a pair of yoked oxen pulling a milk sled at a receiving station or creamery on Meadow Street in Williamstown. The man with the oxen is Russell M. Jeffords. In a time before refrigeration, milk was turned into cheese or butter before it spoiled. Most creameries had an area where the milk was received, tested, weighed, and separated. They also had a detached icehouse. As home and business refrigeration became more common, icehouses disappeared. (Courtesy of Ruth Whitney.)

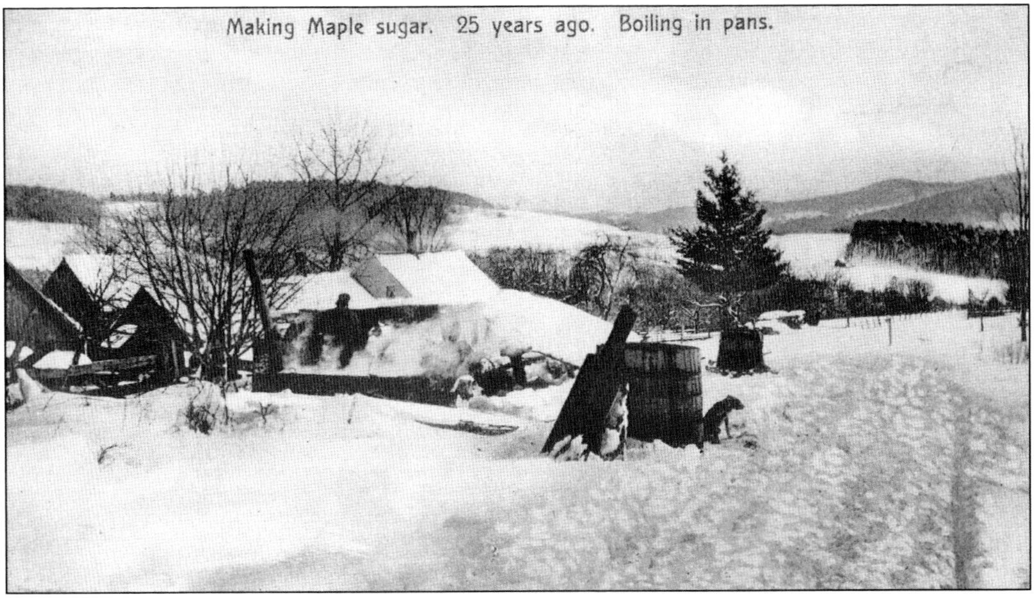

The old way of boiling maple sap in the woods required evaporating the water from the sap by heating and cooking. Today's high-tech equipment using reverse osmosis removes three quarters of the water content from the sap. The new technology is faster and more productive than traditional methods and results in a 50 percent higher yield of sap. (Photograph by Green Mountain Card Company.)

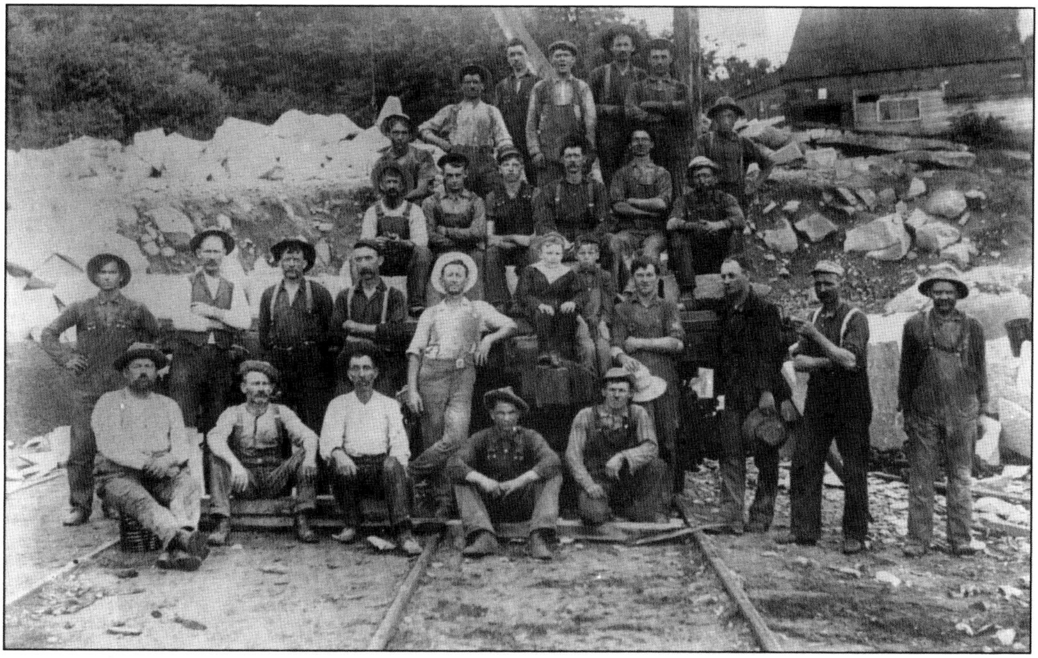

In 1882, the James K. Pirie Quarry opened. In 1955, it was sold to the Rock of Ages, located in neighboring Barre, Vermont. In the first row, second from the left, is James K. Pirie standing with his three sons, James George Pirie (standing third from the right), Ellio J. Pirie (wearing the sailor suit), and Fred F. Pirie (second from the left in the third row, with his arms folded). The rest of the men are unidentified. (Photograph by A.N. Blanchard.)

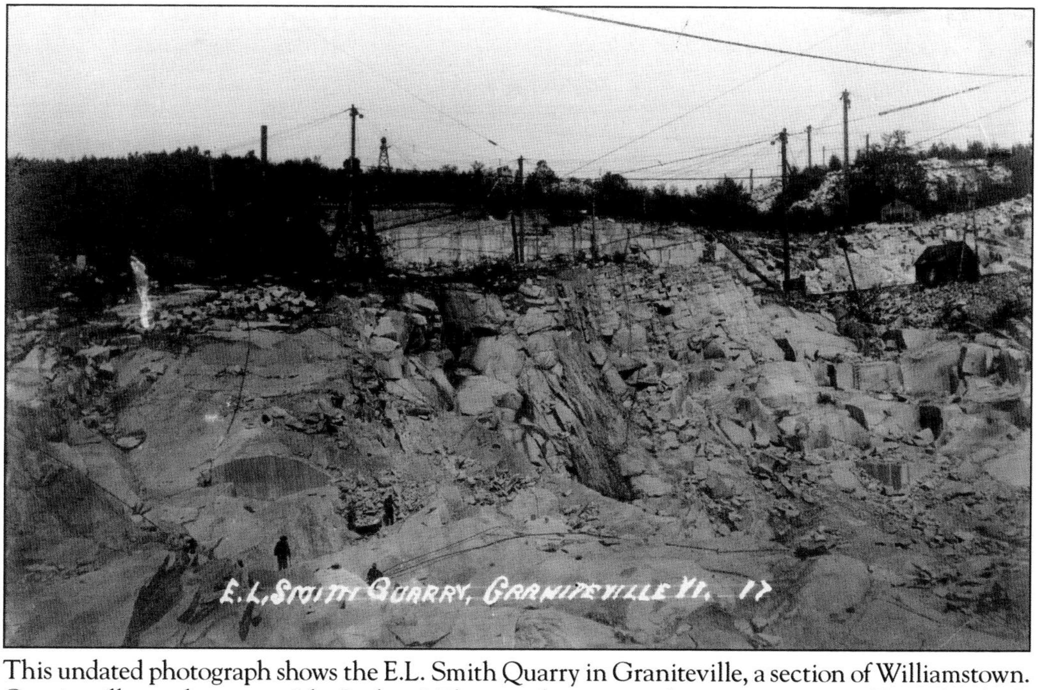

This undated photograph shows the E.L. Smith Quarry in Graniteville, a section of Williamstown. Graniteville was known as "the Ledges." The very first granite business was started by individuals who began cutting large surface granite boulders on their property in Graniteville.

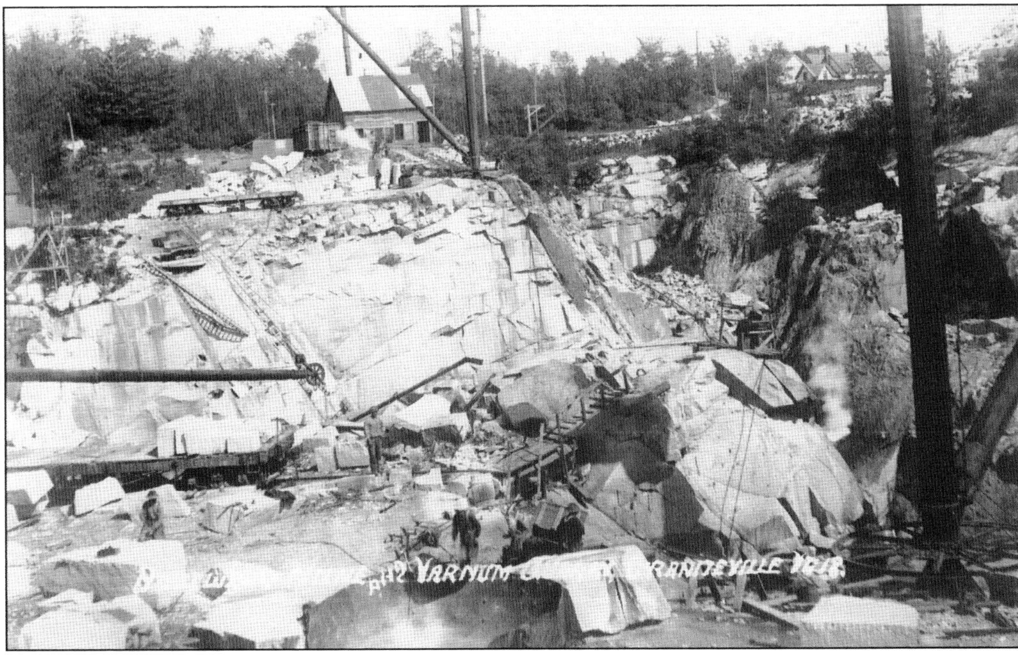

Harvey W. Varnum owned a quarry in Graniteville. Educated as an engineer, Varnum played a key role in developing many railroad lines in Vermont; he is credited with improving traveling and business opportunities. In 1888, the first train arrived in the Williamstown Village, resulting in an economic boom that lasted for nearly four decades. (Courtesy of Bertha Morgan.)

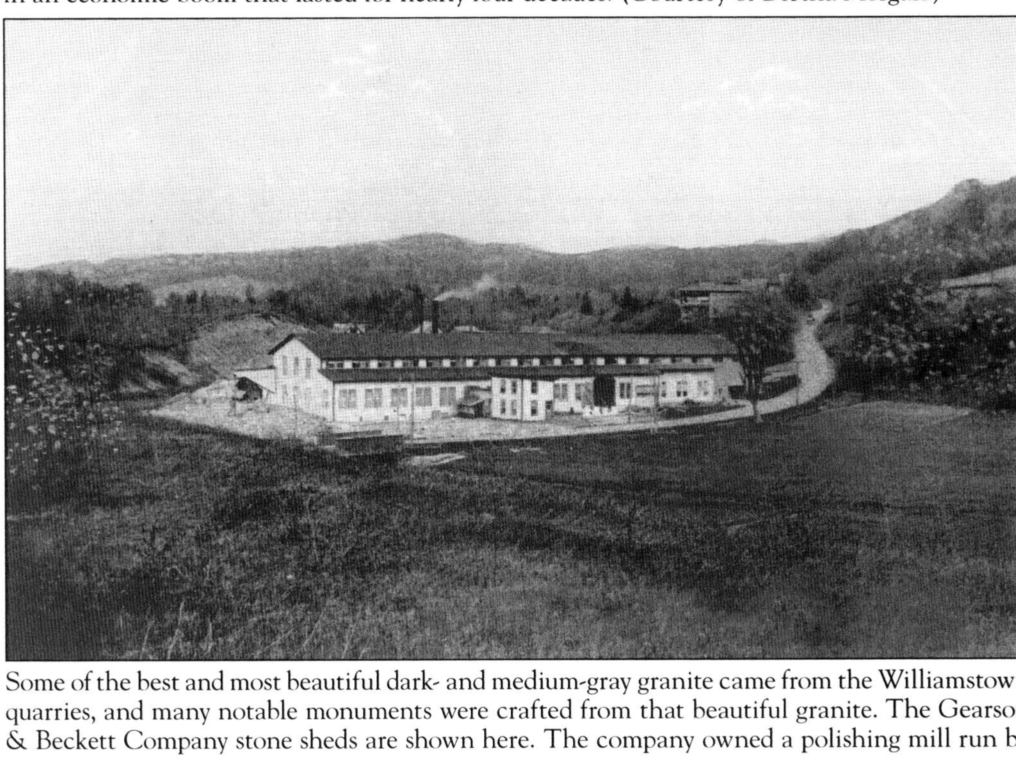

Some of the best and most beautiful dark- and medium-gray granite came from the Williamstown quarries, and many notable monuments were crafted from that beautiful granite. The Gearson & Beckett Company stone sheds are shown here. The company owned a polishing mill run by steam power.

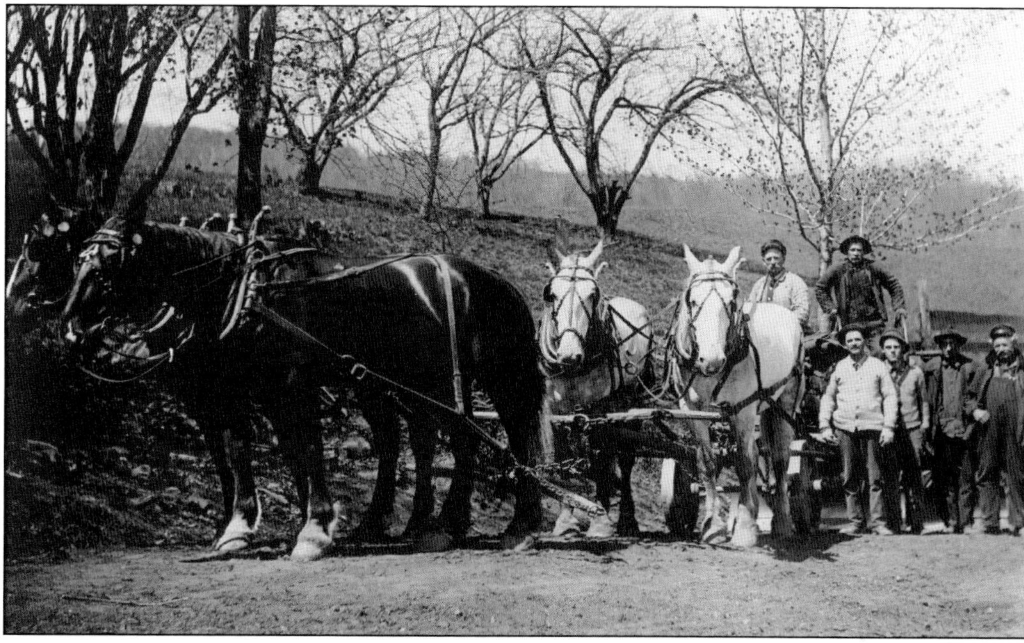

Brimming with memories of the past, this photograph shows how granite was hauled from the quarries in the early 1900s. Two quarry men, James K. Pirie and Ernest Riddle, were originally from Scotland and worked together for a short period of time. Eventually, Riddle separated to begin his own quarry business.

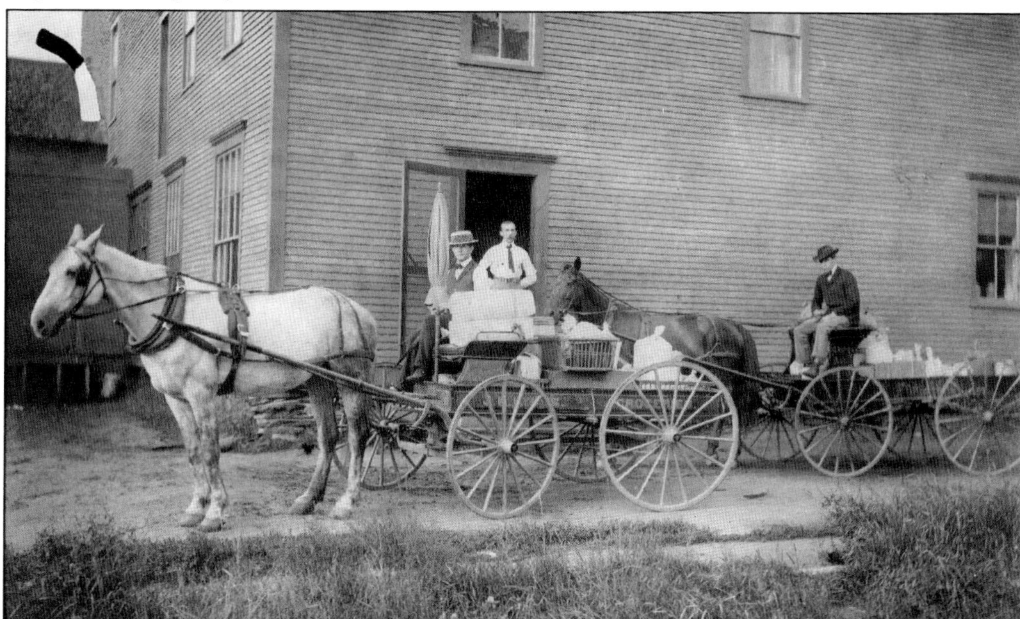

Shown here is a team of horses ready for the trip to the quarry. Two men are stocking up with a day's supply of goods purchased from the Old Lynde Store in the early 1900s. Frank Downs is shown at left in the straw hat, George Edson is standing by the door, and Tom Marshall is wearing a darker-colored felt hat at right. Note the closed umbrella hitched to the wagon, which was used to shade Frank from the hot summer sun.

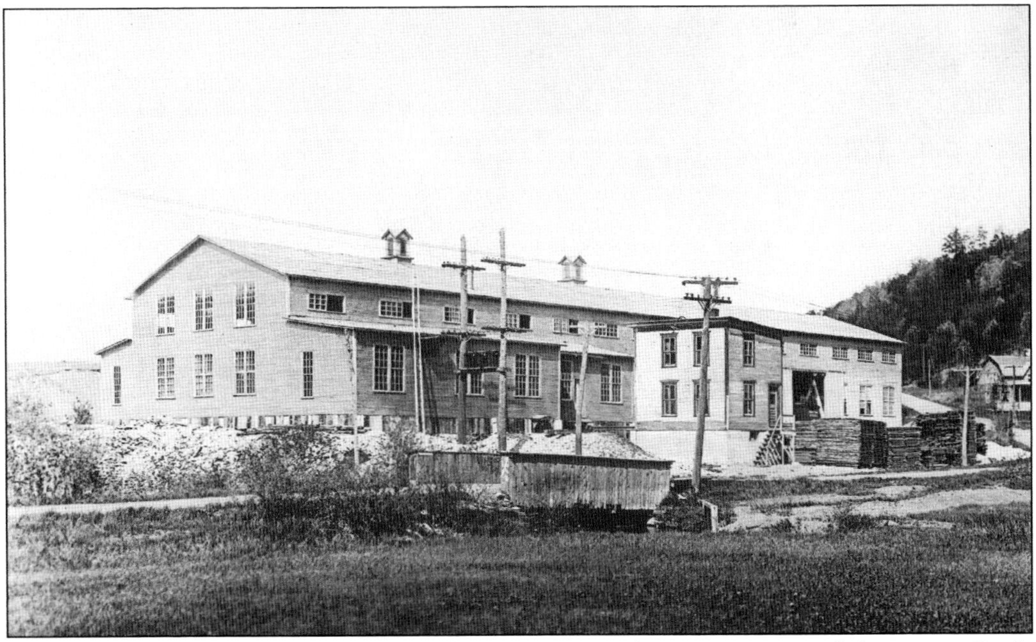

The William B. Jones granite shed opened in 1914 on Meadow Street, currently known as Circle Street. Machines used in the sheds had to be constantly monitored because they became very hot. This building burned down on May 31, 1914, and was immediately rebuilt. (Photograph by E.D. McAllister; courtesy of Carrie Lewis.)

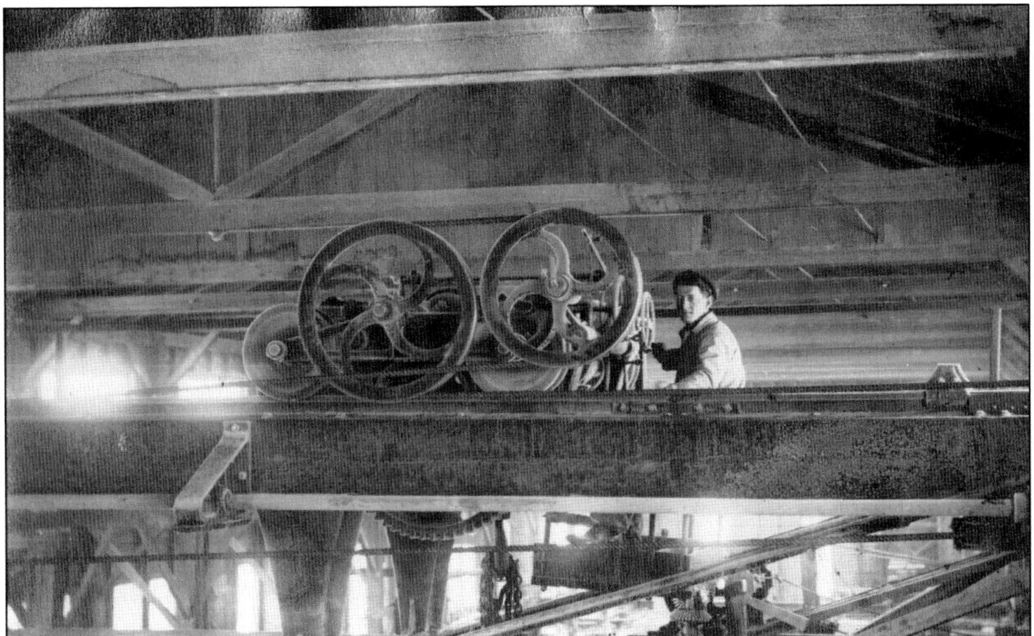

The photograph shows Bert Guild running the crane at the Grearson & Beckett plant. In 1913, the Grearson & Beckett plant burned to the ground.

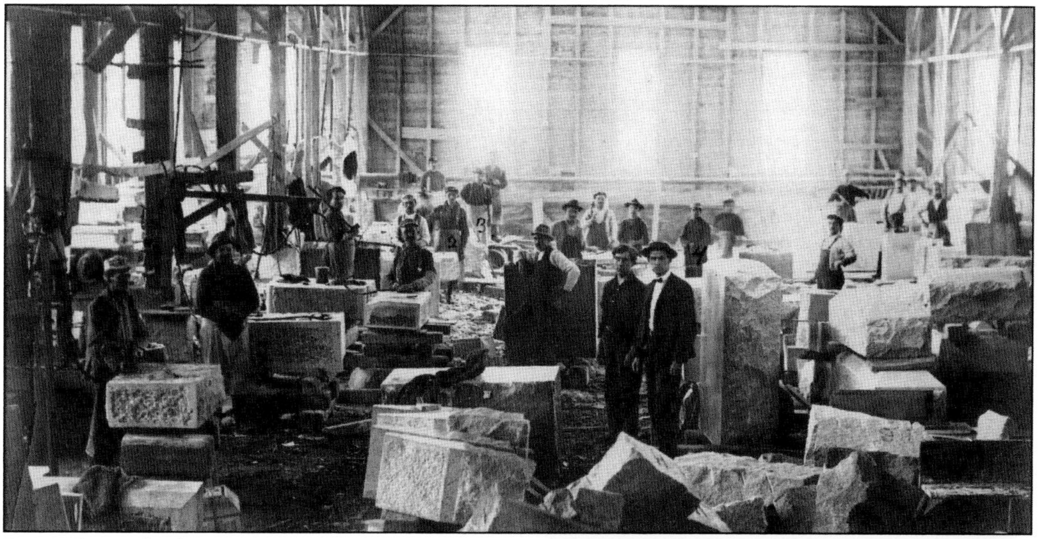

In 1915, inside the W.B. Jones plant, employees are ready to begin work on blocks of gray granite. Pictured are, in the right foreground, Neal Godfrey (left) and Walter Kendrick. Seated in the center are, from left to right, George Matt, Clinton Wilfore, Windsor Ditty, and Burt Guild. (Courtesy of Carrie Lewis.)

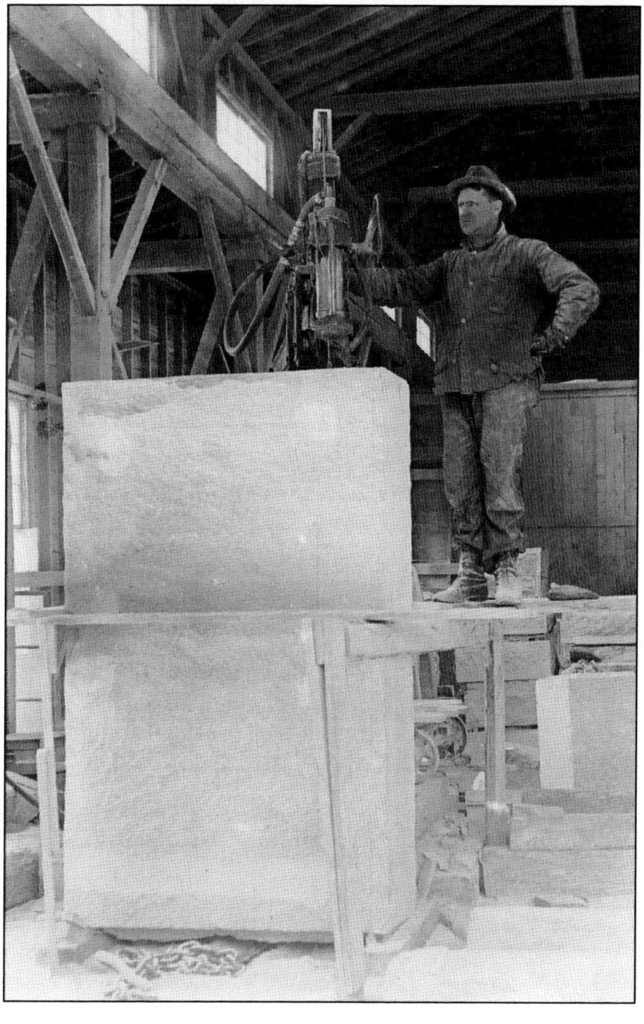

Pictured is Will Lougee, a craftsman at W.B. Jones plant, using modern tools of the trade. Early craftsmen used chisels and hammers. The plant was located at what is presently the town garage lot.

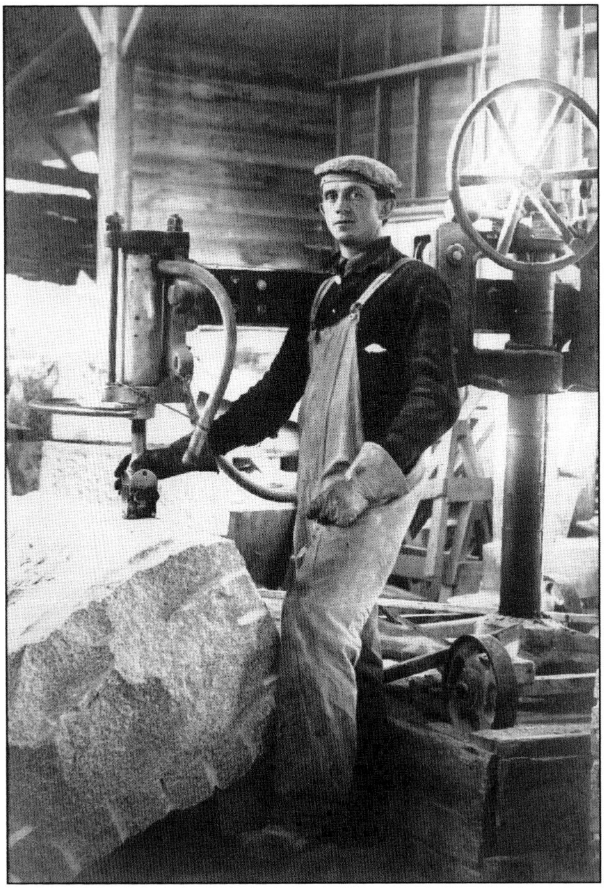

The pioneers in the granite-cutting business were the Elliot brothers; they leased the Williamstown Granite Co. occupied by Gearson & Beckett. Shown is Nelson Vassar in a stone shed in the early 1900s. Once quarried, granite was transported to neighboring Barre, Vermont, and sculpted into monuments, doorsteps, fence posts, boundary markers, and other fine products.

This is the monument of Cornelius Lynde erected in the Williamstown Village Cemetery on Route 14. The monument was crafted in one of the local stone sheds.

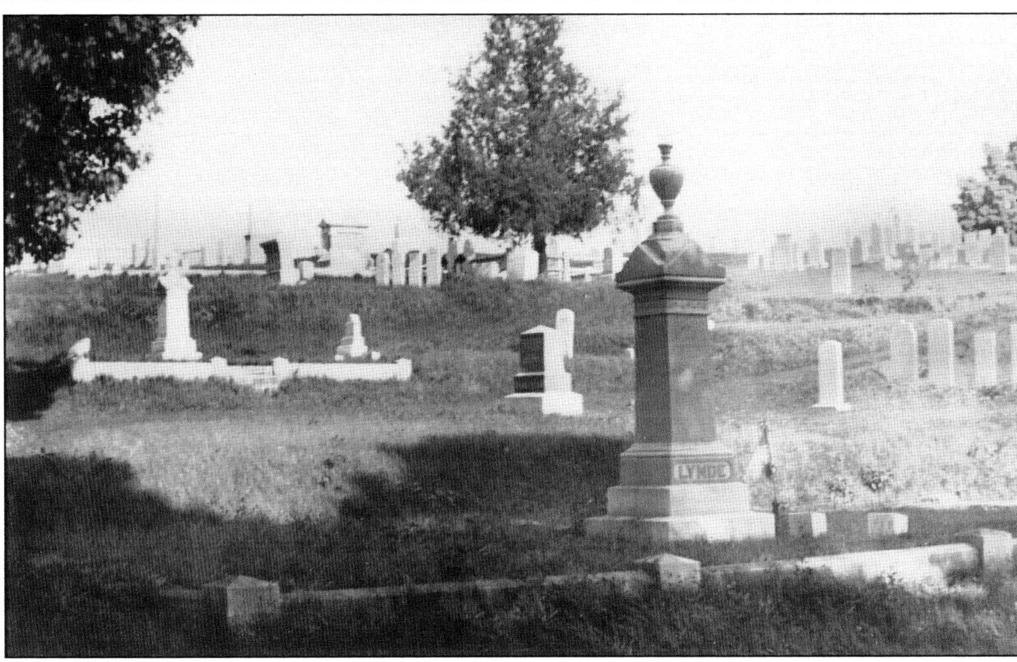

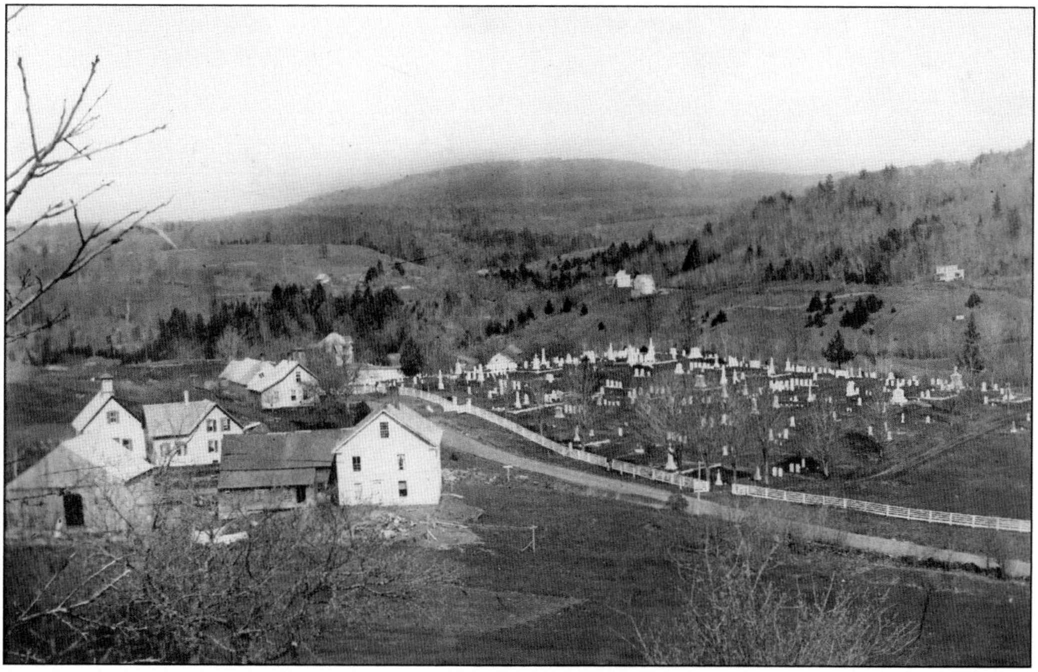

On April 27, 1983, several members of the garden club gathered at the village cemetery to plant and dedicate four flowering crab trees in memory of Ruth Whitney. Another flowering crab was planted in memory of Barbara MacDonald, president of the Williamstown Garden Club, who had died earlier that month in a car accident. This picture shows the full view of the village cemetery at an earlier time, since trees are not present.

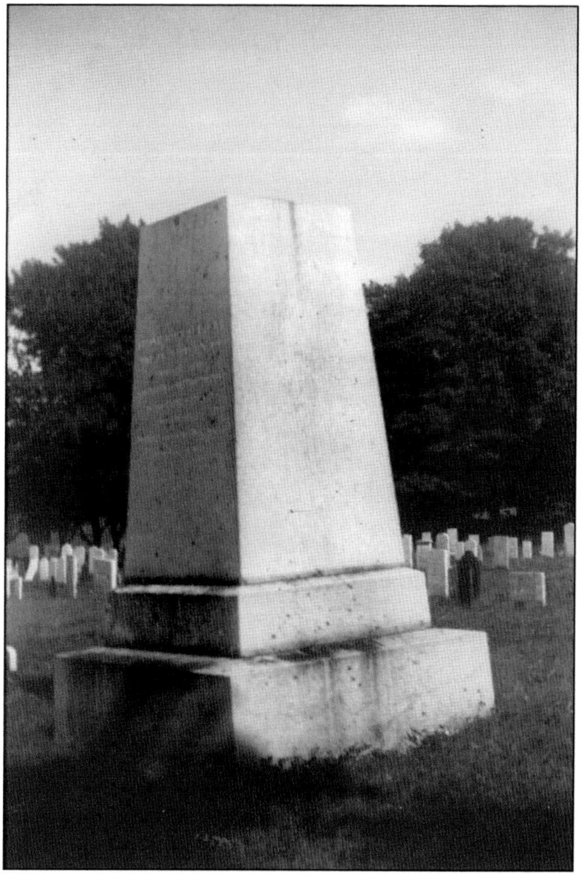

Here is the Elijah Paine monument, as shown in the West Hill Cemetery. Granite headstones found in cemeteries are made from natural granite that was formed hundreds of millions of years ago from molten lava. Today, skilled craftsmen and artists utilize the benefits of modern technology to create works of art worthy of memorializing departed loved ones. (Courtesy of Ora Whitney.)

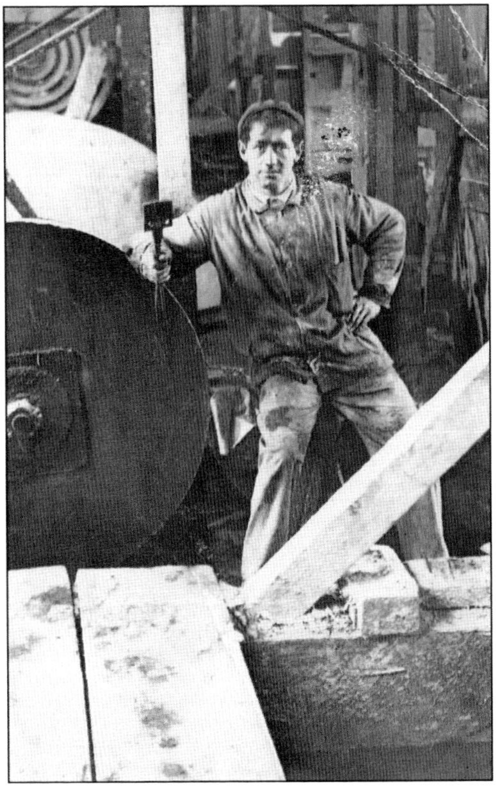

Many of the men who came to sculpt granite were highly educated artists and craftsmen. The Aldrich Public Library reports that many of the Italian designers, sculptors, carvers, artisans, and manufacturers can trace their ancestry back to medieval times. Pictured is Bert Guild in the granite shed.

This photograph shows how granite was transported in the 1890s. The Barre Granite Association reports that huge blocks of granite were laboriously transported by means of drays drawn by 30 or more oxen. The heavier operations were left for winter when the blocks could be drawn over the snow with sleds.

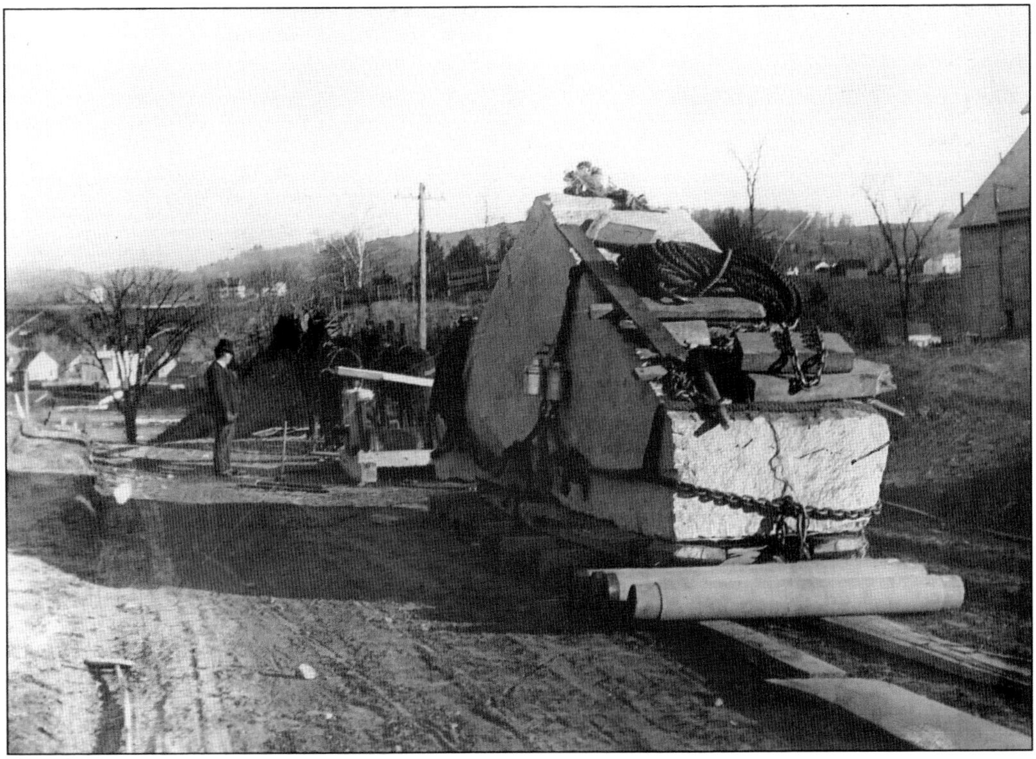

Six

Tourism and the Romantic Era

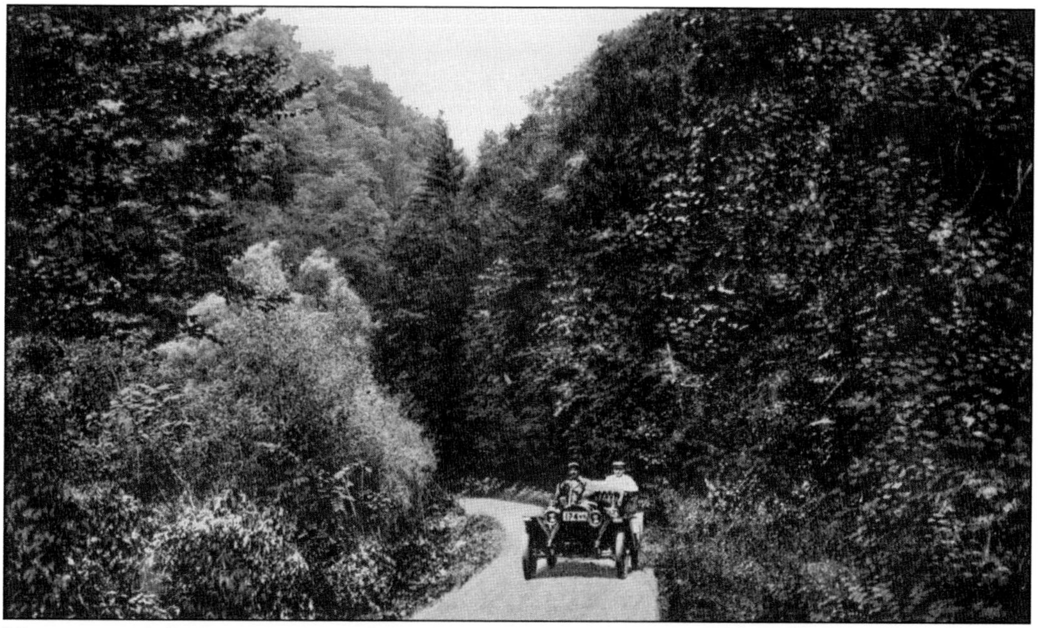

This postcard shows tourists traveling in a horseless carriage through the Williamstown Gulf, a direct road from Boston to Barre, Vermont. The romantic era elevated an appreciation of the arts and the picturesque qualities of the untouched wilderness. People wanted to escape the effects of industrialism and busy city life. (Photograph by Buswell's Bookstore.)

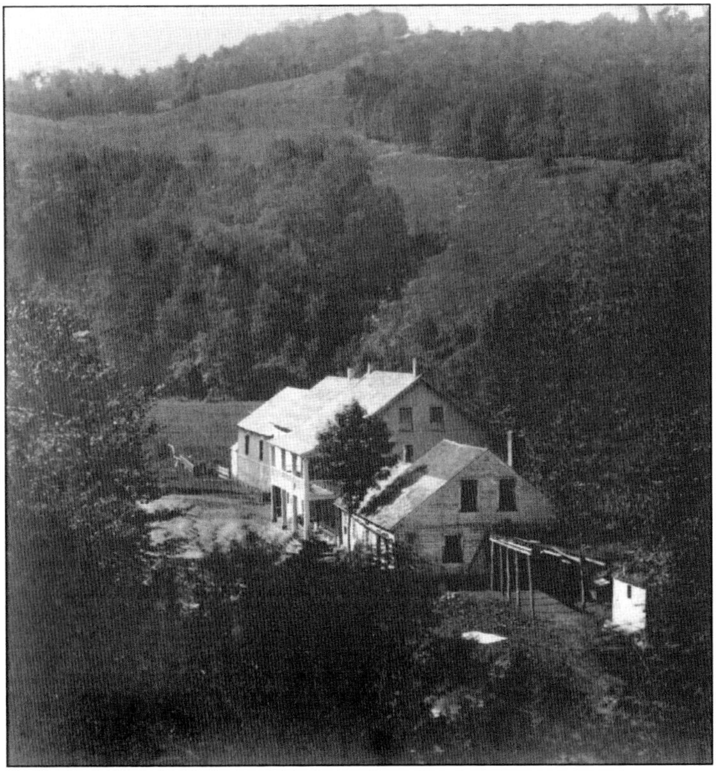

In 1847, after Porter Flint discovered a medicinal spring on his farm property, he decided to build the Gulf Spring House. The natural sulfur springs attracted visitors desperate for a quick cure for their aching joints or just to avoid the hustle and bustle of city life. The resort and spa soon became a favorite spot to visit during Vermont's first tourism boom. The first Gulf Spring House burned down in 1890.

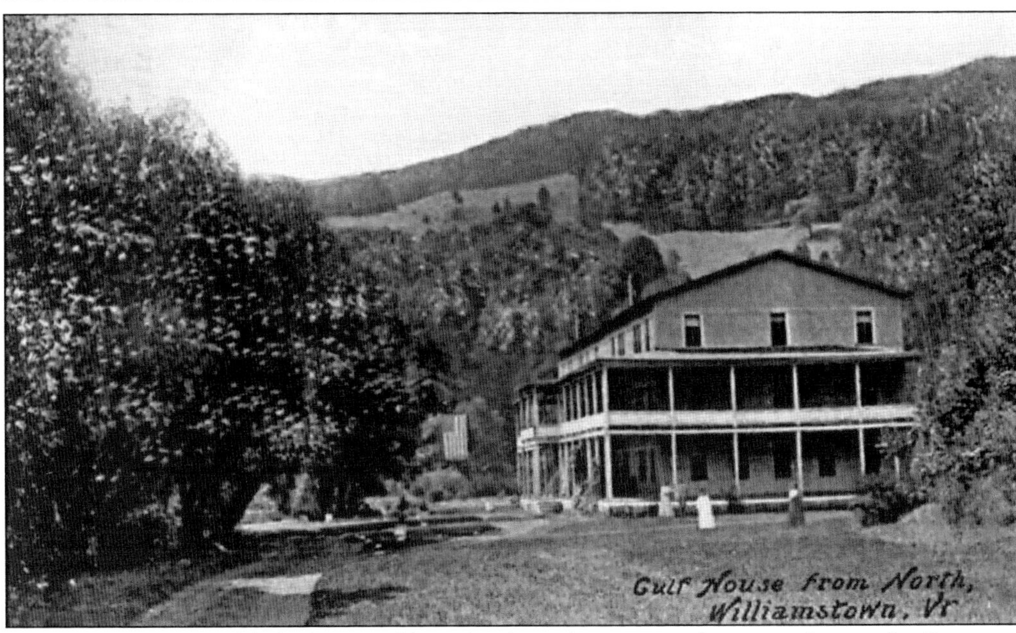

Williamstown has yielded substantial benefits from the increased tourism during the Romantic era. Pictured is a group of women cavorting on the lawn after soaking in the pure, mountain spring water at the second Gulf Spring House. Days were spent playing various games, like croquet, quoits, cards, checkers, ball, and riding, as well as reading. The second Gulf House was torn down in 1913. (Courtesy of Ruth Whitney.)

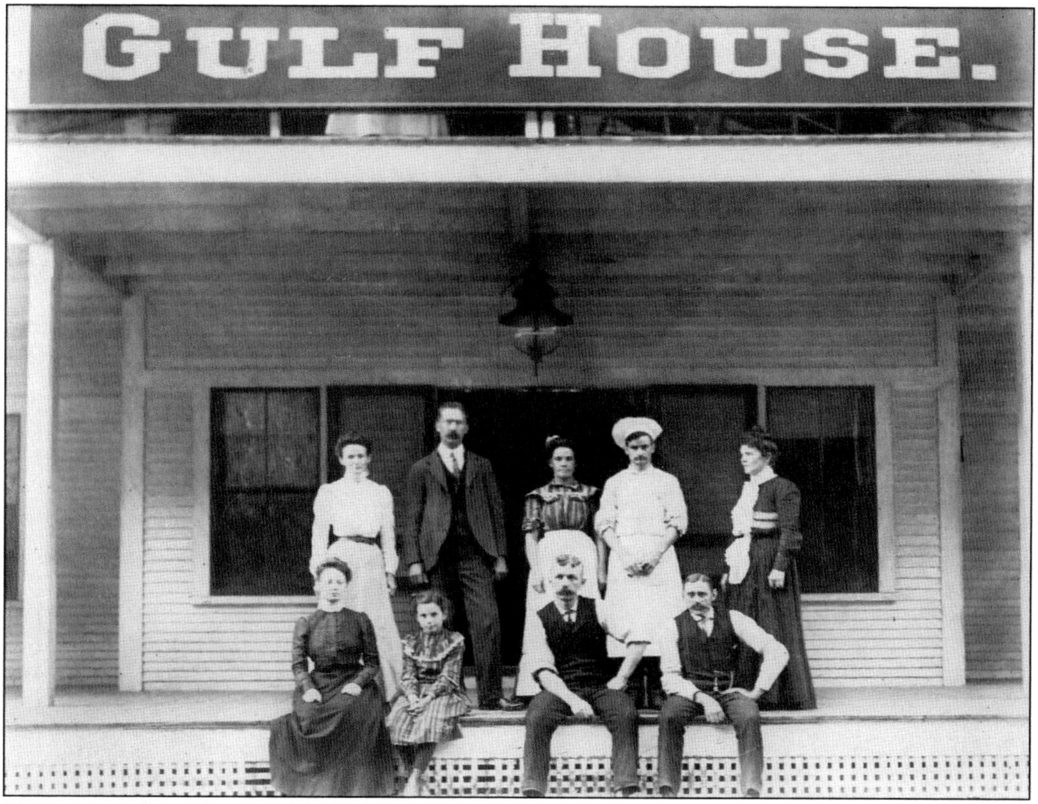

This group of people, most likely the staff and owners, are sitting on the porch of the second Gulf House (1900–1913). Note the four-by-four windows and the hanging light on the porch.

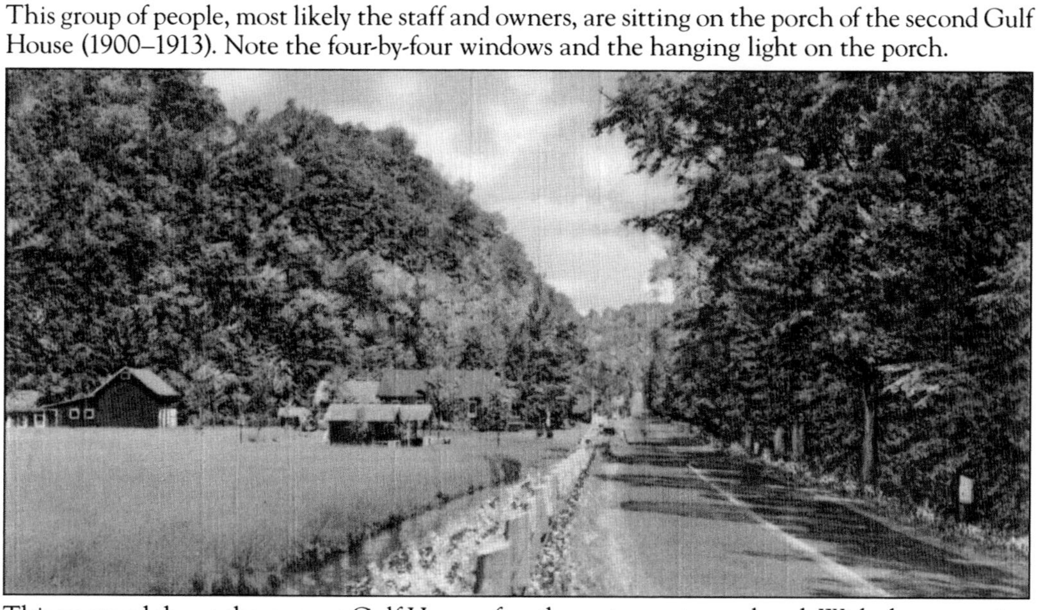

This postcard shows the current Gulf House after the restaurant was closed. With the expansion of the railroads into remote areas and increasing demand by wood product industries, forests were stripped of their trees at a rapid pace. In the 19th century, Williamstown lost an enormous amount of its trees. The gulf was somewhat protected from the clear cutting of the industrialism era because of its steep hills and slate.

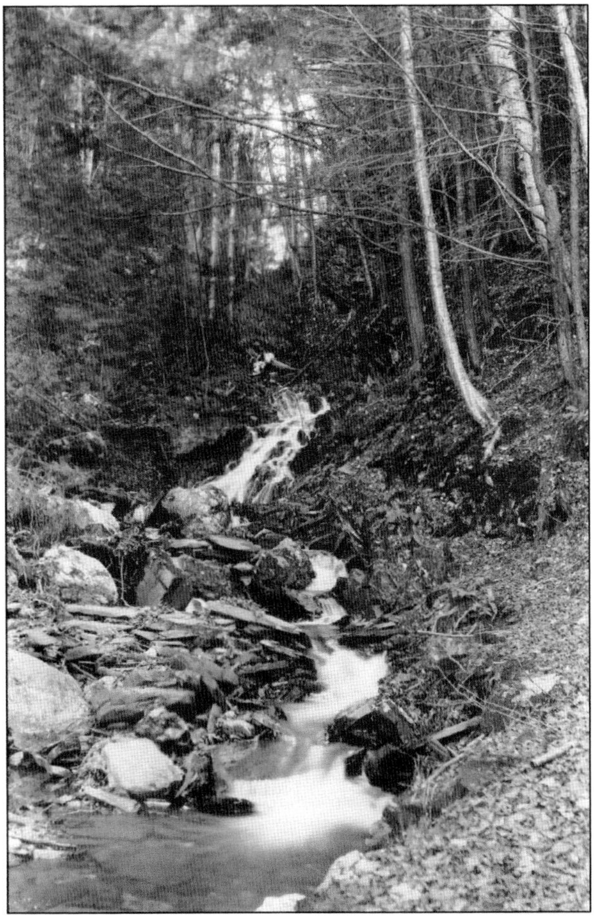

Waterfalls rush down the verdant green banks of the Williamstown Gulf. In the spring, there is a series of powerful cascades that drop about 200 feet into a wooded setting just south of the Gulf House.

Limehurst Lake campground and Limehurst Pond are shown in this postcard. Traveling south from the village, tourists would have noticed a distinct break in scenery and recognized that they were moving into a more rural area. The countryside stretches out below with its hills, lakes, wetlands, and open pastures.

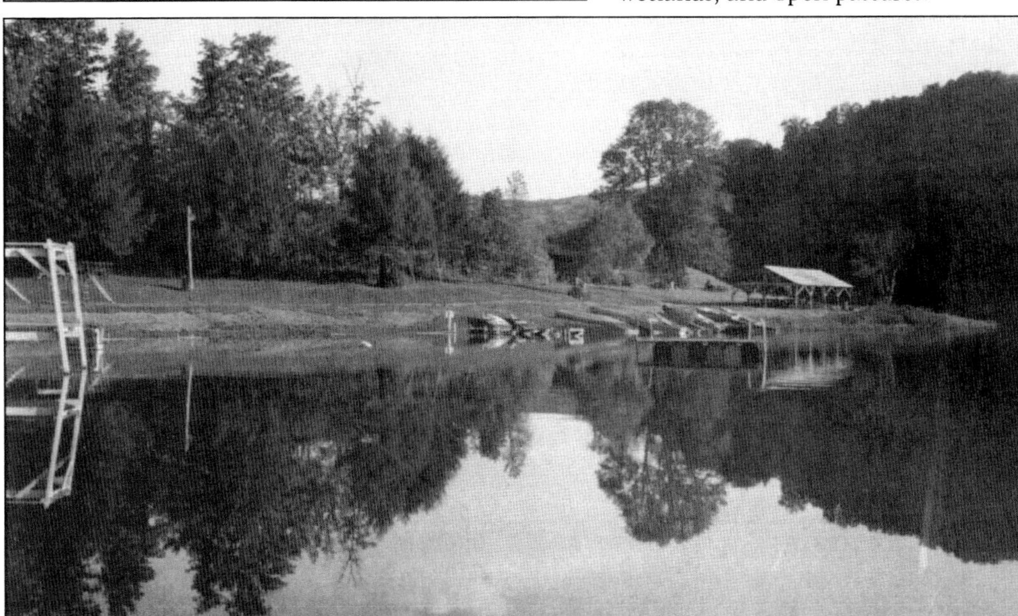

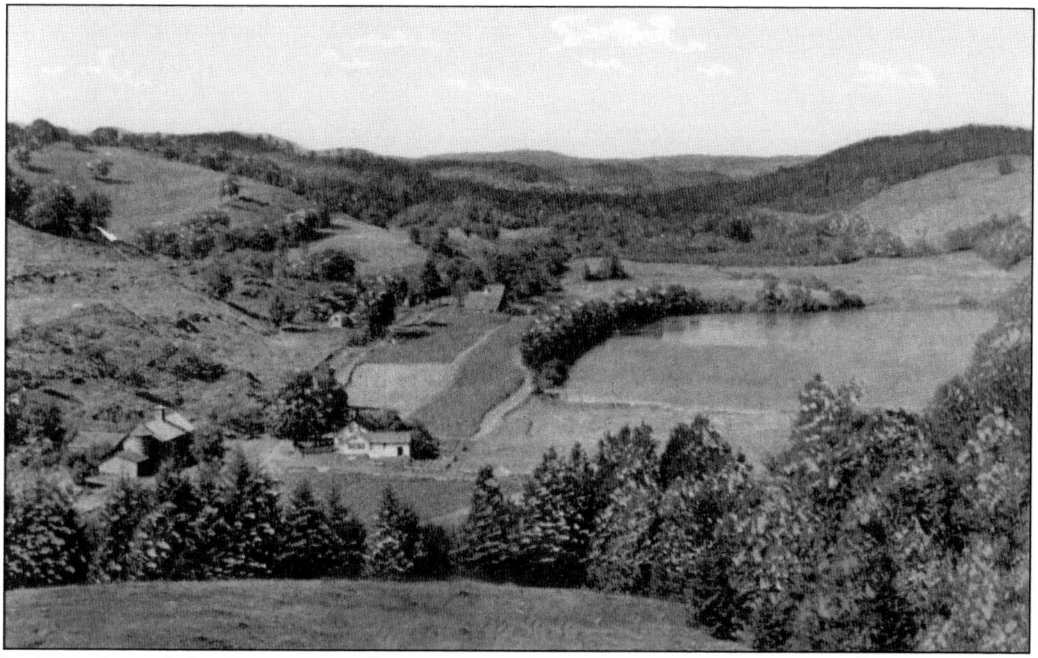

In 1952, Lotus Lake Camp opened as a summer day camp on two former Martin dairy farms on 300 acres of diverse habitat surrounding an 18-acre lake, Lotus Lake, also known as Cutter Pond on Vermont maps.

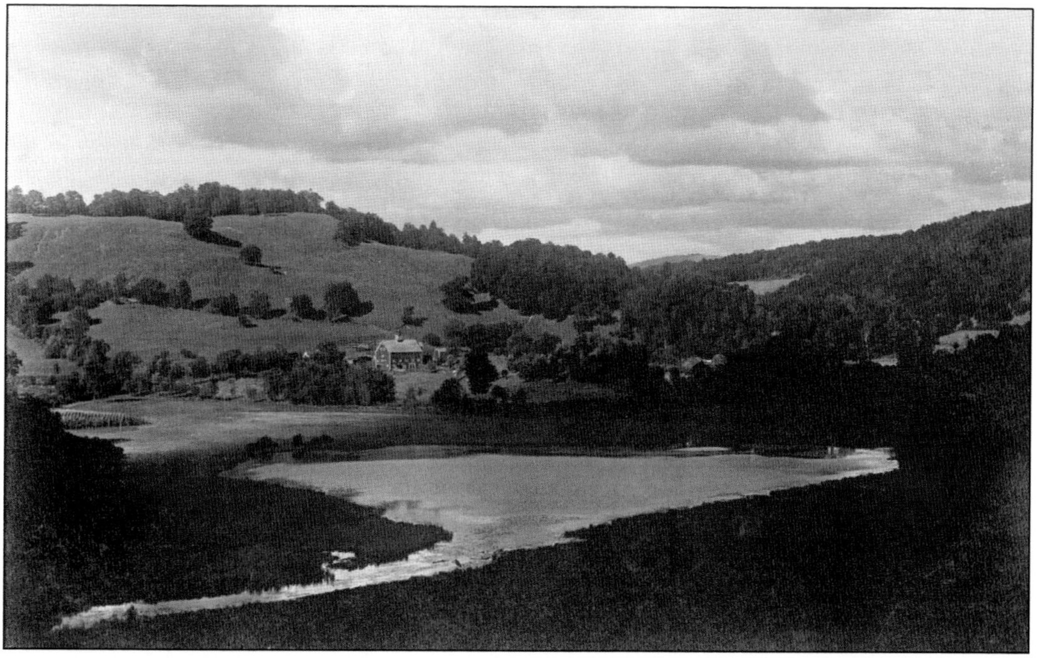

This postcard shows Staples Pond in the foreground and the Tripp Barn in the background. The postcard was sent from Frances (Martin) Lynde "With loving thoughts and hearty sympathy to Etta Martin Covell in 1911."

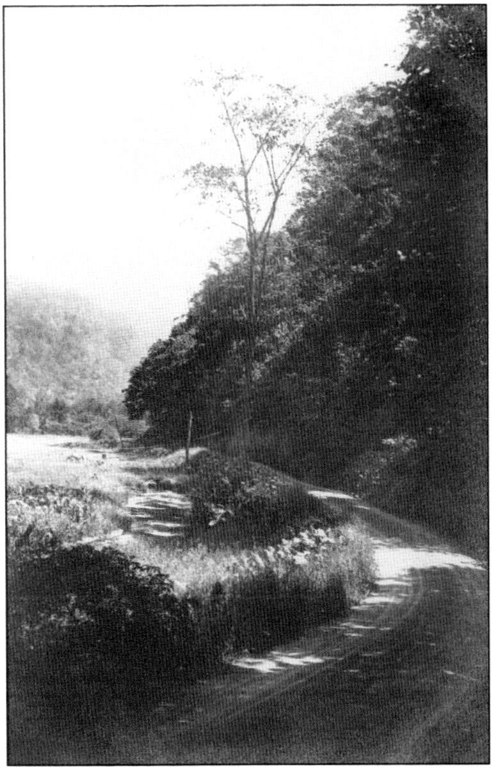

The Williamstown Gulf is shown here as an unspoiled wild place. The road passes through a long valley deep below high mountain ranges. During the romantic era, the gulf delighted tourists and still does today.

Campers could enjoy the beauty of the great outdoors at Ainsworth State Park. In 1926, when Mary Waterman gave the state land, it came with the stipulation that it be named Ainsworth (State) Forest Park. There are no records explaining why Mary chose the name "Ainsworth" except that Mary Waterman and Laura Ainsworth were both members of the Vermont Bird Club. Evidence of early structures (foundation walls, water pipes, and remnants) can still be seen in Ainsworth State Park.

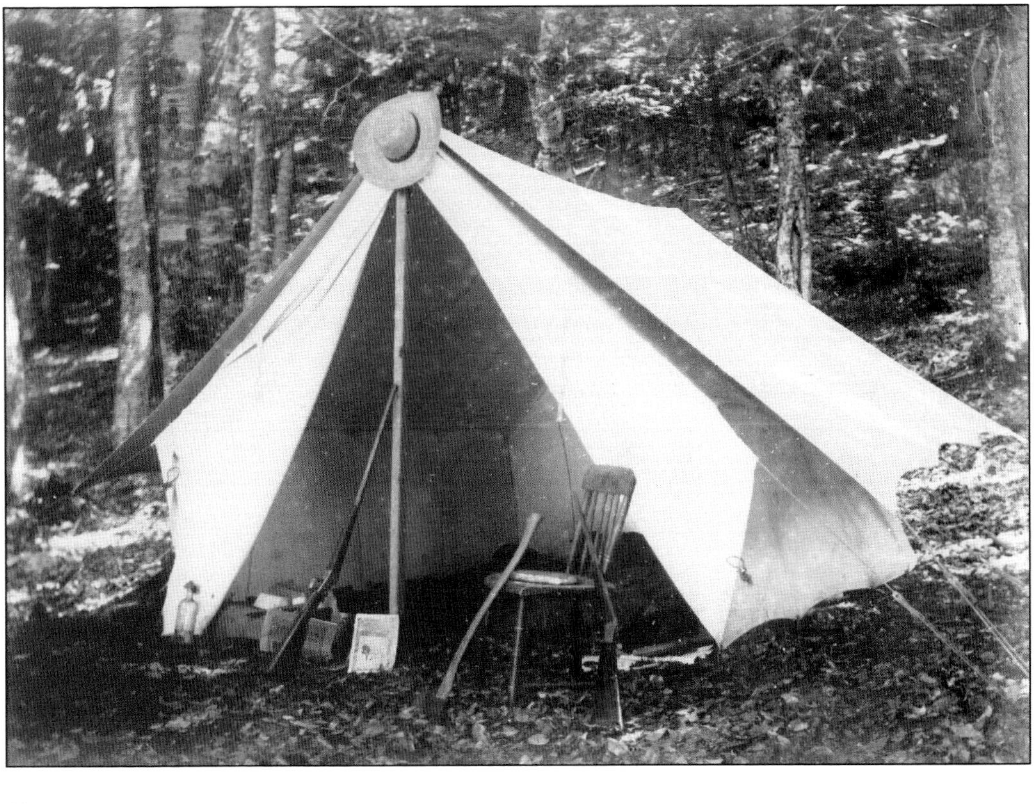

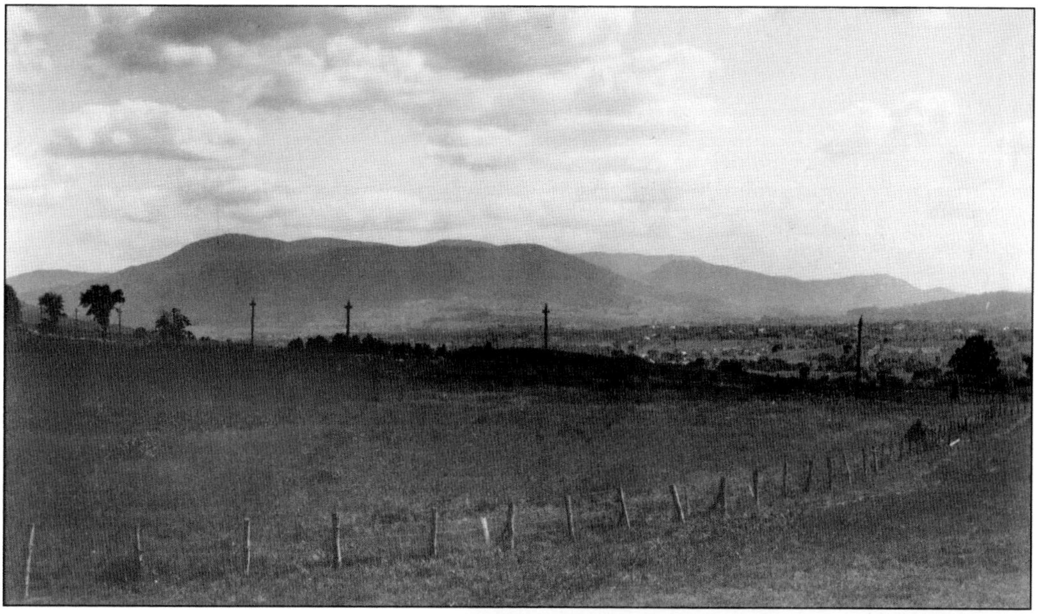

On lazy days, a camper could sit around a campfire and get lost looking at the rolling hills below. The scribble of thin black handwriting on the back of this postcard reads, "This is the view that we get from the camp looking over Williamstown to the mountains." Then and now, the undeveloped slopes contribute to the picturesque views.

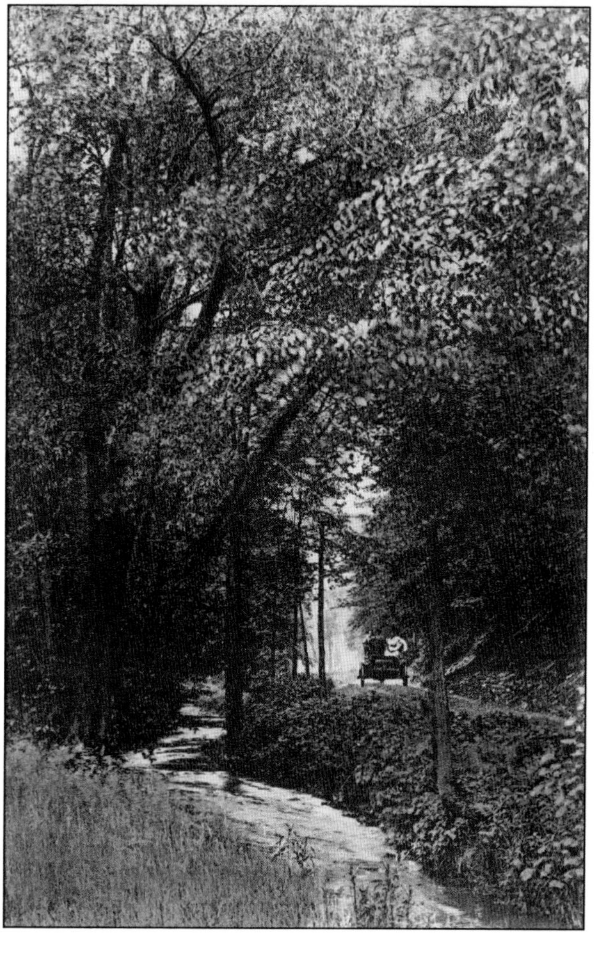

This photograph shows tourists driving north along the gulf's long winding road, which follows the bend of the river. If the day had been hazy, these tourists would have seen a beautiful fog rising from the wetlands in this area. This couple may have encountered a moose and beaver on their trip through the gulf. This colored postcard photograph was taken in the early fall because the trees' leaves have started to turn yellow and orange with a backdrop of red. The water from the river would have been rushing over its banks in the spring. The area remains enchanting to the traveler. (Photograph by Green Mountain Card Company.)

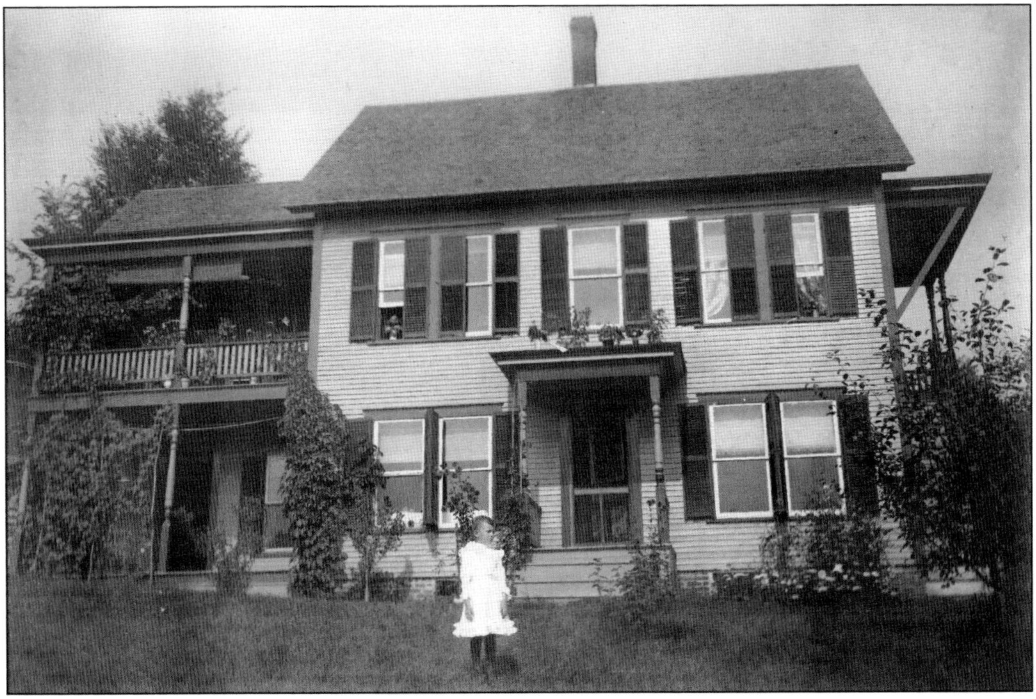

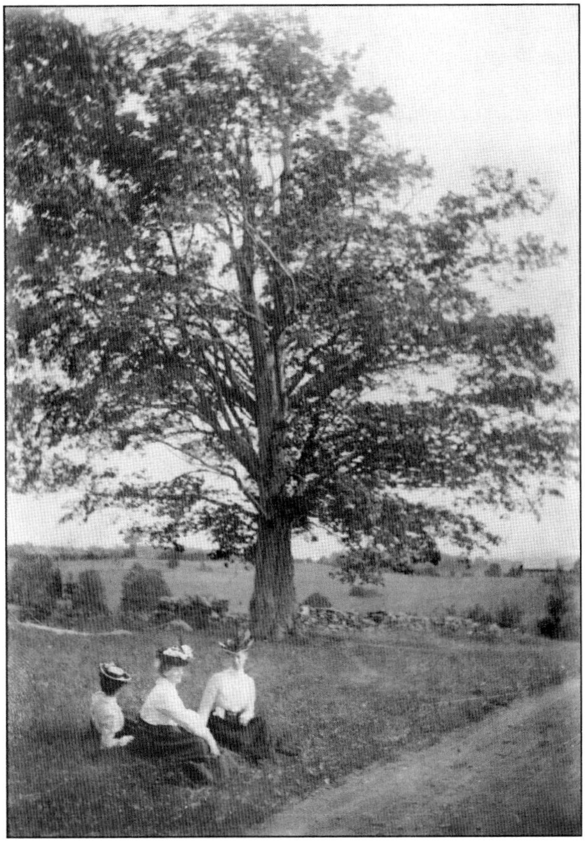

Spiderweb Farm is located at the end of Spiderweb Farm Road in the Williamstown Village. Tourists came from all over the country to visit the farm and purchase a unique gift of a spiderweb mounted and framed. Today, the Spiderweb Farm is still a popular tourist site. Note the potted plants on the porch roof.

Mary Seaver (facing front) and two unidentified women took a leisurely walk from the Seaver farm. During the romantic era, people promoted the wild and untouched land, and Williamstown profited from tourism. During the early 1900s, it was common for political leaders and residents to be educated in natural sciences. Many were aware that the beautiful, untouched land had been stripped of its trees and that all of its wild animals had been eradicated. Eventually, the land and animals were restored.

Seven

Celebrations, Customs, and Fun

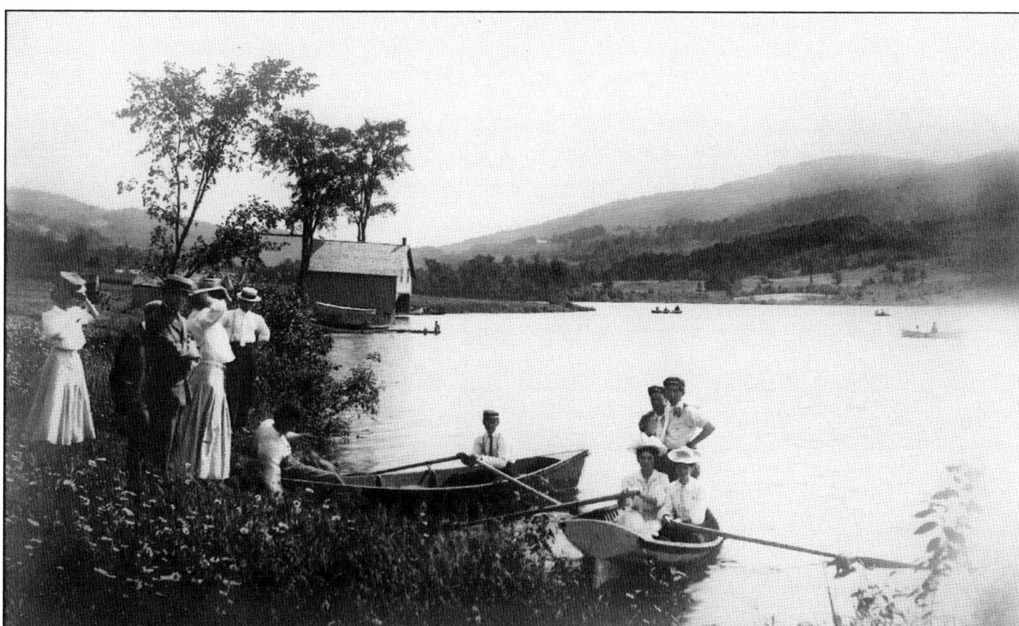

The traditions of the town are reflected in the arts and crafts, annual events, activities, and festivals, like old-fashioned fiddlers, skits at Gilberts Hall, and parades during Old Home Week. Over the years, there were many clubs including the Rural Good Luck Club, Birthday Social Club, Happy Moments, Home Study, Home Project, Eastern Star, and Summit lodge. This photograph shows members of Williamstown's Rural Good Luck Club with their rowing boats headed out on the water at Berlin Pond. (Courtesy of Bertha Morgan.)

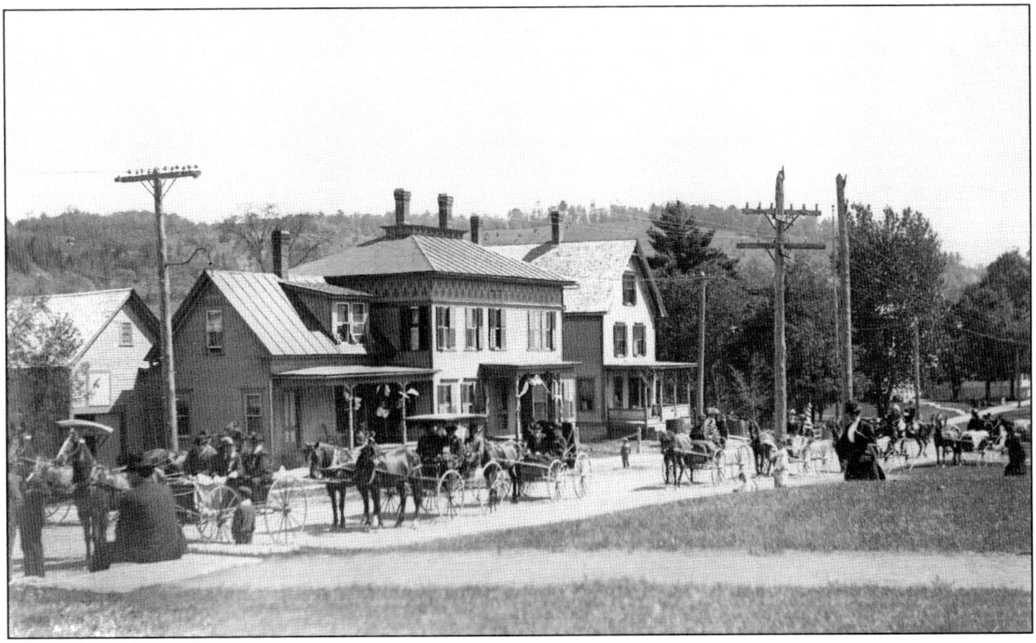

In 1910, Jason Johnson sits in the first wagon at Old Home Week festival, and Nathan and Mary Robinson are in the single carriage. On the right, Carrie McAllister walks across the lawn. Old Home Week is a festival to bring back individuals from out of town to their "old home" town. Events traditionally include a parade, a town dinner, ice cream social, class reunions, and walking tours provided by the Williamstown Historical Society. (Courtesy of Ruth Whitney.)

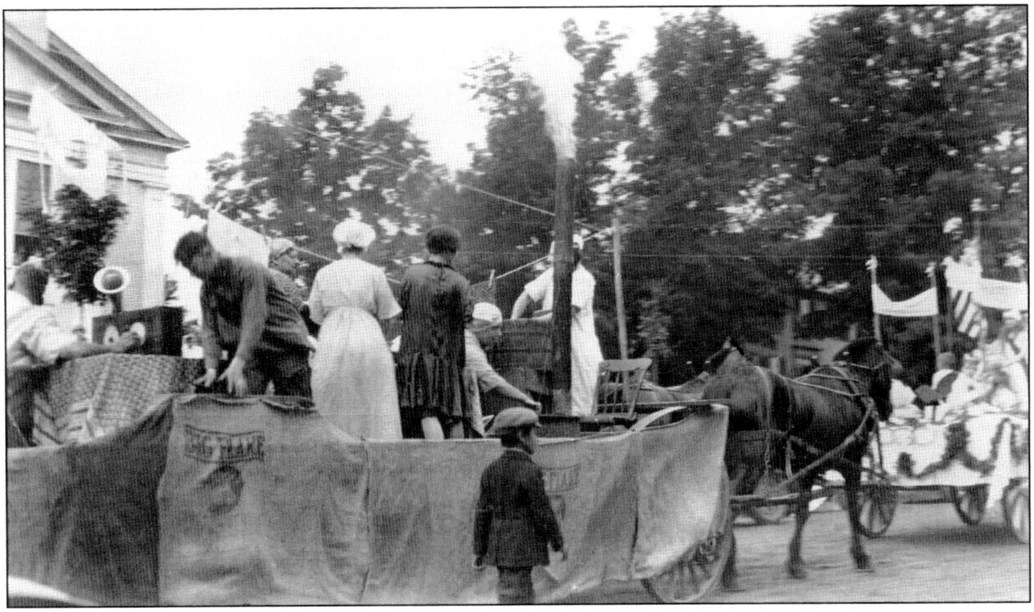

This photograph of Old Home Week was taken in the early 1900s. Leon Poor's team of horses is pulling the parade float, titled "Everyone works but father." In the front of the float, Annie Nixan is putting wood on the fire. Blanche Poor is dressed in a white dress and bonnet with her back toward the photographer, while Leon Poor fine-tunes the phonograph. In the back of the float is Ida Seaver with Ernie Seaver.

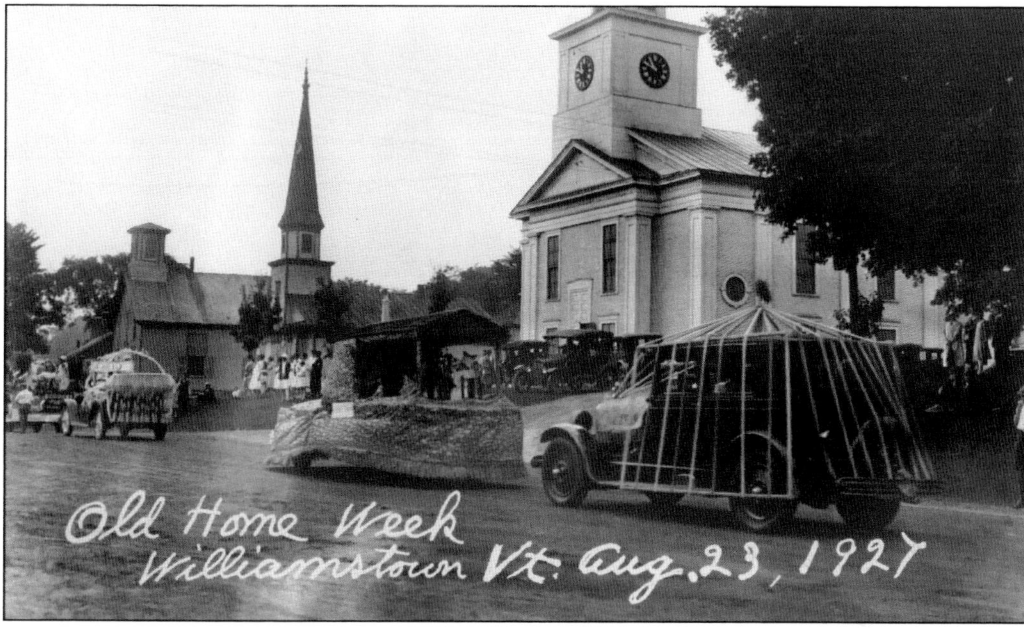

Old Home Week had its beginning in the 19th century when it began as a municipal effort. Over the years, it has been called by many names, such as the Old Home Church Sunday. The festivals always brought a large crowd. The most enjoyable part of Old Home Week festivities is the parade where residents lined the street to view horse-drawn carts, old cars, and fire trucks.

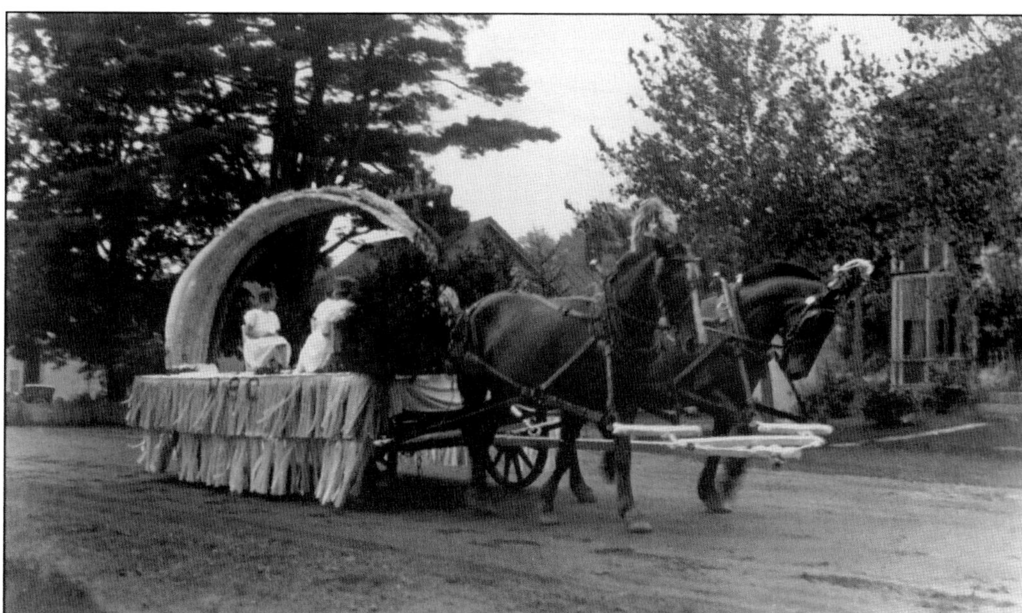

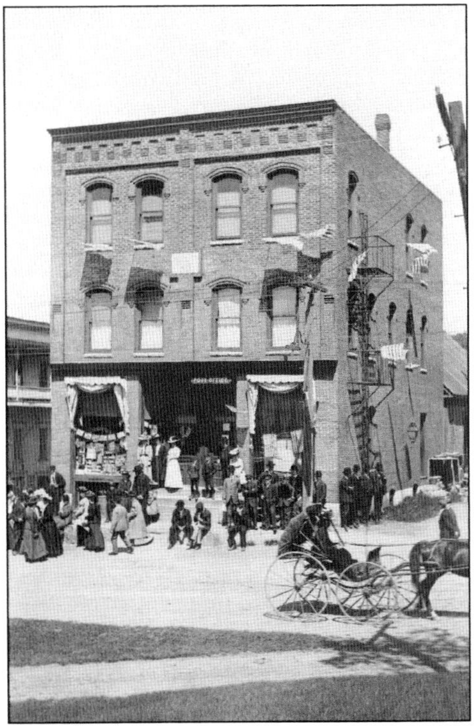

Shown here is a Fourth of July celebration in the early 1900s, when patriotism knew no bounds. Millie Drury stands on the drugstore's porch. Note all the flags flapping in the wind on the buildings. The old livery stable was located in back of the building. (Courtesy of Bertha Morgan.)

In the 1890s and early 1900s, the Shepard family from Royalton gave many concerts in Williamstown that were enjoyed by all. The sign at their feet and below the violins says "Shepard Family Concert Company."

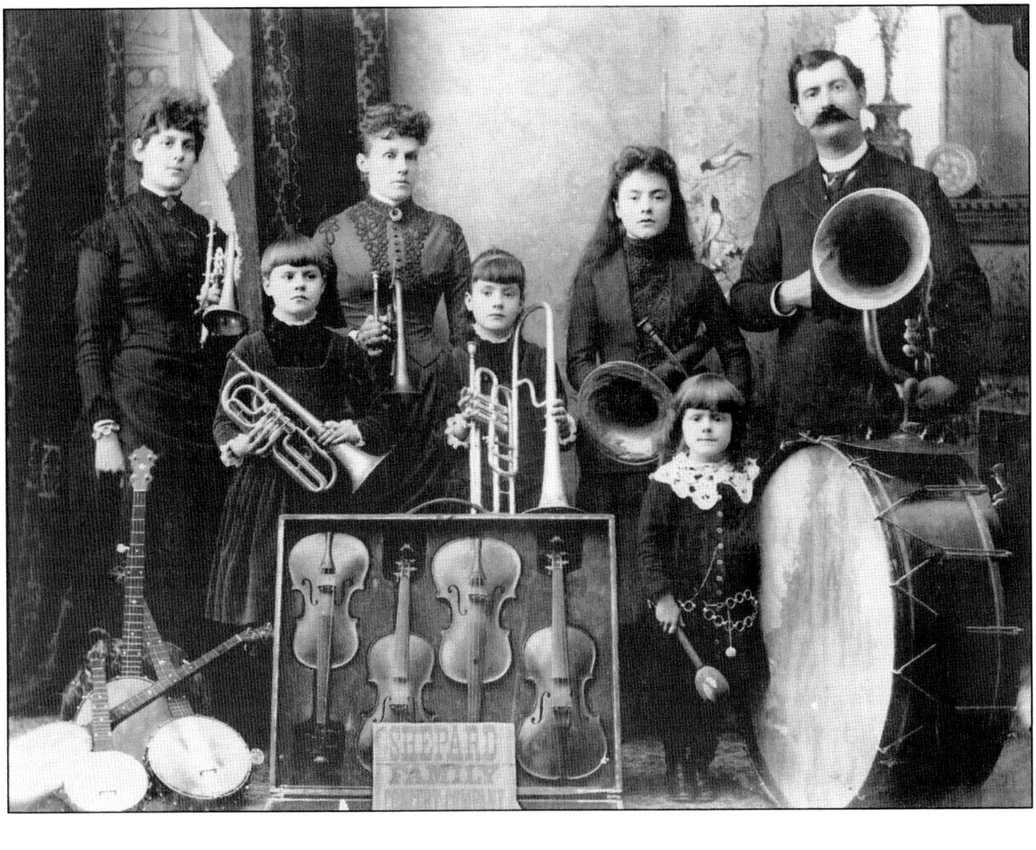

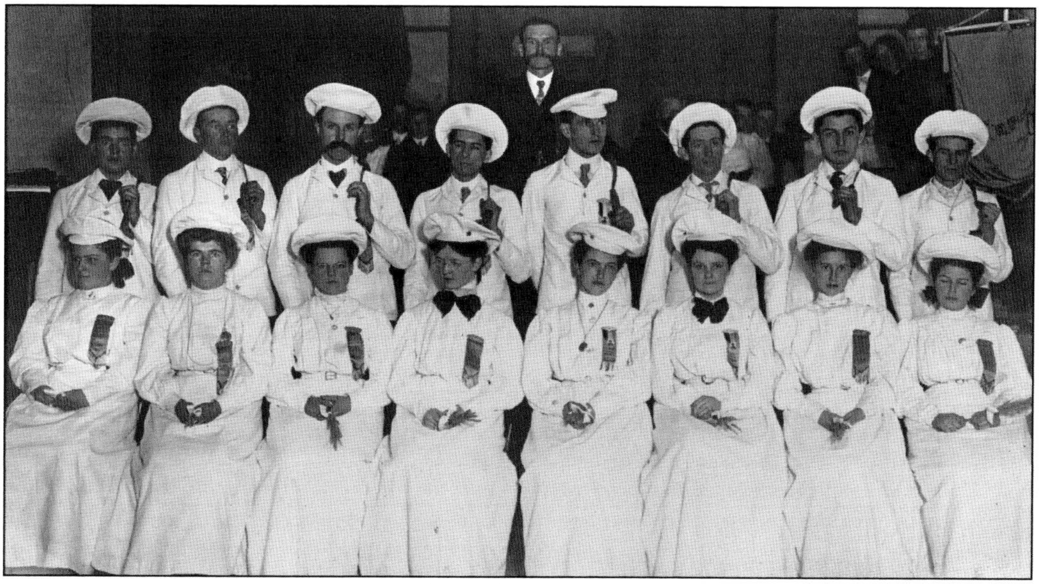

The Grange No. 81 was established in the 19th century to promote farmers' interests in political and economic causes. This 1910 photograph shows the Williamstown Grange Degree Team. They are, from left to right, (first row) Blanch (Nixon) Poor, Minnie (Hebard) Alexander, Ethel Poor, Katie Carlin, Dora Bancroft, Susie Peake, Grace McAllister, and Sara Poor McAllister; (second row) Wilbur Thompson, Paul Alexander, Fred Poor, Archie Cram, Dr. Ernest Bancroft, Jack Jameson, Clinton Wilfore, and Forest Cram. Alone in the back row is Clinton Cram.

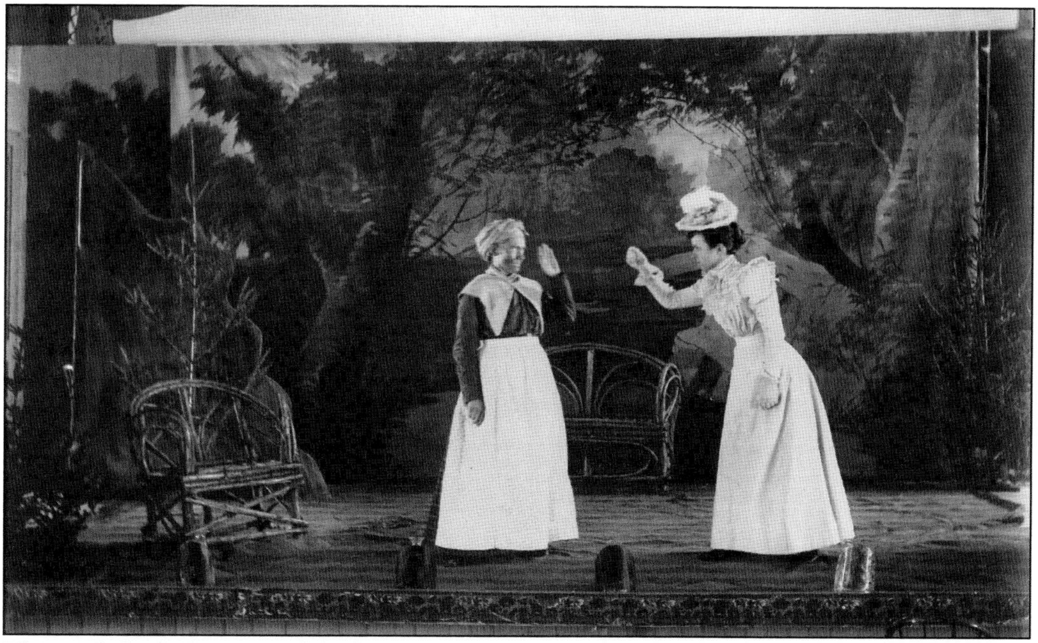

The newly built Grange Hall had a stage and dressing rooms on the second floor. In 1899, Helen Kimball and Marie Seaver acted in a skit, "Millie the Quadroon," given by the Williamstown Grange. The grange offered many other festivities including concerts and dances. They held an annual Grange Fair, where delicious chicken pie suppers were served. Booths in the main hall were well supplied with a variety of articles for sale.

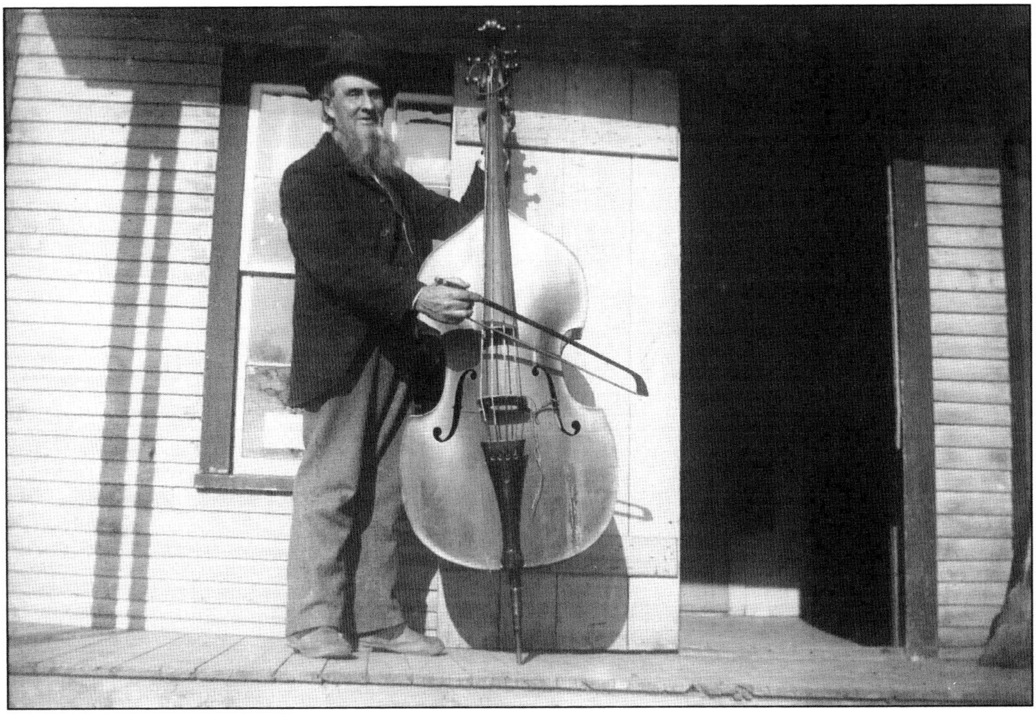

Daniel Bean Jr. (1840–1906) was the son of Daniel Bean Sr. and Hannah Jeffords; he lived his entire life in Williamstown. He was a very accomplished violinist and bass player, thus music flourished in Williamstown for many years. He played for dances and sang at the old Methodist church. He stopped playing for the church in 1866 when they purchased an organ. Occasionally, he mended shoes for others.

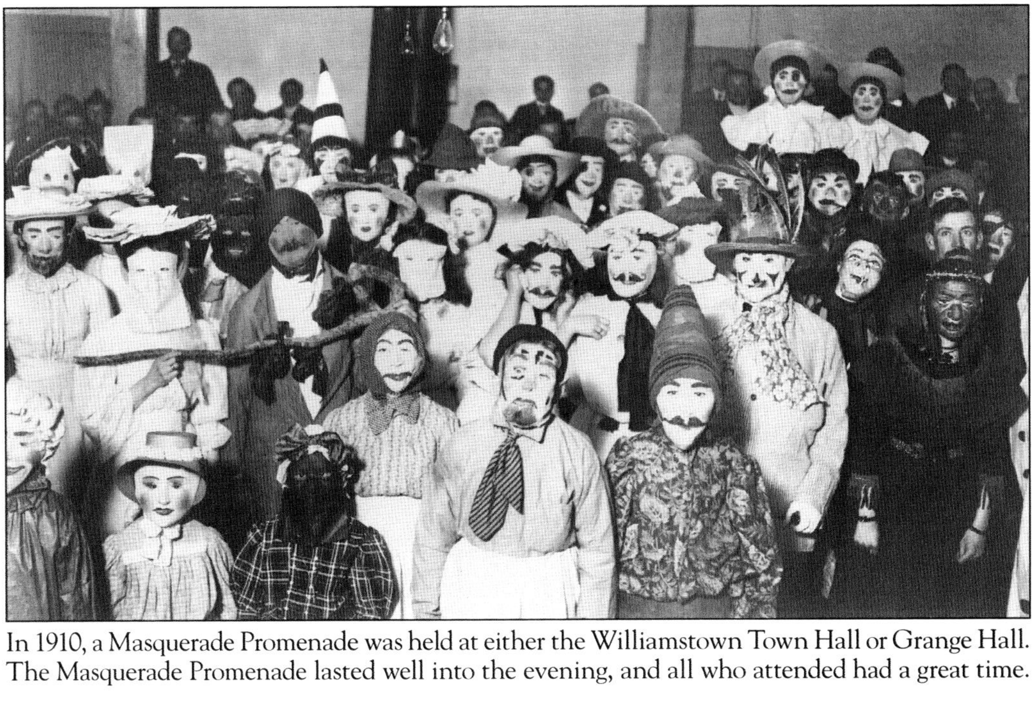

In 1910, a Masquerade Promenade was held at either the Williamstown Town Hall or Grange Hall. The Masquerade Promenade lasted well into the evening, and all who attended had a great time.

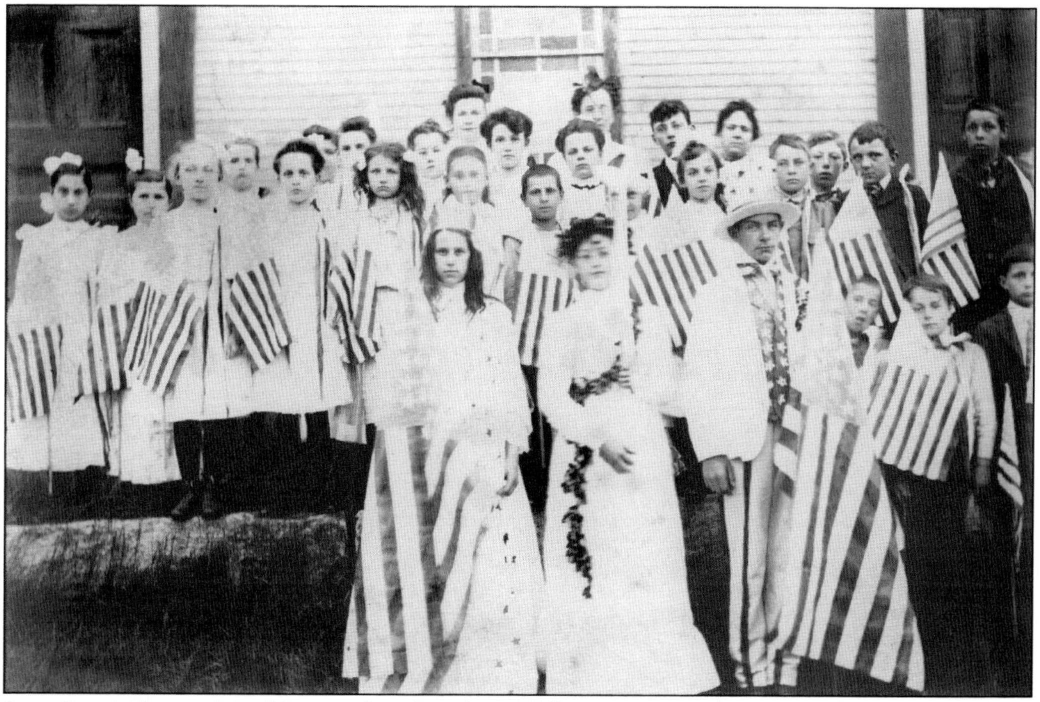

Standing in front of the Universalist church in Williamstown in the spring of 1904, Decoration (Memorial) Day observers are dressed in red, white, and blue.

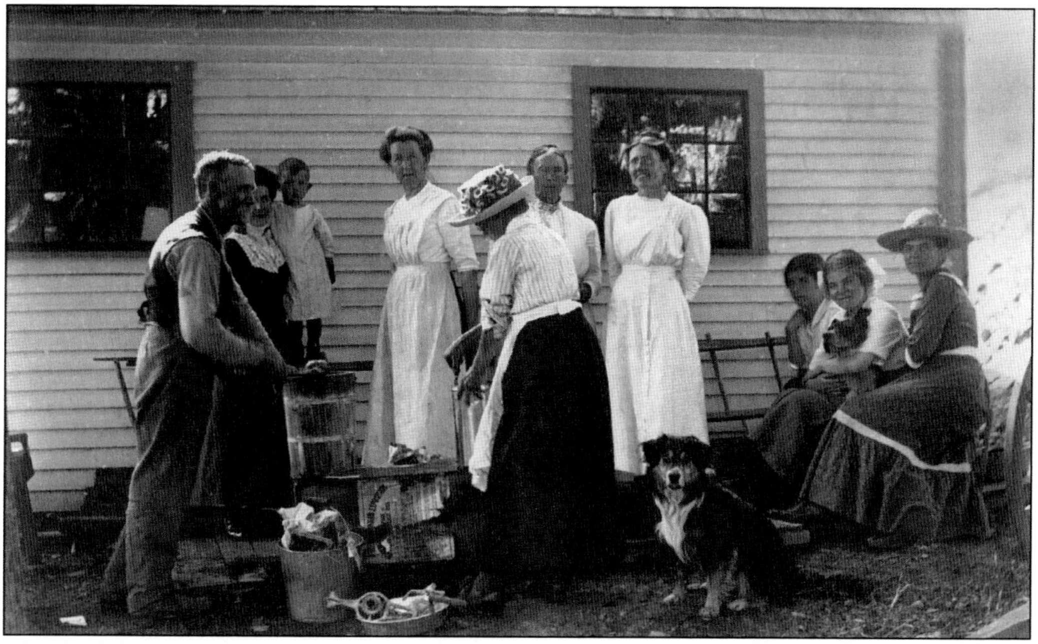

The Birthday Social Club of East Hill held picnic dinners, where members also played games. The *Barre Daily Times* reported that the club held meetings at M.W. Hyland's picnic grove in the evening, after which ice cream and cake were served in the house with the party breaking up about midnight. The picture shows the Gaudy Ice Cream Party before their planned lawn party. Note the wooden ice cream maker being cranked.

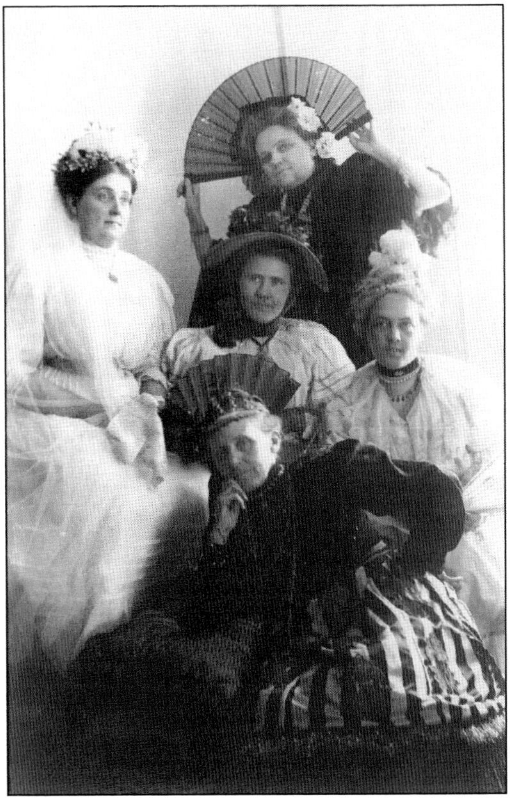

This photograph, taken in 1899, shows Rev. Frances Kimball (center), who was the pastor of the First Universalist churches of Williamstown and South Barre, Vermont. The woman at bottom is identified as the reverend's sister Helen Kimball. Note the wedding dress on the bride. The women in the middle are unidentified.

Taken in the early 1900s, this photograph shows the baseball diamond on the corner of what is now Seaver Field. Drawn from their daily chores, the boys head outside to play with their friends.

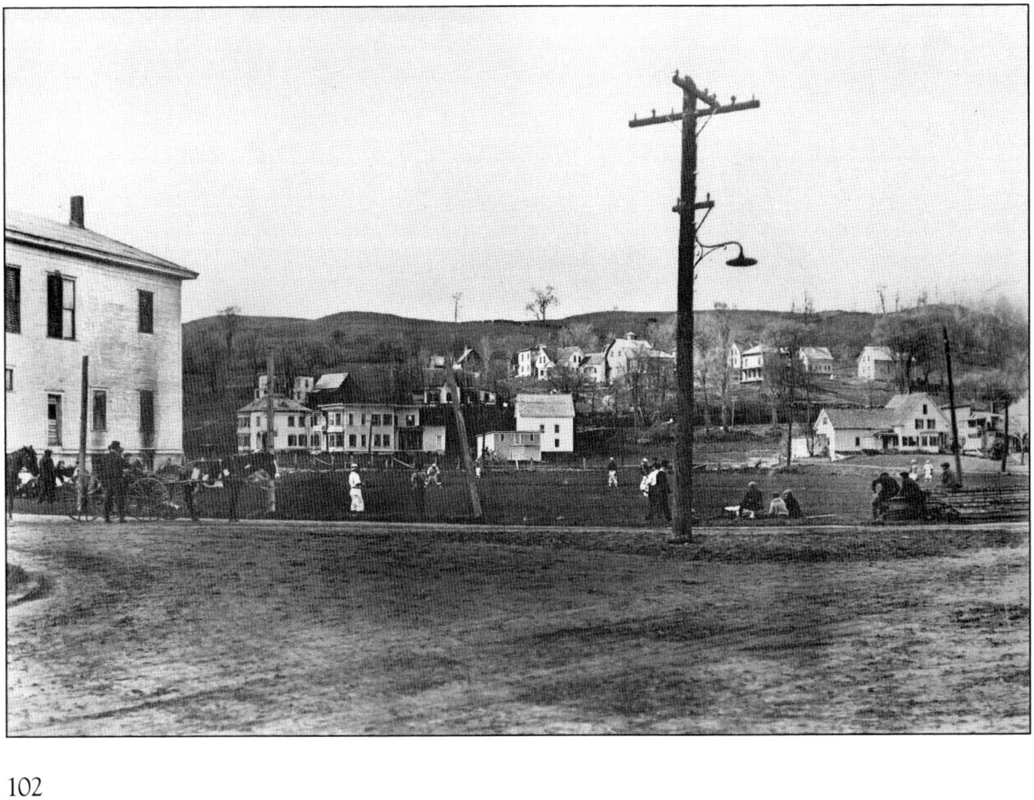

Eight

Neighbors and Friends

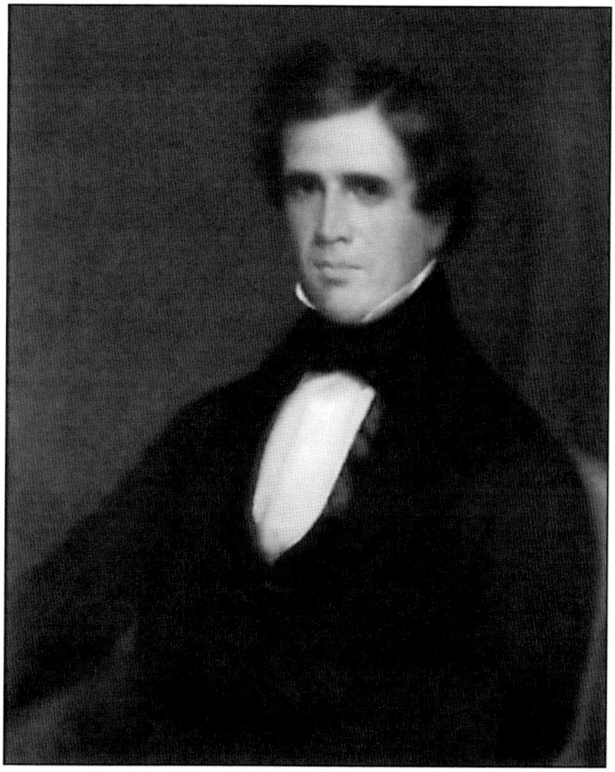

Born in 1799, Gov. Charles Paine was born in Williamstown. Paine was the son of pioneer US senator Elijah Paine. After graduating from Harvard in 1816, he managed his father's woolen mill business. He founded the Vermont Central Railroad, becoming its first president; as governor, he signed the charter of his Vermont Central Railroad. He was elected governor of Vermont in 1841 and 1842. This portrait is hanging in the senate chamber inside the Vermont State House in Montpelier. (Courtesy of the state of Vermont.)

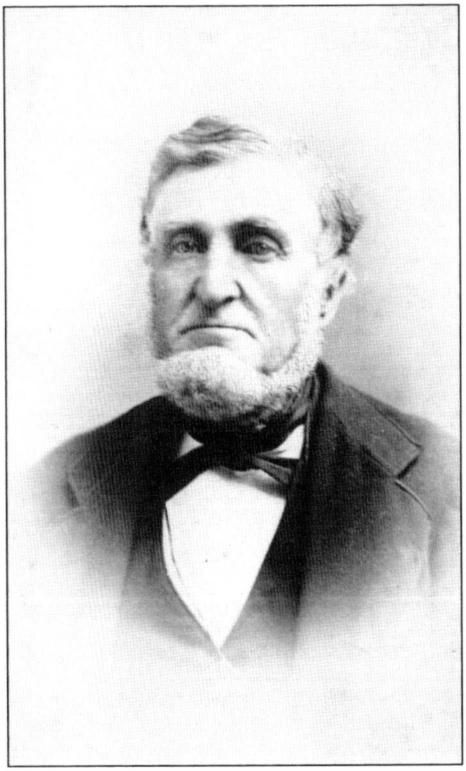

Born in 1810, John Lynde was Rebecca and Cornelius's youngest son. During the summer months, he worked on the family farm. According to the *Williamstown Herald*, special Williamstown edition, "Eventually, he purchased land and started his own farm on what is known as Lynde Hill." He served in numerous capacities including selectman, lister, justice of the peace, county judge, state representative, and senator. (Photograph by H.H.H, Langill; courtesy of Ruth Whitney, Fanny Martin Stewart.)

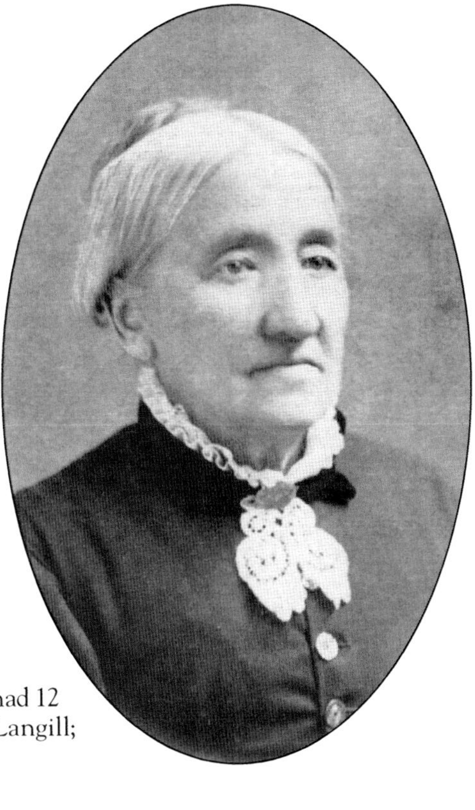

Dolly Smith married Judge John Lynde in 1822; they had 12 children. She died in 1881. (Photograph by H.H.H, Langill; courtesy of Ruth Whitney, Fanny Martin Stewart.)

Born in 1858, Dr. Cornelius Lynde was the son of Judge John and Dolly Lynde. Dr. Cornelius treated patients in his practice in Minnesota after becoming a doctor. He died in 1926. (Courtesy of Fanny Martin.)

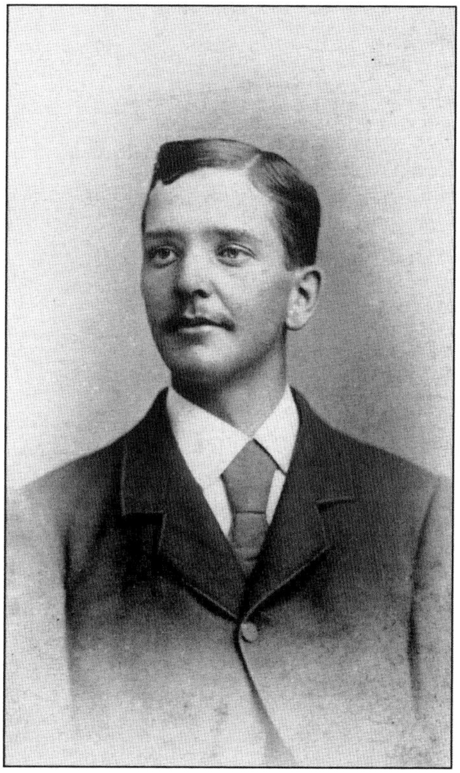

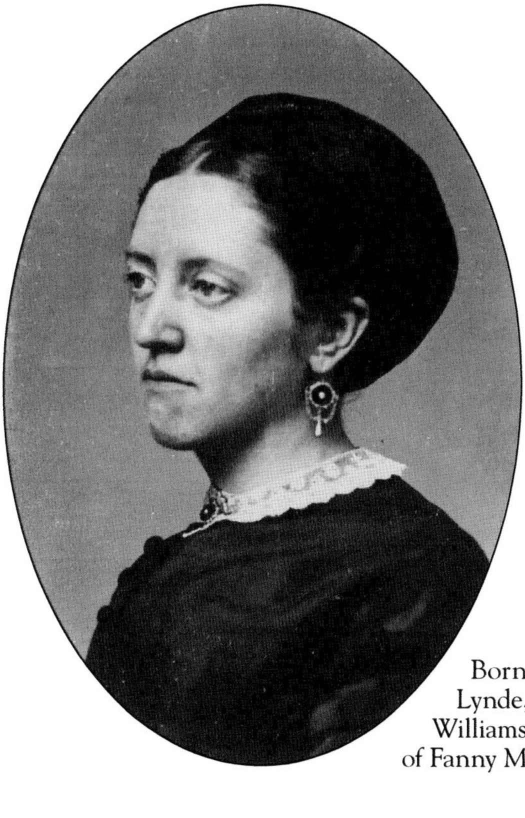

Born in 1846, Rebecca Lynde, daughter of Judge Lynde, married Nathaniel Simons; they remained in Williamstown. (Photograph by S. Vincent Allen; courtesy of Fanny Martin Stewart.)

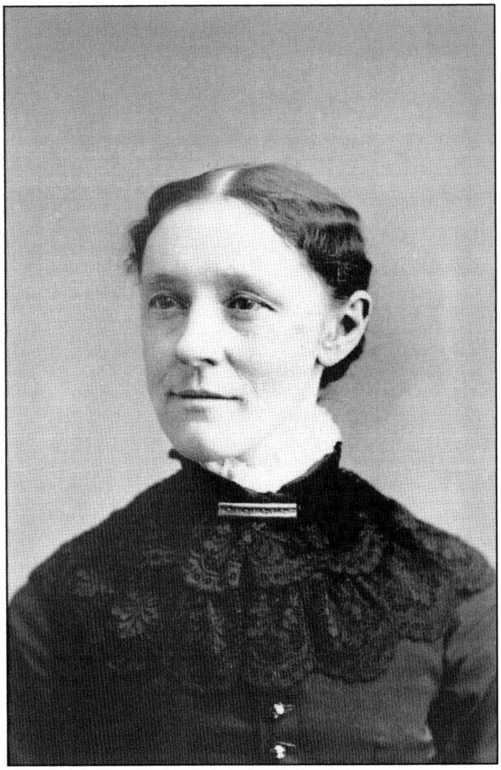

Born in 1845, Laura E. Davis Lynde married Judge John Lynde in 1882. She was the daughter of Norman Davis Sr. (Photograph by Harlows; courtesy of Fanny Martin Stewart.)

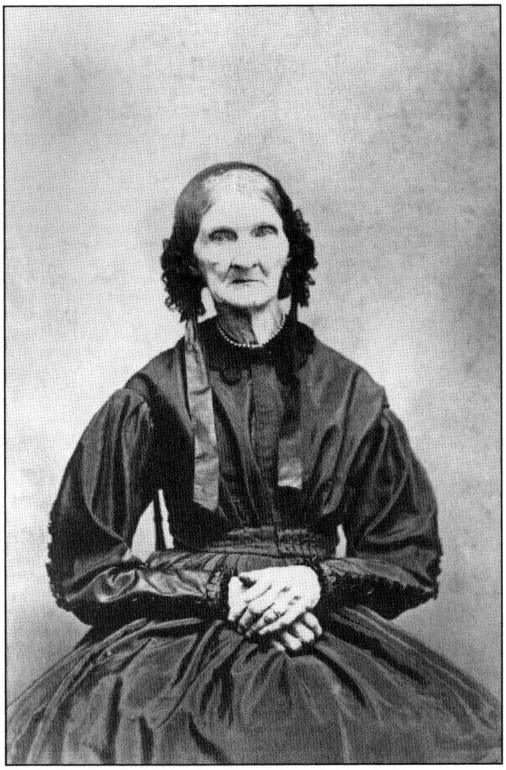

Born in 1788, Polly Burnham Martin was the third wife of Aaron Martin of Clyde Perry Farm, which was settled in the 1700s. (Photograph by Union Davis; courtesy of Fanny Martin Stewart.)

Alma Martin Perry was the sister of Harrison Martin. She married James Perry and was the mother of Dean Perry, daughter of Allen Martin, and granddaughter of Aaron Martin of Clyde Perry Farm. (Courtesy of Fanny Martin Stewart.)

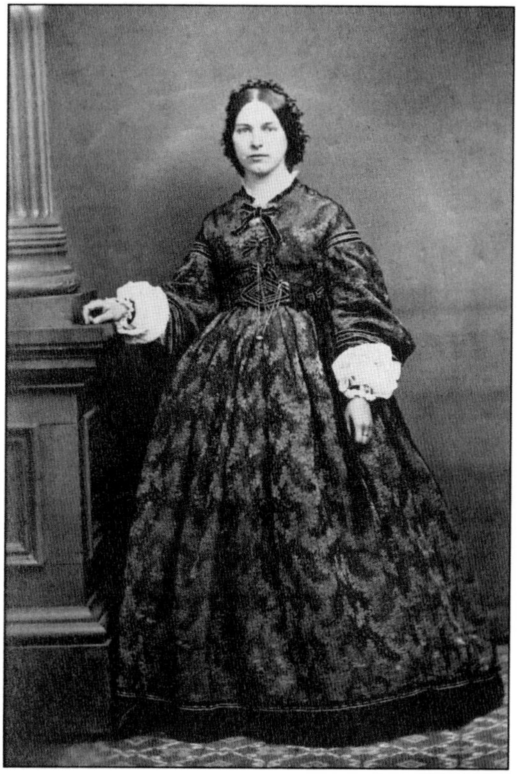

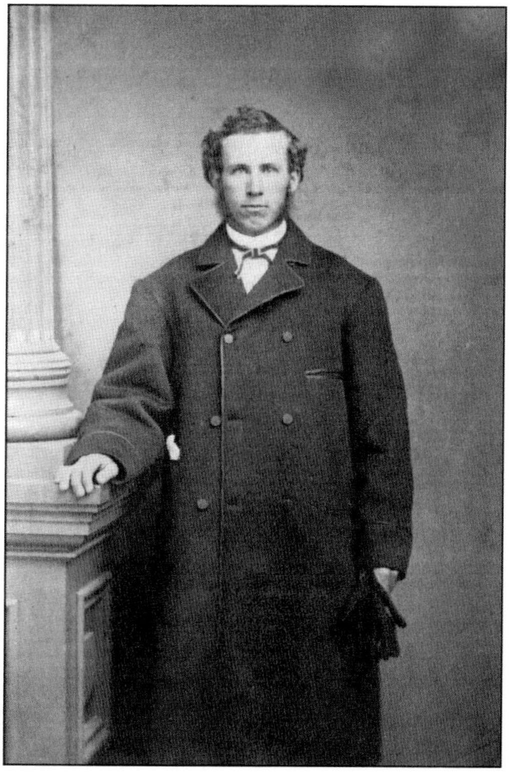

Born in 1839, Harrison Martin was the brother of Alma Martin. Harrison is wearing a winter knee-length topcoat. (Photograph by Union Davis; courtesy of Fanny Martin.)

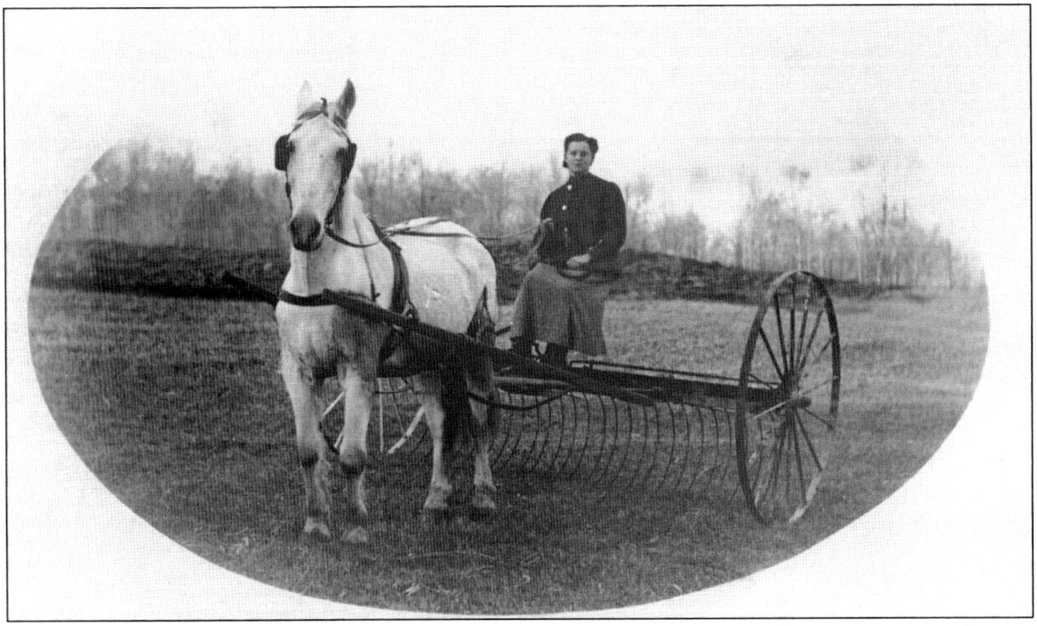

Edith A. Holden was a sister of Ethel Poor. Early on, farm wives like Edith spent most of their time doing household chores, including hand scrubbing and hand sewing clothes, canning, churning butter, hauling water, cooking, and taking care of the family. Wives also pitched in with the physical work. Edith is pictured atop a hay rake pulled by a strong white horse. Haying has shaped the Williamstown landscape for over 200 years. (Courtesy of Bertha Morgan.)

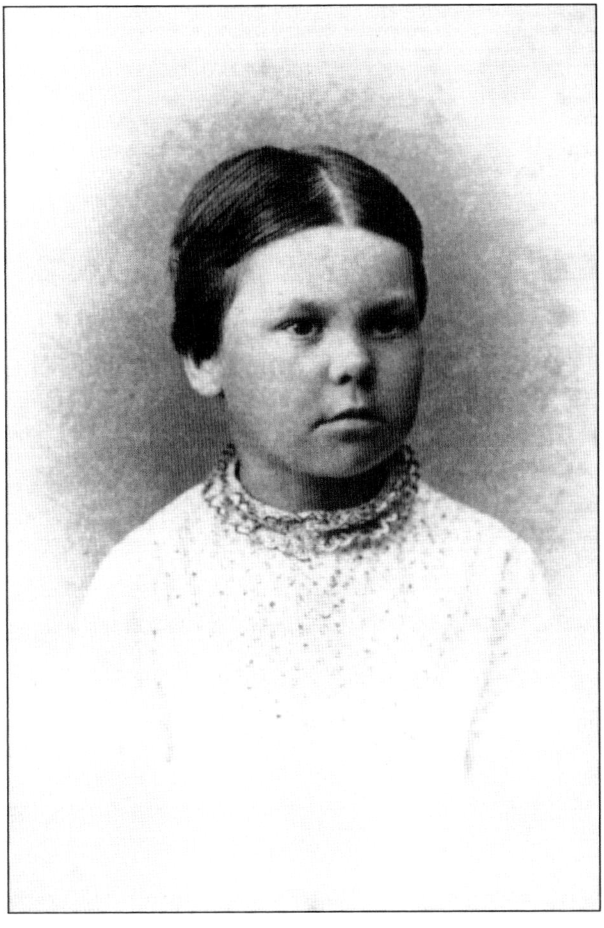

Lora Simons married Rev. Edward Carey in 1901. She was the daughter of Nathaniel Simons and sister to George and Walter. After the Careys' marriage, they went to Turkey as missionaries. Five years later, Lora died during childbirth. On the back of this picture, her mother scribbled that Lora combed her own hair in this picture. (Photograph by C.H. Masters; courtesy of Fanny Martin Stewart.)

Harriet Smith, sister of Deacon Edwin Smith, died of diphtheria in 1890. The American colonies were affected by an outbreak in the 18th century. The College of Physicians of Philadelphia reported that the antitoxin against the bacterium was identified in the 1890s, around the same time Harriet died. The first diphtheria vaccine was developed in the 1920s, and cases of diphtheria have significantly decreased. (Photograph by A.N. Blanchard; courtesy of Fanny Martin Stewart.)

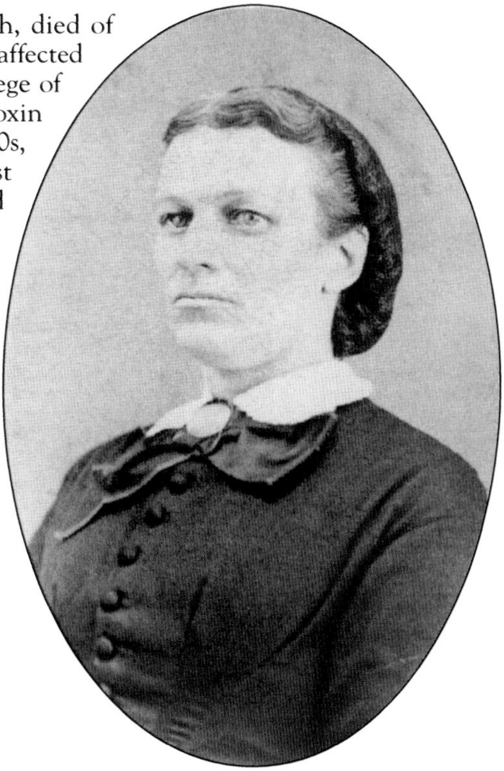

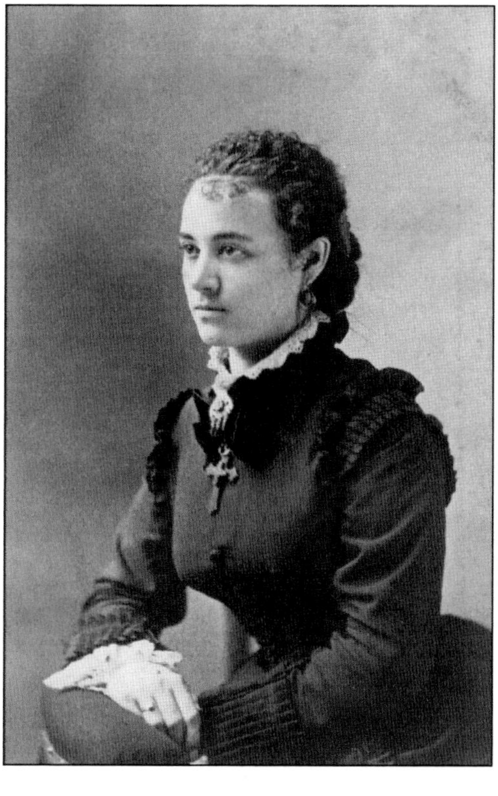

This photograph, taken in 1877, shows Elisha Martin (1856), the daughter of Emma Seymour, posing with a large pectoral cross hanging from her neck. Churches became a primary vehicle for transmitting cultural as well as religious identity. (Photograph by A. Johnson, courtesy of Fanny Martin Stewart.)

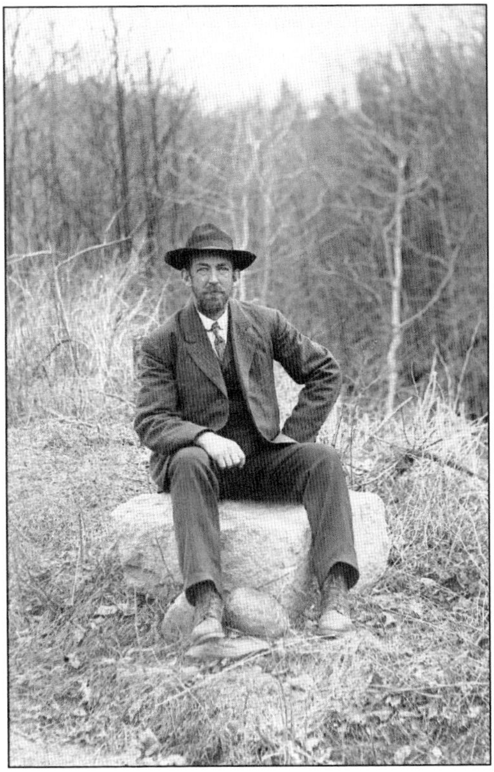

The name Seaver is more represented in the town than any other family except for the Martin family, according to the *Williamstown Herald* of June 17, 1896. Carl Seaver, father of Howell Hugh, poses for a photograph on a boulder with a thickly wooded background.

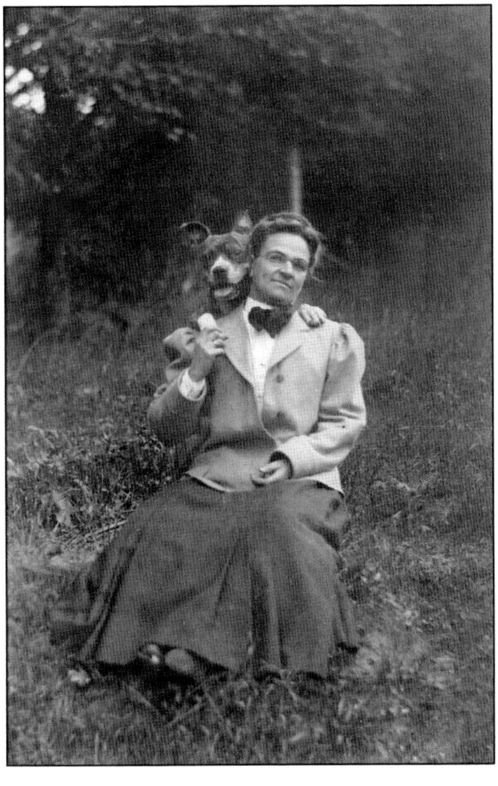

Millie Drury poses with her dog, which is gently wrapping its paws around her neck. There are many loyal friends in Williamstown who like to run, romp, play, and woof.

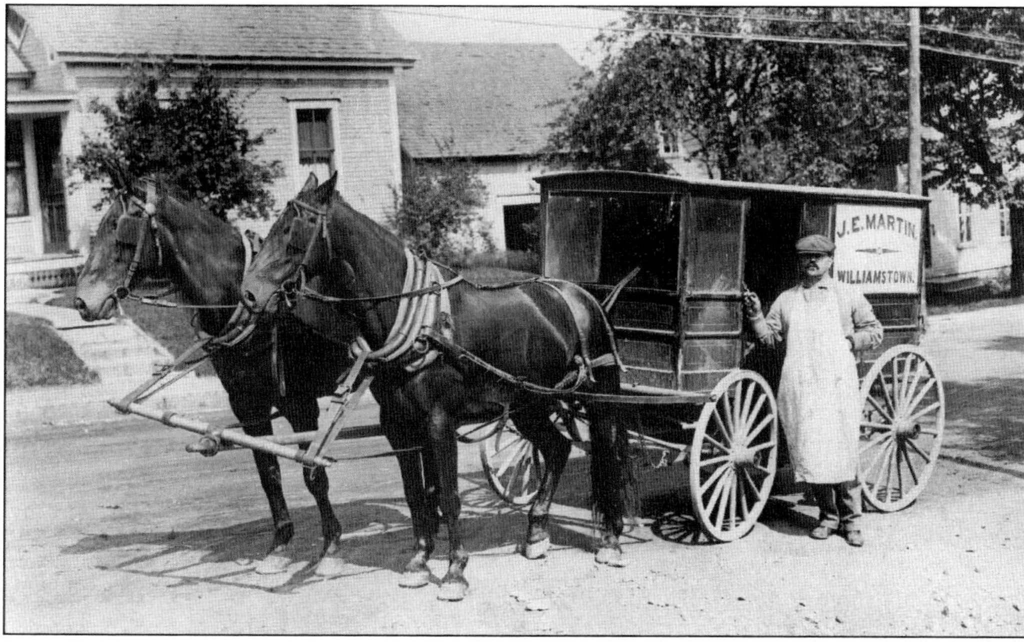

Jason E. Martin poses with his meat wagon pulled by a team of horses on Beckett Street. His meat market was located in this area but burned in 1921. Jason is wearing the white apron of his trade. (Courtesy of Ruth Whitney.)

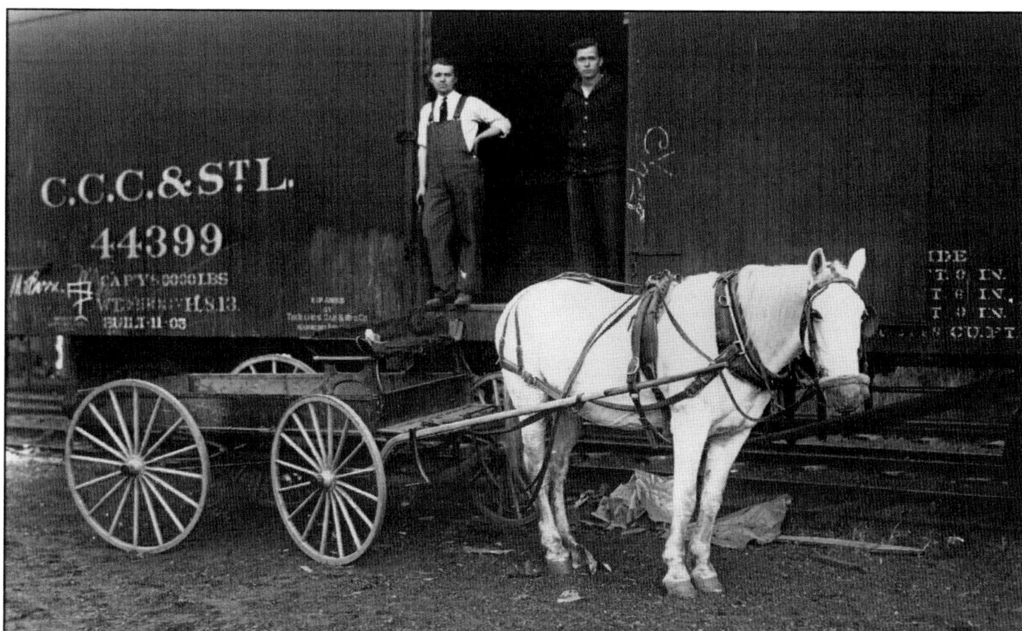

Shown are Glenn and Leon McAllister standing inside a Central Vermont Railroad boxcar sometime in 1915. They were most likely picking up supplies from the train to take back to their grocery store in the village. (Courtesy of Ruth Whitney.)

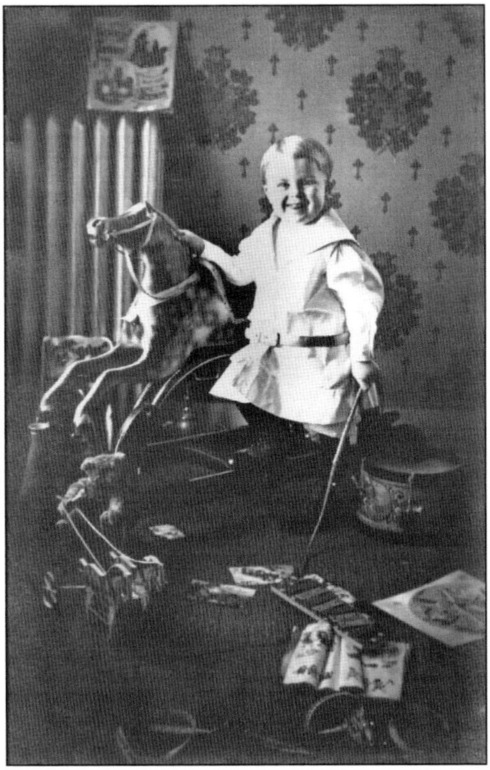

Ellenworth Morgan, daughter of Lester and Bertha Morgan, sits on her rocking horse looking over her treasure of toys, including drums, teddy bear, music makers, wooden horses, and books.

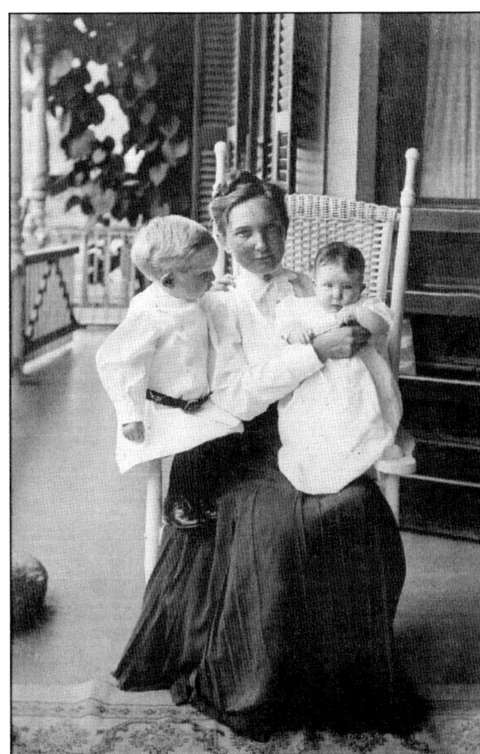

Musette Seaver balances her daughter on her lap while William (left) perches on the arm of the rocker gazing at his little sister. Note William's little black shoes and matching black belt.

Gertrude Jeffords, sister of Worth Jeffords, is dressed in her warm winter coat. With a loving smile on her face, she lingers for a moment to pat her large black dog Trixie. On her left are her cherished sled and her tossed tasseled hat. As the winter sets in, a silence seizes the land except for the laughter of children.

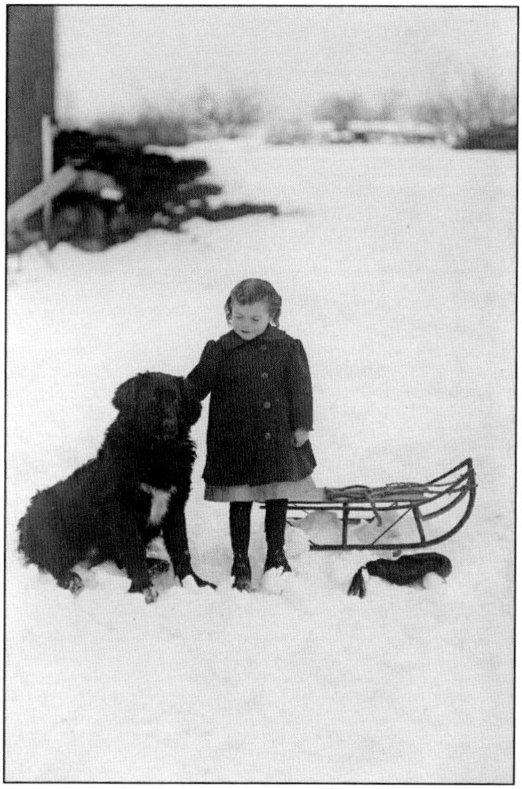

Pictured are, from left to right, (first row) Nettie Cheney, Minnie Perrin, and May Webster; (second row) Horace Farnham, Harry Cheney, Fred Austin, and Charlie Edson; (third row) Nellie House, Myron Flint, Myrtie Katham, Don Earle, Inez Flint, and Ella Benedict. (Photograph by A.N. Blanchard, courtesy of Leo Edson.)

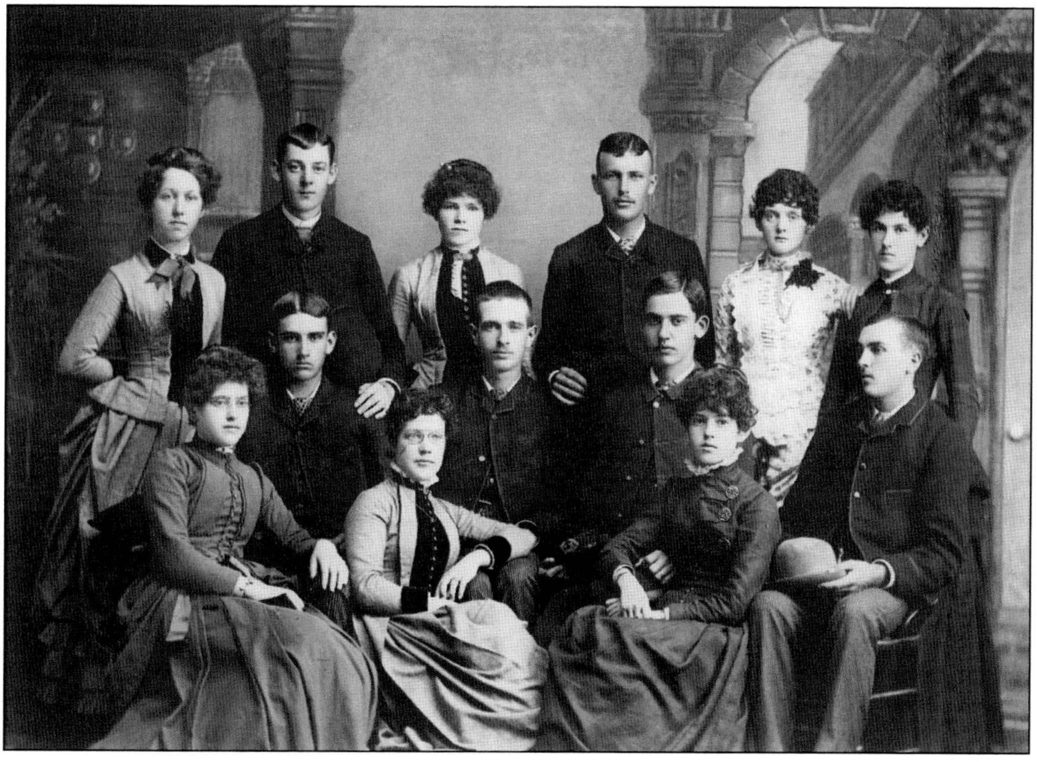

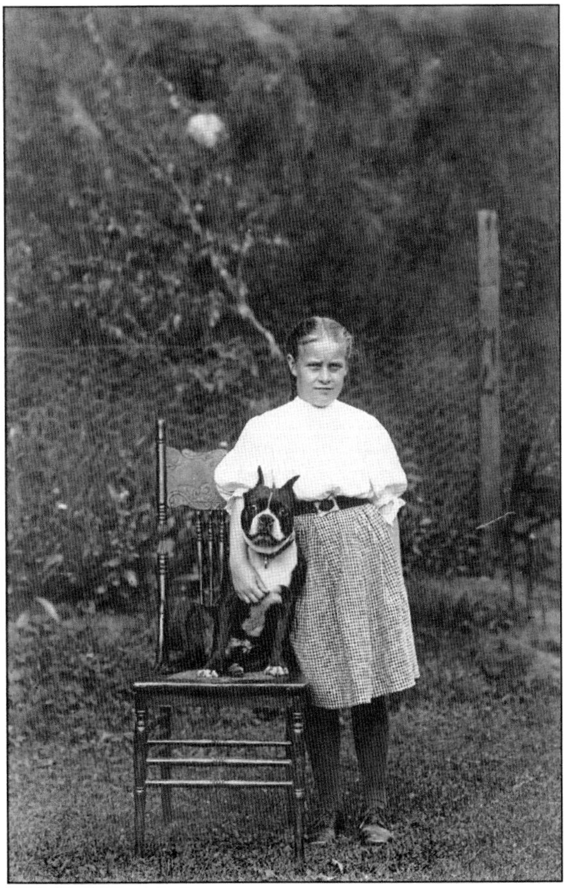

At the Gulf House, the cook's daughter holds Teddy the bulldog. Teddy belonged to the owner of the Gulf House. Note the chicken wire attached to posts in the background.

The unidentified daughter of Alph and Merle Howe giggles while holding her foot. She sits on the porch of her house.

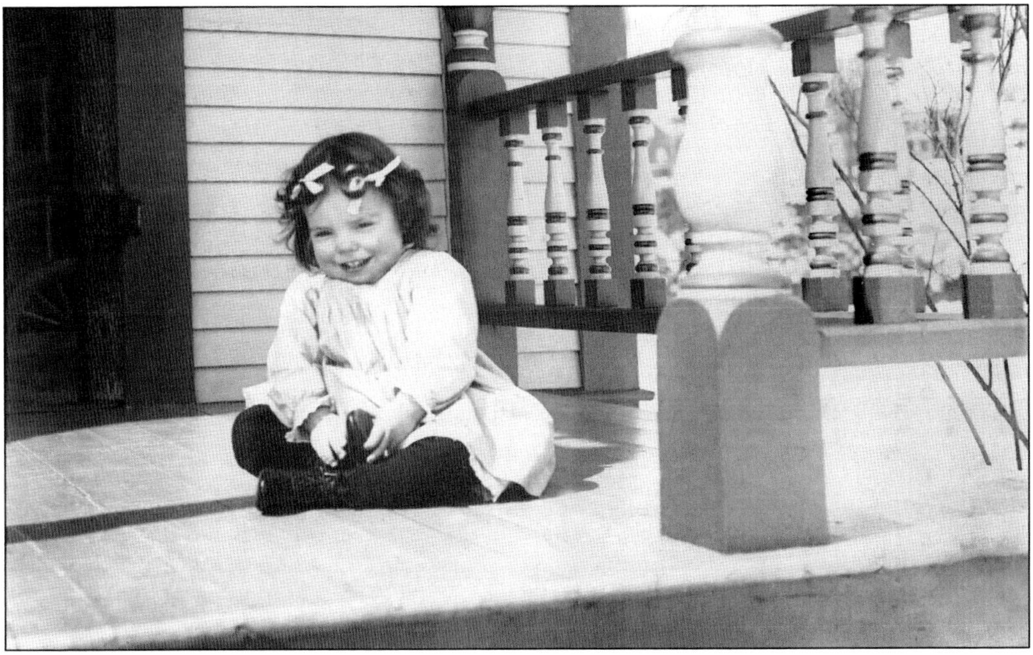

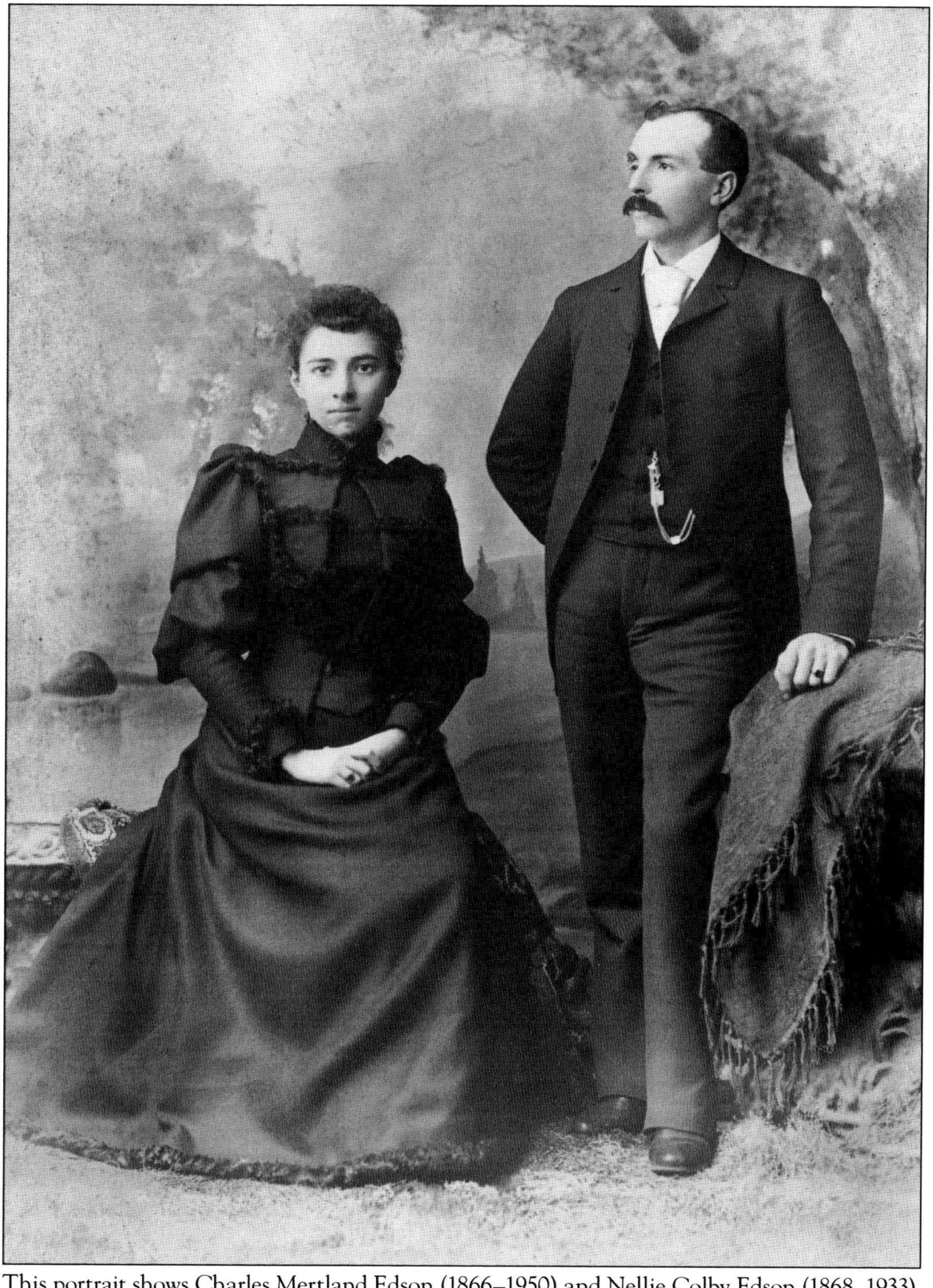

This portrait shows Charles Mertland Edson (1866–1950) and Nellie Colby Edson (1868–1933), husband and wife. (Photograph by Arthur Pepper, courtesy of Leo Edson.)

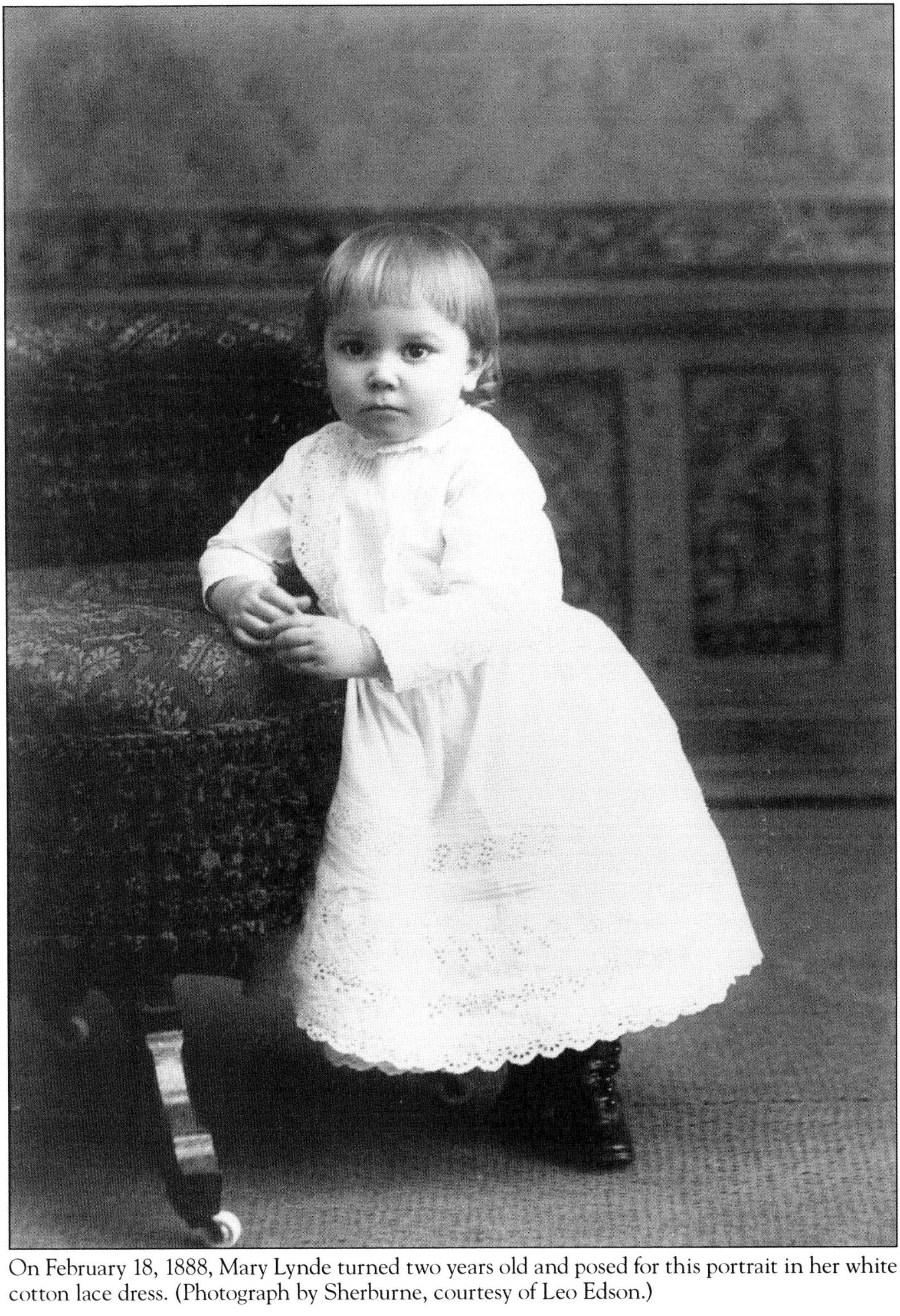

On February 18, 1888, Mary Lynde turned two years old and posed for this portrait in her white cotton lace dress. (Photograph by Sherburne, courtesy of Leo Edson.)

Winifred (Waldo) Jeffords was educated at Williamstown High School; she later married Rev. Erskine Jeffords. According to *Jeffords Family in Williamstown, Vermont* written by Percy J. Jeffords in 1962, the family name Giffards-Jeffords can be traced back to when William the Conqueror came to England at the time of the Norman Conquest in 1066.

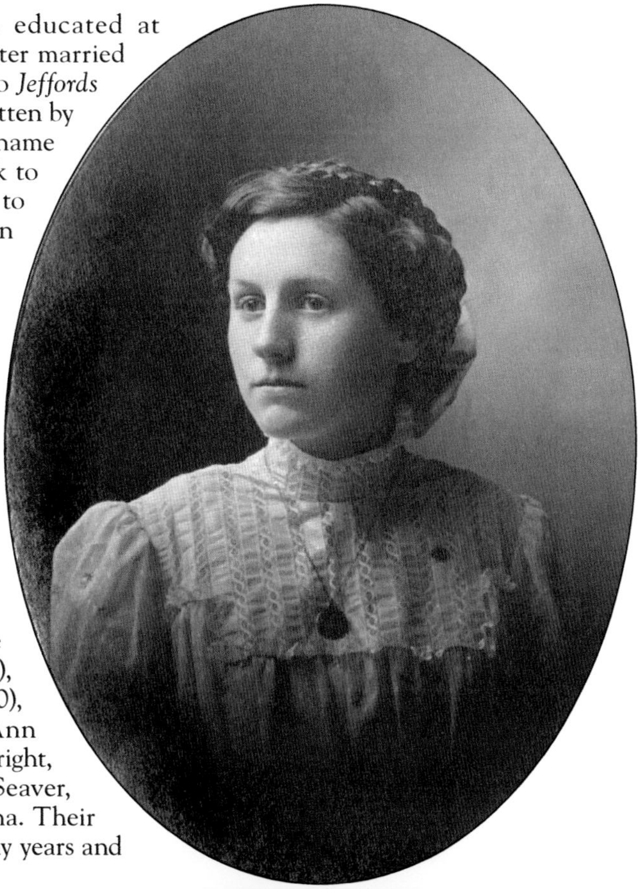

Mary Ann Jeffords (1826–1865) married Lyman Works (1822–1899) of Williamstown. They had five children, Sarah Chastina (1851–1920), Julia (1855–1936), Hattie (1858–1940), Alma (1861–1923), and Elizabeth Ann (1863–1932). Pictured are, from left to right, Alma Hattie, Tina Seaver, Lizzie Seaver, Julia Blanchard, and Sarah Chastina. Their father Lyman owned a farm for many years and a wheelwright shop.

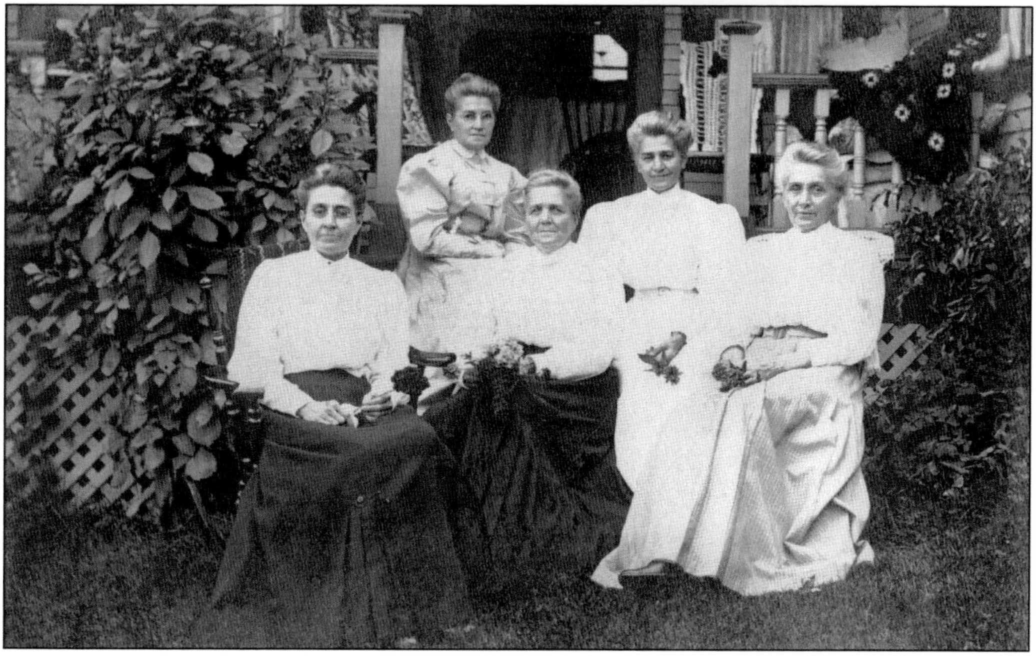

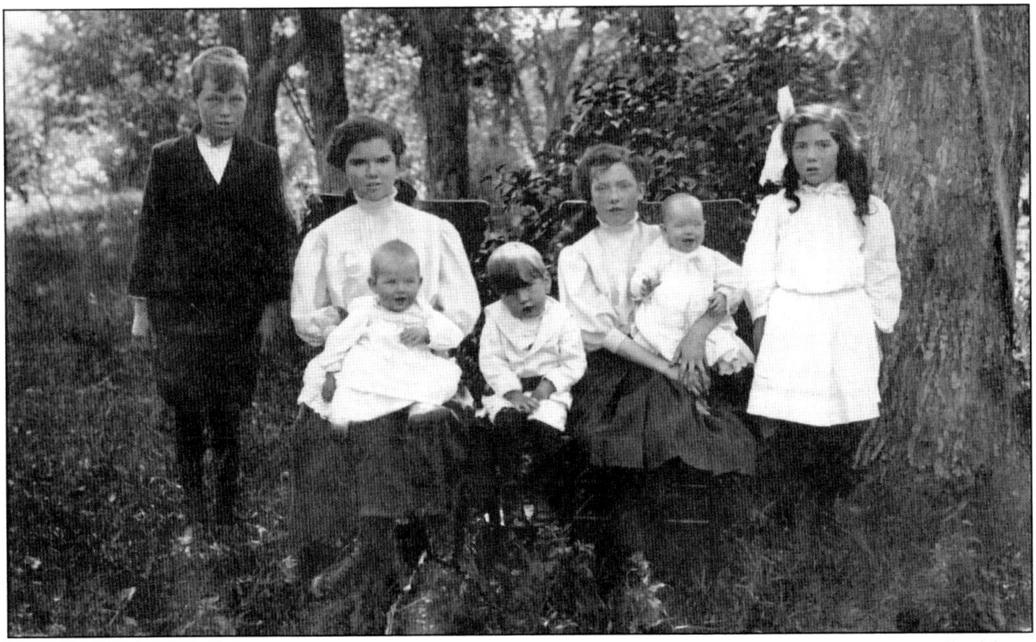

Shown in this group photograph are, from left to right, John McIntyre, Sadie McIntyre (holding Joe McGlynn), Edward McGlynn, Agatha McIntyre (holding Mary Jane McGlynn), and Esther McIntyre. (Courtesy of Edward McGlynn.)

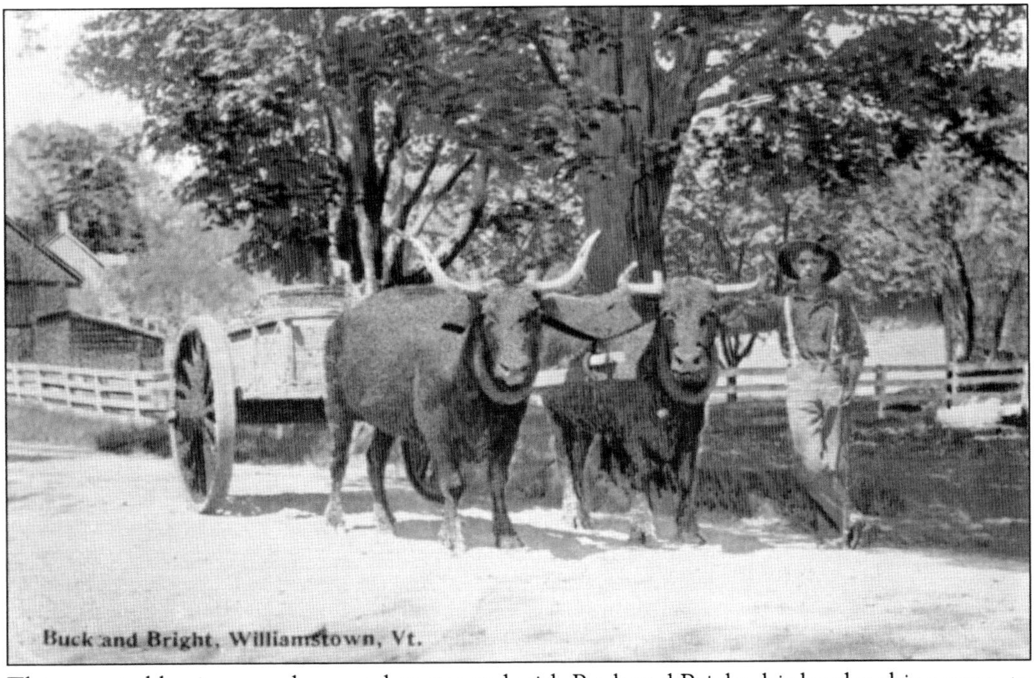

This man in blue jeans and suspenders stopped with Buck and Bright, his hardworking oxen, to have his picture taken.

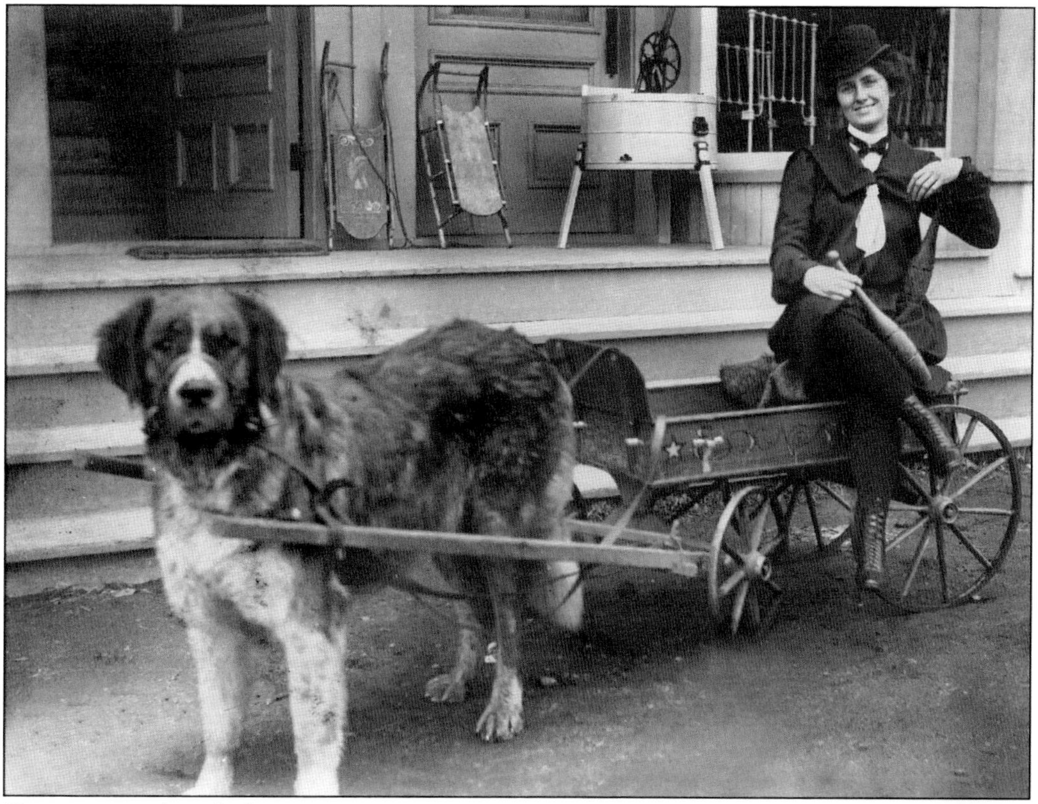

Here is an unidentified woman sitting in a dogcart. Note the items displayed on the porch include two sleds, a churn, and an iron bed frame.

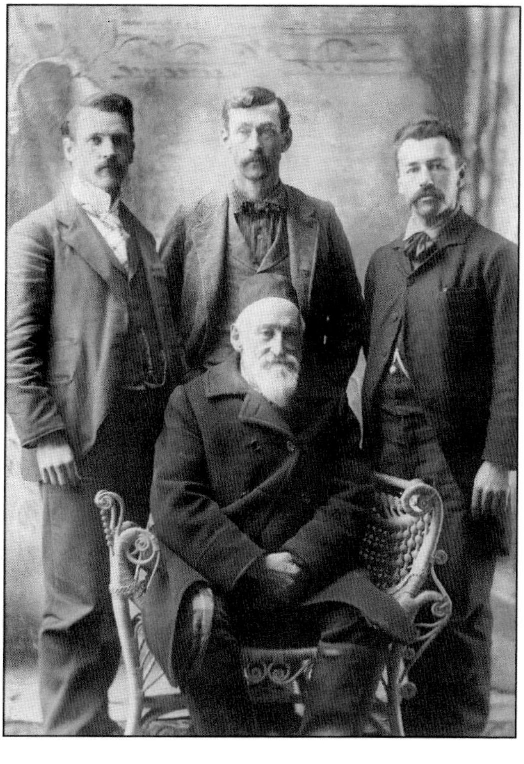

This photograph shows four men named "George" who lived in Williamstown at the same time. They are, from left to right, George Bosworth, George Wilber, George Ainsworth (sitting), and George Goodrich. All four of the Georges were bass singers.

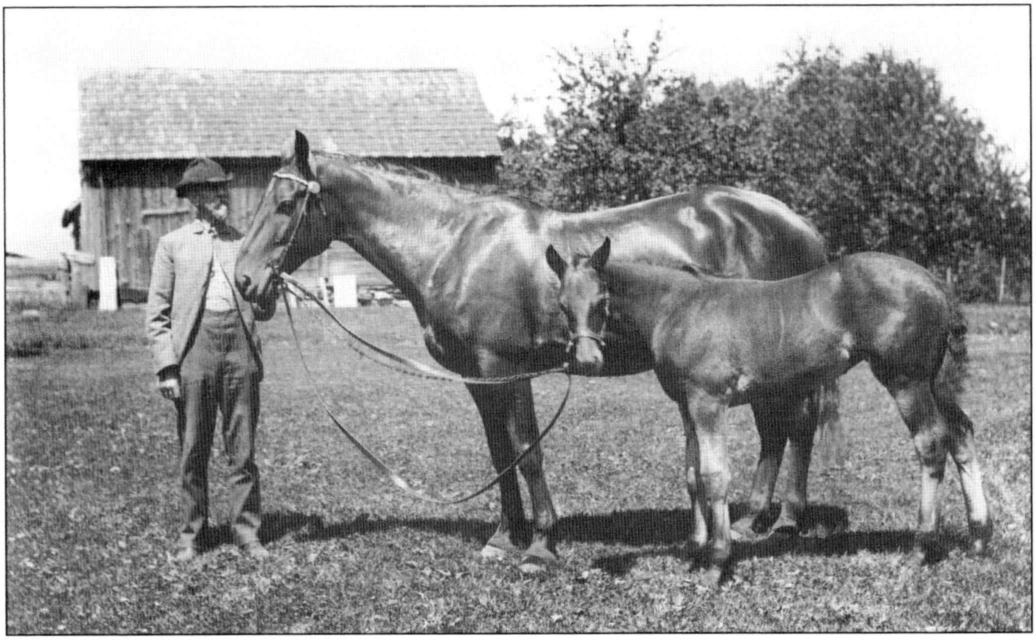

On a calm and sunny day, Dan Townsend proudly shows his Morgan horses. The back of the picture says, "For sale registered Morgan brood mare 10 years old. Height 15 feet 2 inches weight 1200 lbs. Sound and kind. A good driver and good worker - bred and owned by D.L. Townsend of Williamstown Vermont."

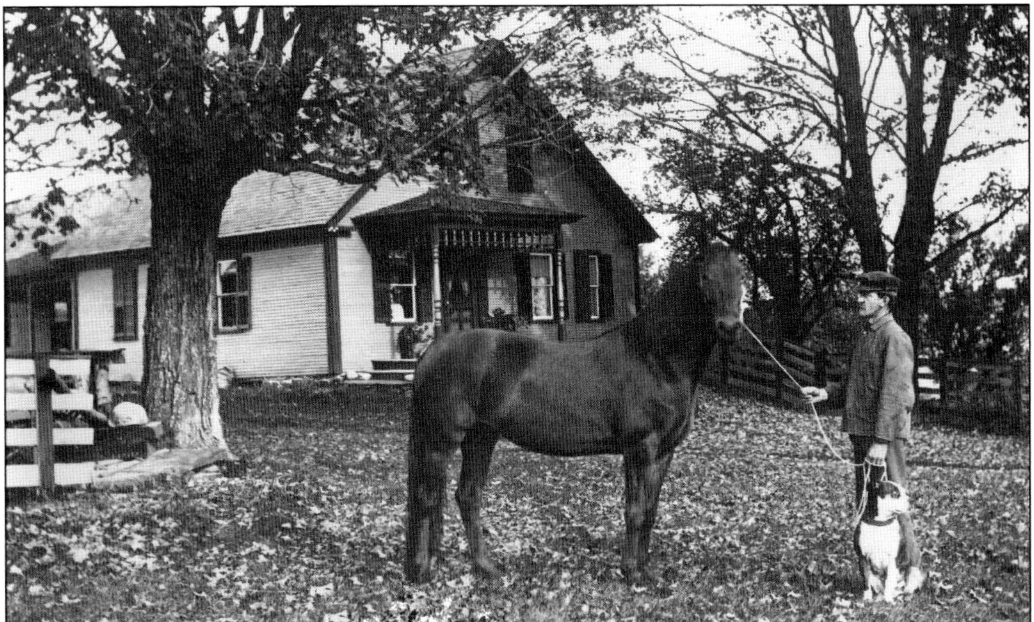

The Morgan horse is Vermont's official state animal. Williamstown was a great breeding town for these fine horses. This postcard says, "Here is a picture of Button. She is a dandy and has grown a lot. I like her very much. She works like an ox and has done half my farm work all summer and quite a bit of driving. I have been plowing with her on the sulky plow. Yours truly, W.P. Briggs."

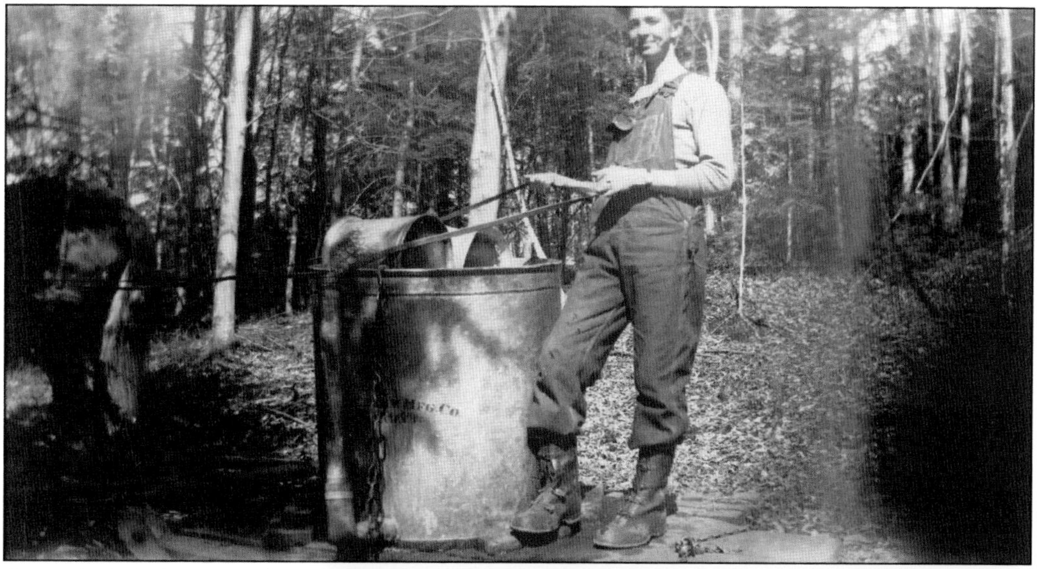

A one-inch hole is bored into a maple tree and a metal spout is driven in. A metal or wooden bucket is suspended by the spout to catch the sap. Here Robert Boyce carries the sap buckets and empties them into a gathering tank. The gathering tank, which sits on the sled, will be pulled by horse to the maple shed. The sweet sap will be boiled down to make maple syrup.

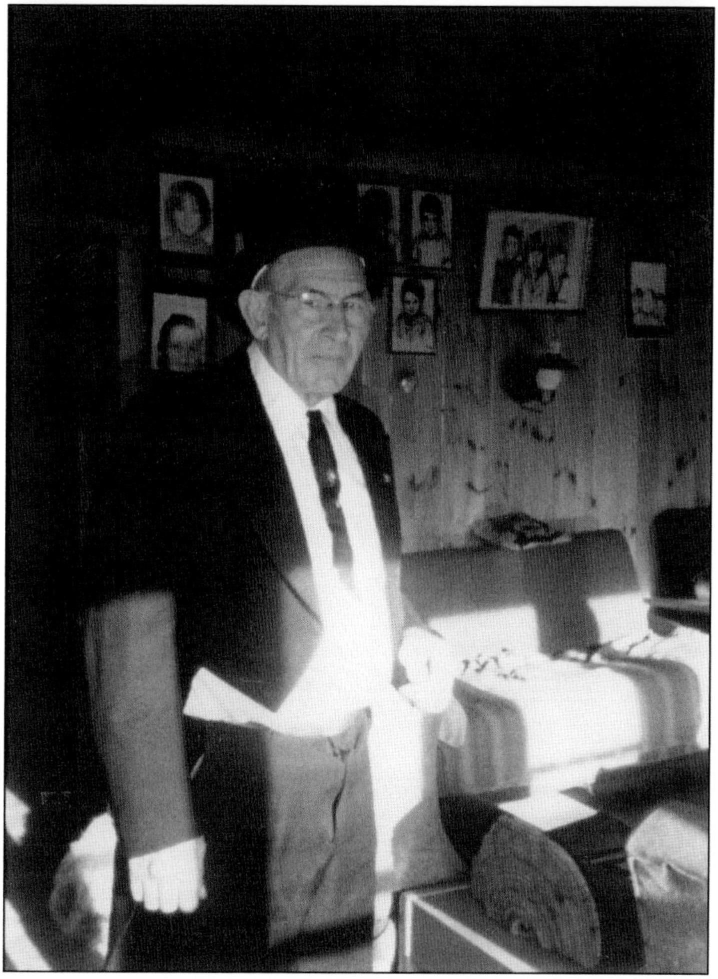

Born in 1916 in Williamstown, Hebert Chambers is wearing his contra dance top hat. He married Mabel (Luce) and moved to Chelsea, where they had four children, Bernice Lee Seaver, Edna Carpenter, Edwin Dale "Red" Chambers, and Winston Chambers. All of his children except Edwin Dale moved back to Williamstown. (Courtesy of Winston Chambers.)

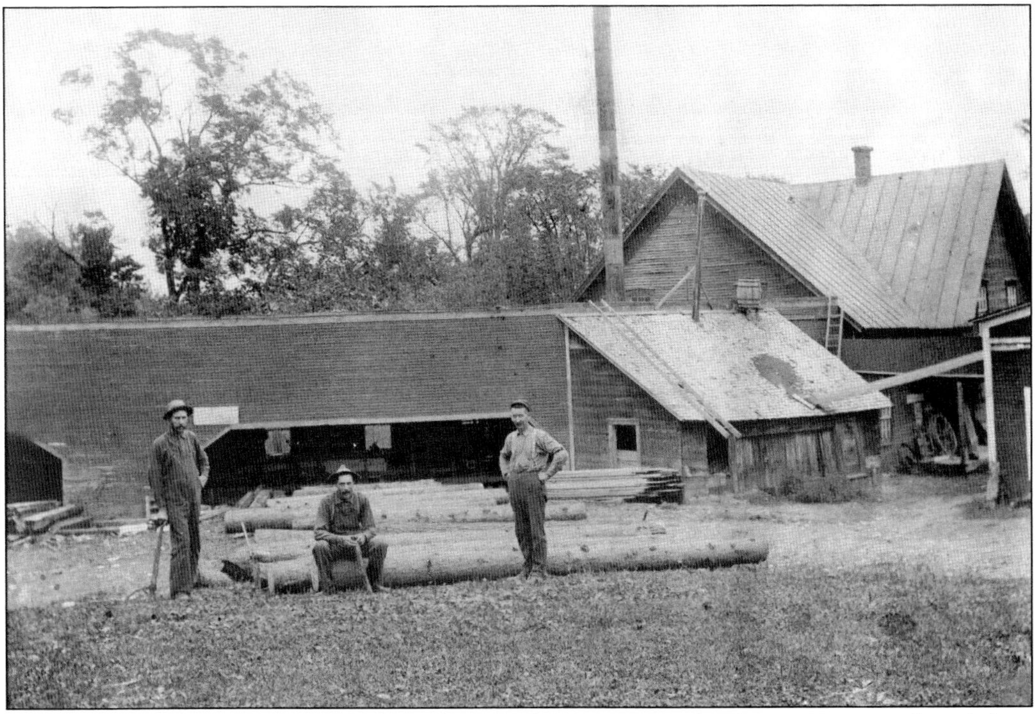

Pictured here is the old sawmill of Lynde and Cheney. Posing for the camera are, from left to right, Will Carpenter, unidentified, and Arthur Davenport.

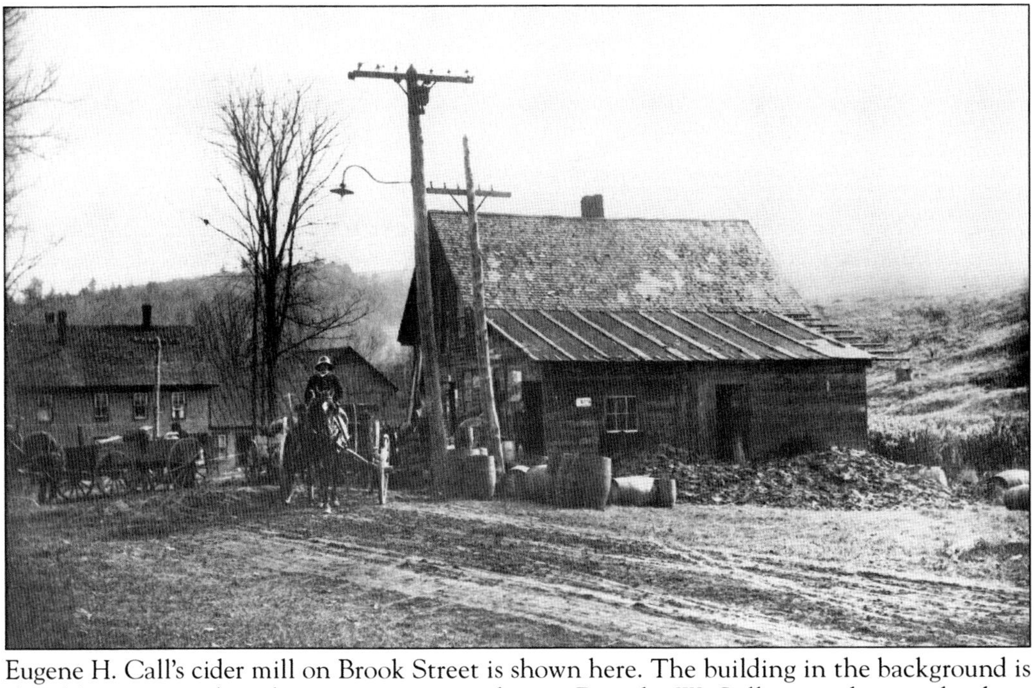

Eugene H. Call's cider mill on Brook Street is shown here. The building in the background is the old tannery; it later became a tenement house. Dorothy W. Call is standing in the door. Eugene H. Call stands in the door at right, Ed Poor stands behind the wagon, and Jerry Fifield is on the horse.

Kenneth (left) and Dorothy were the children of Eugene Henry and Alma E. Work Call. Note the contented cat stretched out on the stair next to Dorothy.

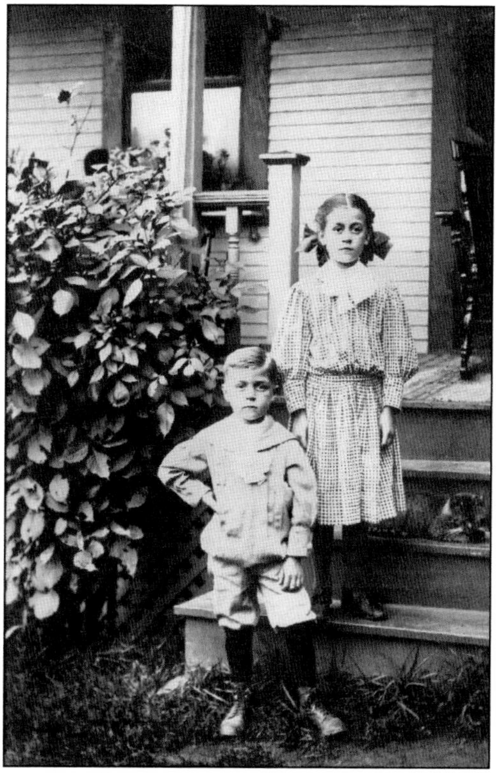

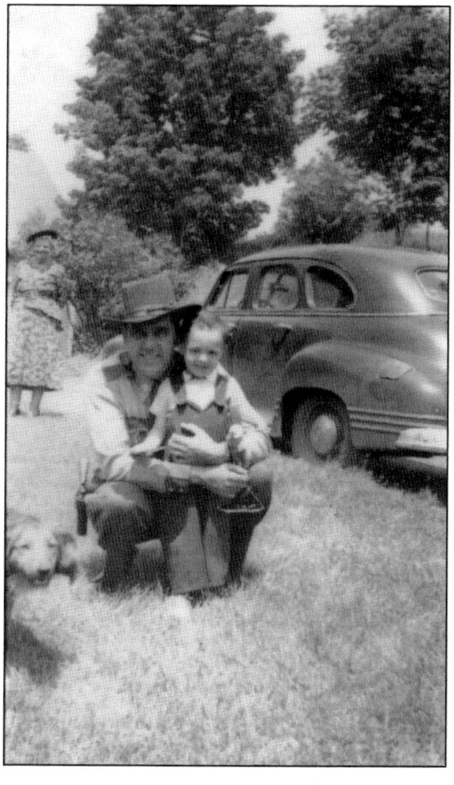

In 1949, the first policeman in Williamstown is seen holding little Robert Jarvis. Note the pistol hanging from the policeman's holster and the floppy-eared dog in the corner. (Courtesy of Robert Jarvis)

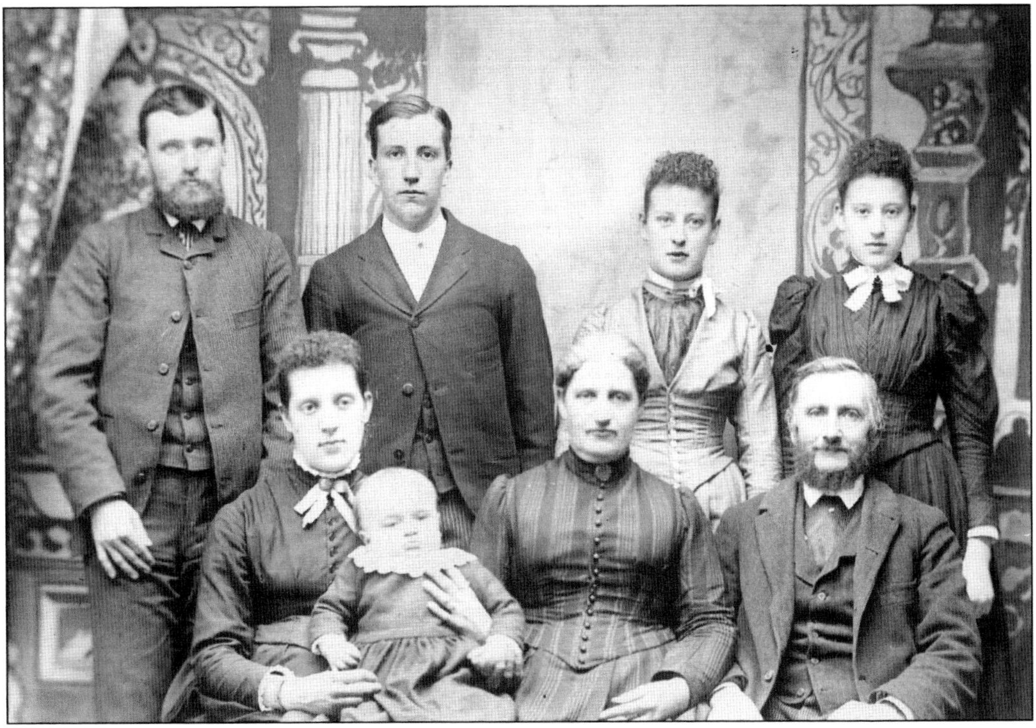

Posing for this portrait are, from left to right, (first row) Eva Seaver (holding Harold Seaver, her first child), Mary Metcalk, and Moses Metcalf; (second row) Forrest Seaver, George Metcalf, Bertha Metcalk, and Hattie Metcalk. (Photograph by Huard and Langlors, courtesy of Donald and Bernice Lee Seaver.)

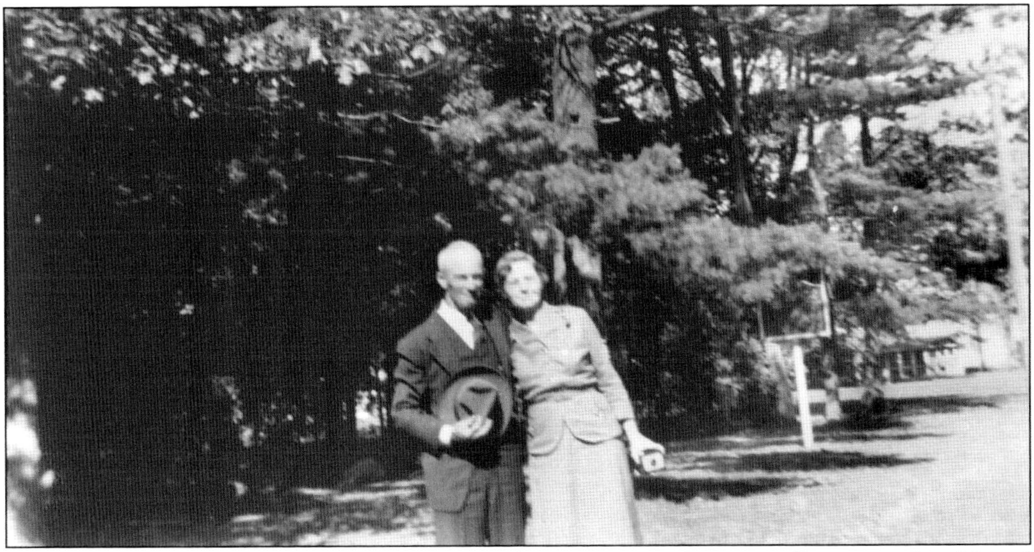

Horace H. (left) and Esther Lasell were married for 52 years. She was well respected and loved by many residents in Williamstown, having lived there for nearly 83 years. She taught at both the Clogston and Seaver Schools. The *Barre-Montpelier Times Argus* reported her role as a local newspaper reporter inspired her to embark on an oral history project for the Williamstown Historical Society, in which she tape recorded interviews with many of the town's residents.

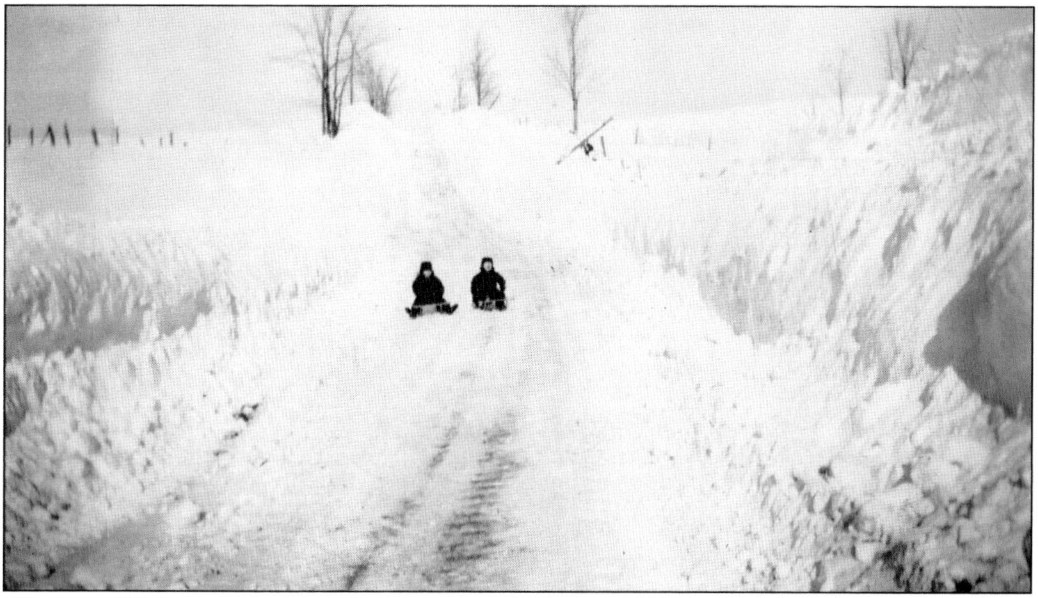

Winter in Williamstown was always a great time for fun. Shown are the Murphy boys sliding down the road on sleds near the Perley Sanders house.

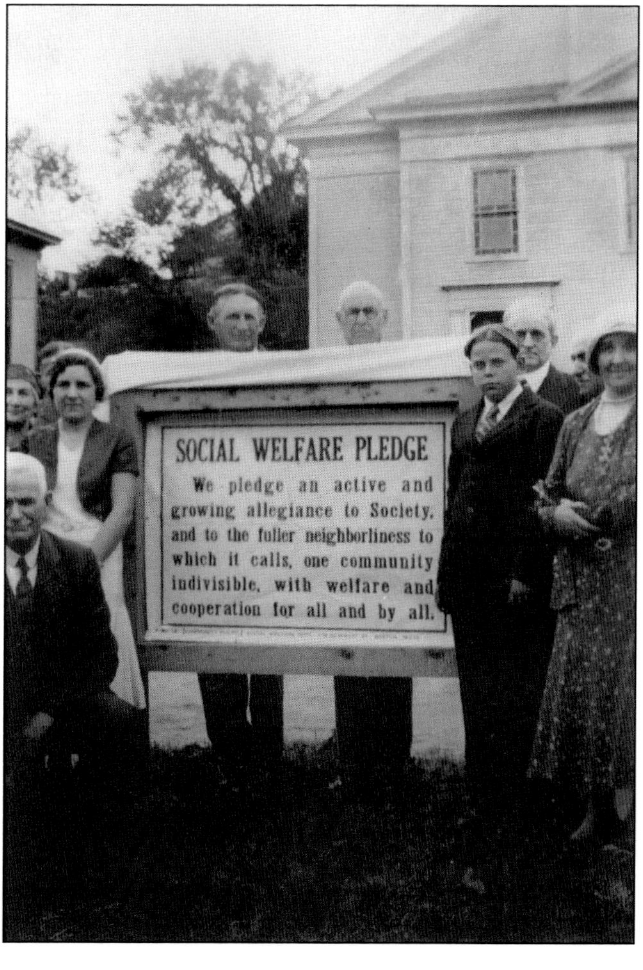

Good friends and neighbors are shown unveiling the social welfare pledge. They are, from left to right, Hiram Drury, C. Malnati, Celia (Wilber) Colby, Stephen Phillips, Rev. John Kimball, Sherwood Poor, unidentified, and Jenny Malnati. Local clubs have undertaken many service activities for the betterment of the community.

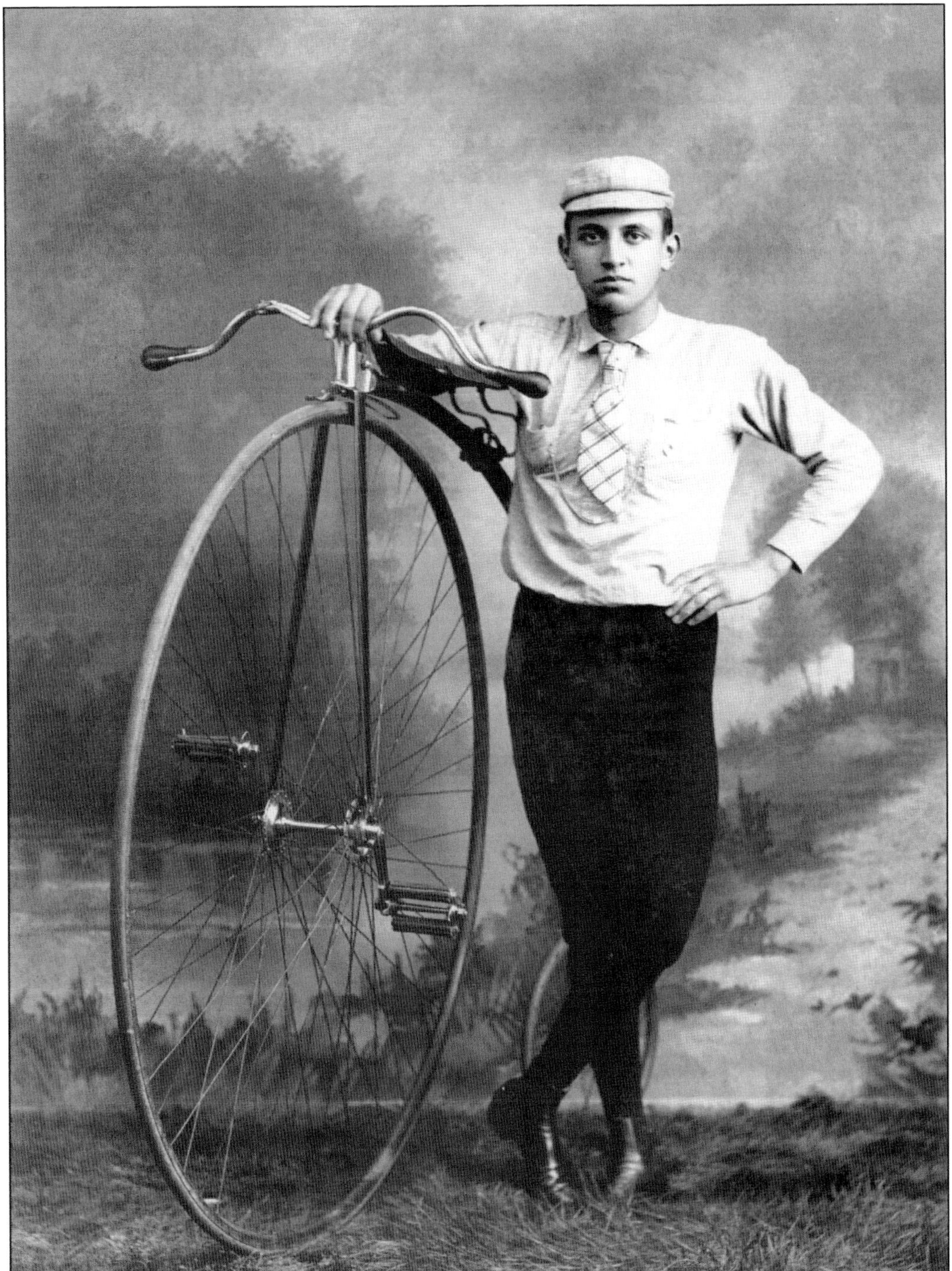

Frank Schofield poses with his bicycle, commonly known as a "penny farthing" or "hi-wheel." He was the son of Rev. William Schofield. The picture was taken in the 1880s. (Photograph by Sherburne; courtesy of Leo Edson.)

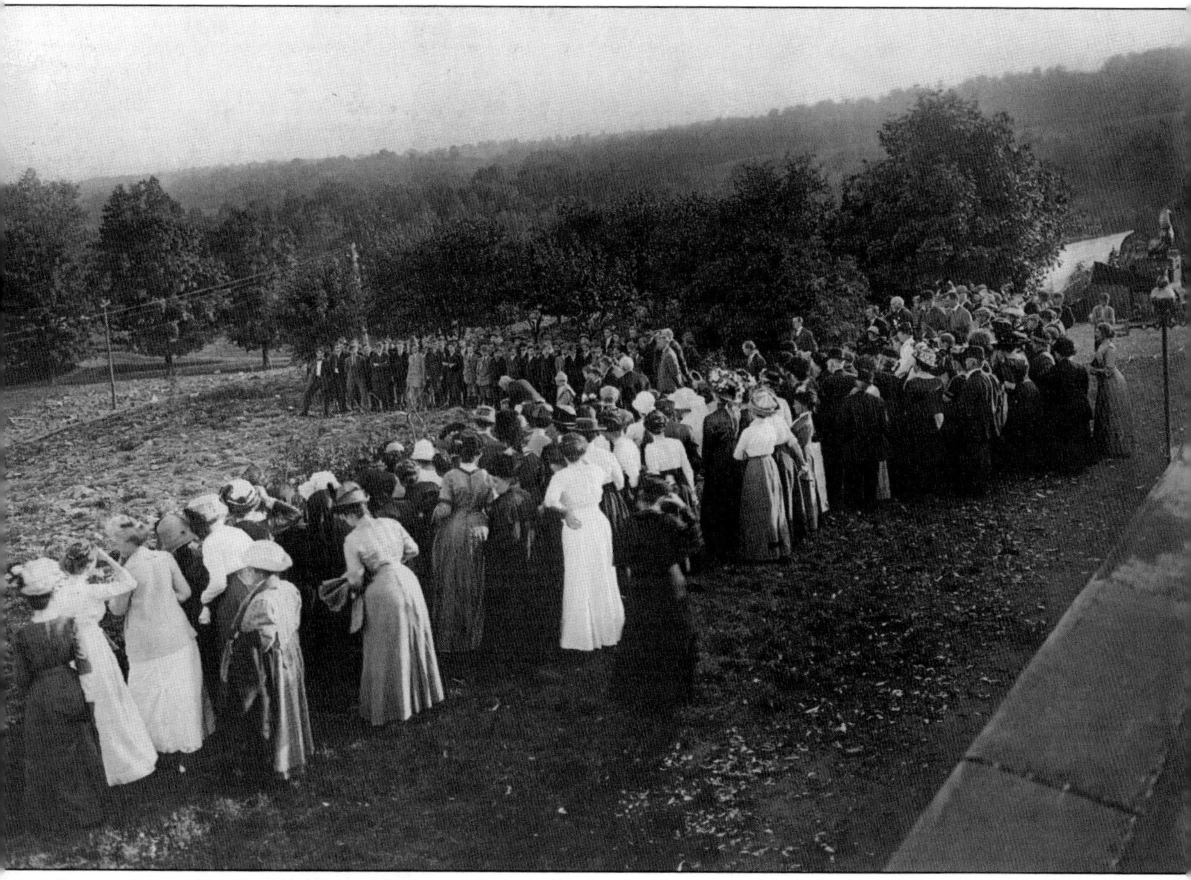

An exciting day for Williamstown residents, this was the ground breaking celebration for the building of Ainsworth Cottage. Note the man bent over his shovel at center.

Consistent with our mission to preserve history on a local level, this book was printed in South Carolina on American-made paper and manufactured entirely in the United States. Products carrying the accredited Forest Stewardship Council (FSC) label are printed on 100 percent FSC-certified paper.

MADE IN THE USA